Dry Ginger

The biography of Admiral of the Fleet
Sir Michael Le Fanu, GCB, DSC

Dry Ginger

The biography of Admiral of the Fleet

Sir Michael Le Fanu,
GCB, DSC

RICHARD BAKER

W. H. ALLEN · London
A Howard & Wyndham Company
1977

Printed and bound in Great Britain by
The Garden City Press Limited,
Letchworth, Hertfordshire SG6 1JS

For the Publishers, W. H. Allen & Co. Ltd.,
44 Hill Street, London W1X 8LB

ISBN 0 491 01788 X

For Prue
and the Three

In the section of photographs between pages 128 and 129, the fifth page should have shown pictures of HMS *Ark Royal* and HMS *Eagle*. The publishers regret that, owing to an unfortunate error, one of these pictures is incorrect. The top one is of the present HMS *Ark Royal* but the bottom one shows, not her sister ship HMS *Eagle*, but the previous aircraft carrier of that name sunk by enemy action off Sicily on 11 August 1942.

Contents

LE FANU, Adm. Sir Michael, GCB 1968 (KCB 1963; CB 1960); Chief of Naval Staff and First Sea Lord, 1968–70; Chief of the Defence Staff from Oct. 1970; *b* 2 Aug. 1913; *s* of Capt. H. B. Le Fanu, Royal Navy; *m* 1943, Prudence, *d* of late Adm. Sir Vaughan Morgan, KBE, CB, MVO, DSC; two *s* one *d*. Served in HM Ships Aurora, Howe and US 3rd/5th Fleets, 1939–45. Commanded HMS Eagle, 1957–58; Third Sea Lord and Controller of the Navy, 1961–65; C-in-C Middle East, 1965–68. US Bronze Star, 1945.

Taken from *Who's Who, 1970*

Author's Preface

'You Lee Kwan Yew, Prime Minister of Singapore. Me Lee Fan Yew, British Admiral.' With these words, Rear-Admiral Michael Le Fanu, Flag Officer Second-in-Command Far East Fleet, is alleged to have introduced himself to the Prime Minister of Singapore at their first meeting in 1960. The joke was shared between the two men whenever they met subsequently, and it earned the subject of this book one of several nicknames : to many a matelot he was 'The Chinese Admiral', just as he was 'LeF' or 'Leffy' to most of his contemporaries and 'Mike' to countless numbers of other friends from every walk and station of life. Indeed it could be disconcerting, as I found at an Admiralty House party in 1969, to be introduced to the professional head of the Navy and be instructed forthwith to 'drop the "sir" and call me Mike'—especially if you happened to be a two-ringer in the Royal Naval Reserve.

It was hardly less surprising when, in the midst of some two hundred high-ranking officers from foreign navies interested in what Britain had to offer in the way of defence equipment, Michael opened the jacket of his lounge suit with the muttered aside : 'Do you think I've got the right idea?' Sewn inside the jacket was a poster which read, in bold lettering and several languages, 'NAVY FOR SALE'.

Of the many remarkable men who have reached high rank in the Royal Navy since World War Two, Admiral of the Fleet Sir Michael Le Fanu was perhaps the least orthodox. His premature death from leukaemia in 1970 deprived the nation of a Chief of Defence Staff who would have brought to the supreme

9

Defence job an exceptional humanity and commonsense, and who would no doubt have championed the cause of the three Services with the flair he had already shown as tri-service Commander-in-Chief in Aden during the critical period of the British evacuation.

Michael's two years as First Sea Lord and Chief of Naval Staff certainly boosted the Navy's morale. Such was the tonic effect of his personality that even the abolition of rum—perhaps the most controversial and most publicised event during his time at the top—took place without dampening the enthusiasm of the Service, and without diminishing the sailors' regard for a boss who cheerfully shouldered the blame by assuming another nickname : 'Dry Ginger'. It reflected his red hair and ready wit, and provided an apt title for this book.

Most of those who knew Michael even as a small boy could see that he was likely to do something outstanding. He was a born leader. Militarism left him cold, but as a young Lieutenant in the cruiser *Aurora* he proved his potential as a commander of fighting men, a potential which was never put to the test after the war—though the withdrawal of British forces and families from Aden in 1967 with minimal loss of life must surely count as a notable achievement.

In this, as in so many other situations, Michael displayed a democratic style of leadership that was entirely his own. He dealt with men at every level in a direct way which often bypassed Service conventions and shocked those who liked to abide by the book. One day, discarding his badges of rank, he went down to the dockside in Aden to help a party of soldiers who were loading a store ship. He greatly relished being told by the NCO in charge to 'get a move on there, Ginger!'. The incident illustrates Michael's determination always to find out for himself what life was like 'at the rock-face', to focus attention on the achievements of the troops, and, if possible, to inject a smile into the day's work.

This book is full of his imaginative and often amusing gestures. But Michael Le Fanu was a complex man, and to think of him merely as 'a fellow of infinite jest' would be quite wrong. Among other things, he was the author of the initial plan for Britain's

Polaris submarine building programme—by far the most ambitious building project undertaken by the Navy since the last war, and one which was carried through with exemplary efficiency. An easy good humour formed the sparkling surface of a character which could be tough to the point of ruthlessness. Michael also possessed a sharp and original brain, a deep and genuine concern for other people, and a considerable talent for words. This last quality might perhaps be anticipated in one whose ancestors included the ghost-story writer Joseph Sheridan Le Fanu and the sister of Richard Brinsley Sheridan, author of *The School for Scandal* and *The Rivals*.

There was obviously a good deal of the actor in Michael, who loved the theatre and made a habit of collecting performances of *Hamlet*. He read enormously ('anything except rubbish'), visited art exhibitions as well as race meetings, walked with his daughter up the Thames to its source and rode a bicycle to Admiralty board meetings. During the last months of his life, he took a course in bricklaying and navigated the lower reaches of the Thames by solo canoe. All these and many other diverse activities grew out of his prodigious energy, and an irreverent sense of fun which no doubt owed something to an Irish father and a mother brought up in the pragmatic atmosphere of the Australian outback.

If there was a touch of the Australian in Michael's manners, he was no less influenced by America. In 1945, at what was perhaps the crucial stage of his career, he was British liaison officer to Admirals Halsey and Spruance during the final stages of the war in the Pacific, and the experience profoundly affected his outlook. He saw at first hand how decisively the United States had taken over world command of the seas from the Royal Navy and was among the first to face that reality. He did more : as a young Commander, he shocked some Admirals by advocating that the Royal Navy should abandon some of its time-worn traditions and emulate the Americans, particularly in matters of pay and conditions—almost revolutionary proposals which have now been realised in all RN ships.

But it is not enough to remember Michael Le Fanu in naval

terms alone. Although he was dedicated to the Royal Navy (he really did love 'the Andrew') his wife and three children remained in the forefront of his mind, whatever the changing demands of his career. Prudence Morgan—'Prue'—the girl he married as a young Lieutenant-Commander in 1943—was severely disabled by polio contracted when she was seventeen and still at school. To Michael, this was 'no problem' and throughout their life together it was never allowed to become one. The wheelchair went almost everywhere, and where it would not go, Prue went in Michael's arms—into boats, ships, aeroplanes and helicopters, or into the sea on bathing expeditions. Whatever the circumstances, both of them coped with Prue's disability in a way which created universal admiration, and enhanced the affection so widely felt for them both.

In the later stages of his career Michael inevitably spent a number of years in Whitehall, and there are those who think he was not at his best in the corridors of power. That he was impatient with the endless intrigues of politics is certainly true, and some politicians found him intractable. But, others argue, wasn't that just what he *should* have been? In their view, the fact that politicians found him awkward to handle was yet another point—and a substantial one—in Michael's favour. Whatever his relations may have been with those above him, and he himself realised he was 'better loved downwards than upwards', there is no question of his achievements in the final years of his career for the Navy itself.

Michael's predecessor as First Sea Lord and Chief of Naval Staff, Sir Varyl Begg, had had the unenviable task of drastically reducing and re-shaping the Fleet. Begg knew as well as anyone that what the Navy needed then was a boost to its morale. He also knew that no one could better administer this than Michael. He was right. Within days the 'Le Fanu touch' had given the Navy a new confidence in itself and in the future. In fact, for all their regret at the passing of the daily 'tot', Michael Le Fanu is now remembered among Britain's sailors, not as the man who removed their rum, but as the leader who gave them back their spirit.

So here is *Dry Ginger*, a portrait created out of admiration for Michael Le Fanu and his wife—with a great deal of help from his family, friends and fellow sailors, whose generous assistance I gratefully acknowledge. It is dedicated to the memory of a man who delighted in the downfall of pomposity; one who, in the words of Robert Burns, demonstrated that whatever his circumstances in life 'a man 's a man for a' that'.

ONE

The Family Tree

The name Le Fanu (in case any reader is in doubt, it is pronounced Leffanyou, with the accent on the Leff) is of ancient and uncertain origin. One theory links it with the medieval Latin word 'fenutio', which carries the connotation 'red-headed', and it is naturally tempting, in the context of this book, to accept that explanation. Nothing much is known about the family before the sixteenth century, and the earliest recorded member was another Michael—Michel Le Fanu, who graduated in Arts at the University of Caen in Normandy in the year 1536.

He was, according to a contemporary, 'drawn by natural inclination to the study of poetry; but as he saw that this was of no use for the support of his family, and that the portion of a poet was meagre, since verses serve merely to amuse and not to nourish, he applied himself to the study of Civil Law and directed his ambitions towards the Bar'. This was a prudent decision in more ways than one, for Michel was a Huguenot—a Protestant—and the legal profession was one of the few callings he was allowed to follow as a member of what was, at that time, a persecuted sect. However, many people in Caen were of the same persuasion, so Michel flourished and his gift for words found expression in the French and Latin verses which he could improvise with great facility. 'Every subject, no matter how barren or futile,' it seems, 'was an opportunity to display the inexhaustible resources of his imagination.' For Michel Le Fanu, enlivening the routine of the courts of Caen *c.* 1560, read Michael Le Fanu four centuries later, spicing the reports of Whitehall committees with rhyming couplets—thereby ensuring that they were actually read.

Another Le Fanu characteristic came to the fore in Michel's only son Etienne, who developed a marked reputation for honesty, and was probably the first to use the family motto 'Dat Pretium Candor' which might be loosely translated as 'It Pays to be Honest'. It evidently paid Etienne, for in 1595 he was ennobled by Henri IV—a gesture symptomatic of changing times : three years later came the Edict of Nantes which promised toleration to all Protestants. For a time the Le Fanus of Caen prospered, until there came another wind of change under Louis XIV. Pressurised by the Catholic establishment, he decided to revoke the Edict of Nantes in 1685, and the Le Fanus, like many another Huguenot family, were driven to seek a livelihood elsewhere.

One of Etienne's great-grandsons, Charles de Cresserons, went to Holland. There he joined the army of William of Orange and subsequently fought at the Battle of the Boyne, a service rewarded by a pension of two shillings and sixpence (later raised to three shillings and sixpence, quite a reasonable sum in those days) on condition that de Cresserons settled in Ireland. When, eventually, he retired from a life of professional soldiering in 1710, Charles set up house in Dublin and lived there in prosperous style until his death in 1738. By that time he had been joined by a much younger cousin, Philippe Le Fanu, who had come over to London from Normandy as a young man. He and his brother Jacques were Charles's heirs, and Philippe—his children survived—became the founder of the Irish Le Fanus.

Philippe's son William greatly flourished as a banker and merchant : he acted as Dublin agent for many of the Huguenot settlers scattered over Ireland, in particular for the Huguenot linen-makers of Northern Ireland, and was given a grant by the Linen Board in 1749 for 'Manufacturing or causing to be manufactured 203 and 606 yards of coarse linen'. But perhaps more significantly for the future of the family he was appointed trustee for the actor, lecturer and playwright Tom Sheridan when, in 1764, debts incurred in various theatrical ventures in Dublin and London drove Sheridan to live for a time in France. This exile did not last, and Tom Sheridan was soon back in London assisting his famous younger son Richard Brinsley in the management of Drury Lane Theatre.

He also re-visited Dublin, where his elder son Charles was eventually to hold a government appointment, and Tom's two daughters, Alicia and Betsy, both of whom had literary talent, were leading members of a social circle devoted to the theatre. So were the Le Fanus. William bequeathed his financial interest in the Theatre Royal, Crow Street, to his son Joseph, and the family as a whole were much involved in the private theatricals so fashionable at the time. Little wonder, perhaps, that after the first Mrs Joseph Le Fanu died, Alicia Sheridan should become, on 11 October, 1781, Joseph's second wife.

A few years later, another link was forged with the Sheridan family when Alicia's younger sister Betsy married Joseph's brother Henry, a match which had to rely for support on the generosity of Richard Brinsley—support willingly enough offered but not always promptly provided. (Fortunately, Betsy had sisterly understanding. 'I am internally convinced,' she wrote, 'that Dick will keep his promise to me, but the hurry he lives in makes him often unconscious of the length of time that passes between his promise and performance.')

However it is through Alicia and her Joseph, solidly employed at the Dublin Custom House but with ample time to follow his other interests, that we pursue our narrative.

The only one of their three children to have a family himself was Thomas Philip, who, in 1826, was appointed Dean of Emly. Apart from his duties in the church, he was a scholar, musician, and a gifted amateur actor. Both of his two sons brought distinction to the name Le Fanu in the nineteenth century. Joseph Thomas Sheridan Le Fanu—or Sheridan Le Fanu, as he is generally known—was called to the Bar in 1839 but devoted his life to journalism and literature. His contemporaries knew him as a Dublin newspaper proprietor and a vigorous Conservative; now he is best remembered for ghost stories like *Uncle Silas* and *The House by the Churchyard*, each of them masterpieces in their own way, like the fine Irish ballad *Shamus O'Brien*.

We are told that Joseph's brother William recited *Shamus O'Brien* to great effect and that on one occasion it 'positively electrified an audience rather disposed to be languid and indifferent'. But it was neither with his histrionic talents, nor with his amusing book of memoirs, *Seventy Years of Irish Life*, that William Richard Le Fanu made his chief impact on Victorian Ireland. As a civil engineer he played a great part in the construction of Ireland's railway network and its drainage system, eventually becoming Commissioner of Public Works. He is also remembered as one who possessed the 'common touch'.

William and his wife Henrietta had a family of ten children, including eight boys, most of whom lived to be remarkable people. Collectively, they inspired the subject of this book to remark, when young, 'it's an awful sweat keeping the uncles well oiled!' Thomas, William's eldest son, followed his father as Commissioner of Public Works in Ireland; Fletcher was a cleric of High Church views who became Rector of St John's Sandymount and chaplain to a convent; Harry also entered the Church and ultimately became Archbishop of Perth and Anglican Primate of Australia; Victor, who was agent to Lord Meath and who never married, achieved seven rugby caps for Ireland and wrote good poetry; and Hugh, the youngest son, entered the Royal Navy at the age of twelve.

It was thanks to the Navy that, during a visit to Western Canada, Hugh met his wife Georgiana, a naval officer's daughter and a member of one of the few pre-Norman Conquest English families, the Kingscotes of Gloucestershire. They married in 1909—and in his marriage Hugh was indeed fortunate; Georgiana (that is how she spelt her name though it was pronounced 'Georgina') was an exceptional person with a heart so obviously made of gold that it earned her the family nickname 'D'or'.

However, luck was not on Hugh's side in the Navy. Somehow he never quite managed to be in the right place at the right time. Once, when coaling ship, a huge piece of coal fell on his head and put him out of action for six months. Later, and possibly due to this accident, he began to go deaf when quite a young man; Then, while the German Kaiser was returning home after a state visit and the Kaiserin noticed that an officer under Le Fanu's command was drunk—Le Fanu had to take the rap.

Quite apart from that incident, some said that in Hugh's case his native honesty had always been a touch too blunt to please their lordships of the Admiralty.

One way and another Commander Hugh Le Fanu had reason to think his chances of further advancement in the Navy were poor, so in 1913 he retired with the rank of Captain to become Chief Coastguard Officer for south-east Ireland, based at the Naval Centre in Kingstown, now Dun Laoghaire. By that time he had three children, Barbara, born in 1910, Peter, born in 1912, and Michael, who arrived at Haywards Heath in Sussex on 2 August, 1913, just in time for the family's move back to Ireland.

TWO

The Green Triangle Gang

In order to be near his office at Kingstown Harbour, Hugh took a house on Killiney Hill, just to the south of the town, and from there was able to free-wheel down on his bicycle every day to the Naval Centre. The duties of Harbourmaster were soon added to his coastguard responsibilities, and these grew greatly in scope when he had to set up a watch for German U-boats in the Irish Sea during the First World War. Those who worked with him respected the absolute integrity of the hard working 'Commander', as he continued to be known, and the energetic, no-nonsense way he would set off, when the day was over, to push his bike up the hill again.

For a child, it was an ideal place in which to grow up. From the house there was a superb view of coastline and sea, and, near at hand, the wild and beautiful Wicklow Mountains. Mrs Le Fanu believed in giving the children freedom to explore, and they used it to the full.

By the age of three, Michael could swim, and was competing with his brother Peter, just a year his senior and close to him in every way, in feats of daring. Together, as they grew older, they and their sister Barbara wandered the countryside—often accompanied by a large Airedale dog; they ran precariously along the parapet of the railway bridge, climbed cliffs and trees. Once Peter fell quite badly and Michael, feeling responsible, took him home, explaining calmly, 'he seems a bit dizzy'. Already this small red-headed, freckled lad with the bright eyes had a reputation for cheerful imperturbability. Everyone liked him, but that didn't keep him out of trouble. Outraged by something or other at the age of five he vehemently exclaimed 'What the juice...!'

and was reprimanded. 'Daddy says it' came the quick reply—and Daddy was heard to remark under his breath on this or some similar occasion : 'That boy will have to watch it—he's got too much push and go!'"

It was certainly too much when the boys decided to experiment with a new set of tools Peter had been given, and the pair of them managed to saw through a thick vine stem which grew along the front of the house, thinking it was an old log. But stupidities of that kind were few, for Michael was generally wary and clear-headed. At the age of about seven, he was walking very slowly with his Uncle Tom to the station to catch a train. 'Come along,' said his uncle, 'the train is due!'

'It's all right,' replied Michael, 'there's no hurry : the train will be signalled from two stations down the line.'

'Who told you that?'

'No one told me,' said the boy airily, 'I learnt it from experience!'

The Le Fanu children were lucky to have 'the uncles' near at hand. Uncle Tom's house, *Abington*, was at the seaside resort of Bray, only five miles away; unmarried Uncle Victor lived near by, at *Ballymorris*, with unmarried Aunts Emmy and Harley; and Uncle Fletcher, who had a protective feeling for Peter and Michael, was not far off either, in his Sandymount vicarage. If the presence of the uncles was to the children a source of treats and outings, their support was needed in more important ways by 'the Commander' and his wife, especially when Hugh retired from the Coastguard Service in 1920. His pension was nothing much on which to bring up what was now a family of four children : Anthony, the 'baby', had been born in 1918.

This was the time of 'the troubles' in Ireland : after the Dublin rising of 1916, the movement for Home Rule rapidly gained momentum. Hardly had the armistice been signed at the end of World War One than a General Election returned an Independent Parliament (Dail Eireann) to Dublin in December 1918, and after three further years of struggle, the Irish Free State came into being. The Le Fanus, like many well-born Protestant families, were firm supporters of the Home Rule movement, but that was not the only reason why, after the formation of the Irish Free State, Thomas Le Fanu was among the very few top civil servants invited to stay on. Clearly others recognised, as his nephew Michael did, that Uncle Tom was 'an incredibly wise man'.

Wisdom was certainly needed when it came to the problem of educating Barbara, Peter, Michael and Anthony. The answer was eventually found in the Harpur Trust, set up by a sixteenth-century Lord Mayor of London, Sir William Harpur. He endowed what was probably his own school in Bedford with land in London's Holborn, thus affording many hard-up parents the chance to give their children what amounted to a public school education for nothing. For the last century or so the Trust has run four schools, providing for girls as well as boys, and for the Le Fanus it offered an ideal solution. The fact that, in order to qualify for scholarship places, a family had to reside in Bedford was no great problem—to Bedford they must go.

Meanwhile, when the boys reached the age of eight, they could start at a local prep school in Bray called Aravon. There, Michael was thought of as 'small, studious and clever—above average but always ready for a lark. He had a good eye at conkers, and with his red hair and freckles was always full of merriment and zest.' The gaiety, though casual acquaintances might not have guessed it, was offset by a stubborn determination —displayed for example when Peter and he tried smoking. 'I didn't like it,' said Peter, 'so I threw my cigarette away. But Michael smoked his to the end.' He already possessed a precocious vocabulary: once, a companion spotted a lad from a rival school and remarked, 'That's the Castlepark cap, isn't it?' to which Michael firmly replied, 'I look upon that boy with the direst scorn'. Once, too, as they passed a brawling group of urchins, he remarked to his mother, 'What can one expect from these untutored country folk?'

Early in 1922, Hugh and D'or went to Bedford to look for a suitable home. First in Cornwall Road and later in Bradgate Road, they were to live in respectable, though hardly affluent, surroundings. Many of their neighbours had also come to Bedford for the schooling: it was an intelligent and congenial community. While their parents were house hunting, Peter and Michael stayed behind to finish the school year at Aravon, living for those few months at *Abington* with Uncle Tom.

In September 1922, about a month after his ninth birthday, Michael and his brother Peter entered Form Ii of the Preparatory School at Bedford, known as the 'Inky' (Incubator) under H. L. 'Minnow' David. Younger than the average age of the form, Michael progressed in the course of his first year from being twenty-seventh in term order to thirteenth, but during his five years at the school never attained any great distinction. 'His work is spoilt by untidiness,' said an early report—though the debates 'Minnow' organised in the prep school were said to have been completely dominated by Peter and Michael, blessed as they were with 'the gift of the gab, together with a generous measure of good humour, logic and blarney'.

In mathematics and physics, Michael was 'a fairly good worker' : in English he made 'good progress', but he needed to be 'more thorough in the preparation of History and Divinity'. Much ground was lost through illness, since both the boys had scarlet fever, but by the time Michael left the school for Dartmouth at Easter 1927 he had pulled himself up into the top ten—'an encouraging result' which 'showed a marked improvement'.

Recalling his Bedford schooldays in a speech many years later, Michael said that for him Bedford was populated always by godlike men, 'tall, athletic, virile, handsome and wearing enormous coloured scarves. I was a fugitive from a Georgian chain-gang. I was one of the submerged tenth, but unlike my contemporaries I never surfaced!'

The struggle to do better at school, however, was not allowed to interfere with what was in other ways a pleasant, even exciting, way of life in Bedford. There was much unknown territory to explore and new friends to be made. John Irving, whose family lived opposite the Le Fanus in Cornwall Road, vividly remembered his first encounter with young Michael. John was playing in the street, and Michael, leaning over the low wall in front of the Le Fanu house, hold out a small paper bag with the greeting : 'Hi, Curly, do you want a sweet?'

Swallowing his hurt pride at being addressed as 'Curly', John succumbed; and so began a firm alliance between the five young Irvings and the four young Le Fanus. They wandered in and out of each other's houses at will, eating their meals on whichever side of the road they happened to find themselves. At Christmas time they would all pore over the excitements of the Gamages catalogue, and as money would not run to large individual presents, essential things like meccano, train sets and air guns would be shared. Then there was the 'Green Triangle Gang'. Full members were Peter, Michael and John Irving, with 'baby' Anthony as messenger. An old bicycle shed at the bottom of the Le Fanu garden—with a triangle and Keep Out painted on the door in green paint—served as headquarters, and here the gang concealed loot captured on nocturnal raids into neighbouring gardens. Michael—or 'Micky' as he was called at this time— was adept at wriggling his small body through tiny holes in carefully loosened fences, and, with his 'diabolical cunning', was also expert at wriggling *out* of trouble if caught. Thirty years later he still remembered the gang's password.

The river Ouse was the great joy of summer life at Bedford. There were family picnics, boating in an assortment of canoes and coracles, and swimming. The children would disappear for long periods, causing no doubt some parental anxiety; but D'or always appeared unworried. The year after the family arrived in Bedford, young Anthony, aged five, went off alone on the river in a canoe and was missing for some hours : they found him eventually among thick reeds, tearful—but only because he couldn't free the boat. D'or was philosophical about such escapades—there was no fuss; though she did once complain when she found the boys were throwing her best pie-dish into the river as an object to dive for, and was perhaps unconvinced by their reassuring shout : 'Never mind, you'll get it back !'

For the older ones it was not too far to venture some twenty miles down the river to Godmanchester near Huntingdon, where a great friend of D'or's, Miss Tillard (regarded by the Le Fanus as an honorary aunt) lived in a house by the riverside; this was the scene of much fun and games on long summer days. There was camping on an island in the river, terrifying climbs on the flimsy roofs of boat-houses, and 'shooting the rapids' in canoes. On one canoeing trip, a future admiral was nearly lost for ever. His canoe capsized and although his companion bobbed up quickly enough, Micky stayed below. When he was eventually hauled to the surface, it was found that his pockets were weighed down with air-gun pellets. Walking along the parapet of the large main-road bridge over the river between Godmanchester and Huntingdon was a specially challenging exploit, but they accomplished it; and through this and similar adventures, acquired a self-reliant, fearless attitude to life.

'Cultivate Courage' was the great motto of Hugh Le Fanu, and one that lodged permanently in his son Michael's mind. Both of them had need of it—not least because they had to face fatal illness in their fifties; in fact they both died when they were fifty-seven.

For some time after the family's arrival in Bedford, visitors found Hugh an entertaining host and enjoyed his sardonic turn of wit. (Once, an ageing cousin expressed the view that everyone over the age of sixty should be put down. 'Darling Eva,' came the reply, 'how we should miss you!') Hugh could tell a good yarn about the old days in the Navy, and the children found him kind, if somewhat austere. But in the mid-twenties, the image of the vigorous retired naval captain began to fade. When people called, he would slip quietly out of the house to work on his allotment. He began to lose weight, though the increasingly thin contours of his face were concealed by the bushy red beard he decided to grow. This was a sign that, whatever was wrong, he had not lost his sense of fun, for he started it as a protest when his wife and a neighbour went and had their hair shingled in the latest style. But all was not well with him, and his health suffered a further sharp setback when he fell on a fishing trip and broke his leg. It was not this however which caused his death : he eventually died of cancer in 1929, after a very long decline.

If D'or had always been the pivot of the household, she was now entirely in charge, and it was fortunate that she was both capable and full of commonsense. She was a large person in every sense of the word, and ahead of her time in encouraging the children to be independent. Her clothes and huge hats were as casually untidy as her house, which although spartan in winter (D'or's north-facing bedroom window had never been known to be closed) had a door that was ever open to young and old. A cheerful voice calling 'step right in' welcomed friend or stranger to a blazing fire and an immediate offer of refreshment.

Though on the Kingscote side she was descended from an old English family, D'or lived as a child in Australia, on a large cattle station owned by her mother's family. This upbringing gave her an Australian accent and helped to explain her total lack of snobbery. When, much later in life, she became partially blind, D'or made a remark which summed up this side of her character. She had asked her doctor whether there was a class in the town for people who had lost their sight. 'There is,' he replied, 'but I don't think it's attended by the kind of people you'd like.'

'I like *everyone*,' replied D'or, quite truthfully.

Always cheerful, she loathed illness (though she nursed Hugh devotedly to the end, and when anyone was unwell could always be relied on to turn up with a basket of goodies); she also hated sanctimoniousness at tragic moments, of which she was to have more than her share. After a well-meaning friend had overloaded her with sympathy on one such occasion she was heard to remark : 'Oh, I get so bored with Mrs so-and-so when she puts on that *obituary* voice'.

D'or was sustained by a deep religious faith which prompted her to many unheralded good deeds, and she was greatly missed when she was no longer to be seen with her broad-brimmed hats bicycling around the streets of Bedford on her various errands. She was knocked off her bicycle when she was seventy and broke her leg. After it healed, she contented herself with walking everywhere, which she did at a great rate, and swaying from side to side with a sailor's roll, for upwards of another ten years.

But all this was in the future. Her immediate problem when Hugh died was how to cope with everything on a widow's pension of ninety-nine pounds per year. She managed it with generous help from Uncles Tom and Victor in Ireland, though she just couldn't resist an occasional 'flutter' on a likely horse—a weakness (if such it is), that Michael was to share in later years, and one of the many features of his mother's character which he inherited. However, when he had a win, he was not quite as liable as his mother was to give away the proceeds. For instance, when a great niece got married, D'or had been unable to afford a wedding present; but six months later she had a stroke of luck and sent them five pounds, with the strict injunction that it was to be spent on 'some sort of spree'. That was typical of D'or.

Naturally she did not burden the children with her problems and Michael retained happy memories of his young days in Bedford where the family, he later said, 'had a super time on damn-all'. Lack of funds did not curtail their activities, and on the unexpected arrival of some dividend from D'or's small invested income, the whole family would jaunt up to London by train to the theatre. Cultural outings unluckily did not settle the household bills, and eventually the family solicitor was forced to become treasurer and parcel out the dividends in methodical monthly sums.

During the Bedford days, there were happy Irish holidays with Uncle Tom or Uncle Victor during which Michael first developed his life-long passion for hill-walking; he made a point of conquering a fresh peak in the Wicklow Mountains every holiday. In Le Fanu style, even Hugh's illness was made light of, so far as this was possible. But below the surface his father's unhappy experiences made an indelible impression on Michael. By the time he was twelve, he had firmly decided that he wanted to be a sailor. In the spring of 1927, two years before his father died, he passed just adequately into Dartmouth 'on an assistance deal' (as Michael later described his scholarship) and said goodbye to Bedford school with the secret intention that his career should 'prove something about his Dad', who in his view had been 'seen off'. That determination, Michael once told a reporter, probably explained 'any slight ambition' he might have had.

THREE

'Them What's Keen . . .'

In November 1969, when he was First Sea Lord, Michael organised a reunion in HMS *President* on the River Thames for members of his term at Dartmouth—the Benbow term, May 1927–December 1930. In the *Who's Who* of the Benbows produced for the occasion, 'Le Fanu, M' was the only full Admiral listed; the chances against any of them reaching the top had been estimated at around three hundred and fifty to one, and the one who made it was not the most likely-looking of the new entry.

Small for his thirteen years and wearing an overcoat that was too big for him, Michael felt convinced, as he began the long trudge up the hill from Dartmouth Station, that 'he'd made a terrible mistake'. Nor were the staff at the college impressed. H. W. U. ('Jock') McCall, who was later Michael's Captain in the battleship *Howe* and became an Admiral himself, was the Benbows' first Term Officer, and, to quote his own words, 'I little thought, when walking round the Benbows for the first time and coming across, in the very middle of the rear rank, quite the smallest and most red-headed boy in the college, that I was sighting one who was to climb to the top rung.'

Michael, whose surname gave rise to some confusion, was quickly nicknamed 'Leffy'—further abbreviated to 'LeF'—by his term mates. Academically he made a moderate start, and soon acquired among the boys a reputation as 'one who would always speak out for what he believed to be right'. Not that he was in any way a prig; in the Benbow Term's Official List of Martyrs (Revised Edition March 1928), it is recorded that M. Le Fanu tied with five others for twenty-first position in the term, having received a total of six cuts for unspecified offences; this placed him about midway in the martyrdom stakes. As a sportsman Le Fanu was below average, which could have made life difficult in the sport-worshipping world of Dartmouth in those days, if he had had no other talents. Praised as 'a useful oar' on the river, he was only passable at cricket and distinguished neither on the football field nor in the boxing ring; however he put immense effort into his rugby and contemporaries long recalled 'the small red-headed figure fighting his way into the scrum like a terrier after a rat'.

But the rugger pitch was not, as we might say today, 'LeF's scene'. Nor was the Term Band, for which he was 'told off' to learn the trumpet. After weeks of conscientious toil he found he could play *A Room with a View*, but very slowly. He would start off in time with the other members of the band, but before long found he was ten bars behind—they had reached 'we'll bill and we'll coo' while he was still at 'no one to hurry us, no one to trouble us'. As the bandmaster wearily told Michael's Term Officer: 'That's Le Fanu, sir, he tries hard, but it's physically against him'—a phrase Michael was to store up and use in more than one speech—it always raised a laugh. No one, least of all Michael, could have foreseen how 'physically against him' things would turn out to be in the end.

Humour was one of his saving graces at Dartmouth. There's evidence of the developing Le Fanu touch in the pages of the *Benbow Journal*, admirably edited by Richard Chichester Beckwith who was killed in HMS *Prince of Wales* in 1941. There LeF appears chiefly as the author of poems about Dartmouth events, and characters such as 'Battleship Bill', a devotee of square-bashing, who inspired a satirical eulogy called *Hero Worship* with the refrain 'my hero, my cave man, my battleship Bill!' Then there were one or two essays in comic mystification —schoolboy echoes of the ghost-story writer Sheridan Le Fanu, his great uncle, but indicating, too, that Michael would always find it hard to be serious for long: 'I am alone, utterly: a soul apart. No ray of sunshine enters *my* life . . . there is only one way out. You ask me where am I? I am near to you, yet I am on a different plane. I am separated by a double door of darkness. Yes, you have guessed right . . . I am in the dark room.'

That kind of thing was enough to win him the Benbow Literary Exhibition (two shillings and sixpence) in 1929, along with the Benbow challenge medallion (a new 1929 penny). More important, Leffy's talent for words attracted the interest of George Barnes, later Sir George Barnes, distinguished in broadcasting and the academic world, who at that time taught English at Dartmouth. A civilising influence in what was then largely a philistine preserve, Barnes offered the boys Bach on his gramophone and introduced them to the English poets, Shakespeare above all. He certainly touched a responsive chord in Le Fanu who remained a great reader, particularly of poetry, all his life.

With the encouragement of George Barnes, Michael, in spite of the fact that he had not done too well in the 'thriller competition' Barnes organised in 1929, went to the top of the 'alpha' class in English. Did it look a trifle like favouritism? A termmate, Jerry Kirkby, was moved to put the following lines into George Barnes's mouth, as it were, in the *Benbow Journal*:

> *Ah, but here is my red-headed ruffian*
> *Whose story does not suit the case, the case;*
> *But he doesn't like thrillers either,*
> *So of course we must give him first place!*

And Le Fanu, not to be shamed, wrote two more verses:

> *Oh, young Le Fanu has come top of the class*
> *For Rose and North-Lewis he's managed to pass—*
> *To him marks ad lib will I willingly give*
> *Though his mind's like a whirlpool, his mem'ry a sieve.*

> *Though he spits and he coughs and he frantically splutters*
> *Though he sulks and he growls and he angrily stutters*
> *I will give him the best parts in all of the plays*
> *And he shall be top till the end of his days!*

With his Sheridan blood it was perhaps to be expected that 'Leffy' would serve on the theatrical committee and take a major share in the ambitious *Midnight Revue* staged in November 1929, in which, among other things, three different versions were given of *The Monkey's Paw* by W. W. Jacobs. Le Fanu played the wife. In that same year, he won the Harold Tennyson Memorial prize for poetry, established in memory of the poet's grandson who was lost in HMS *Queen Mary* during the First World War.

If Leffy showed special promise in the Arts, he did more than adequately on the science side too—his Engineering Officer considered him 'an outstanding boy'; and he was beginning to show promise as a leader, in the role of Cadet Captain. His report for December 1929 describes him as 'a splendid character whose powers of command and influence are increasing greatly' and a year later Le Fanu, M. passed out of Dartmouth second in his term. He went home for the Christmas holidays, and kissed a childhood girl friend during a game of 'Sardines' at a Christmas party at Godmanchester, but never thought seriously of marrying her. 'We have known each other far too long,' he wrote in precocious Noël Coward style, 'for a sudden infatuation'. On 6 January, 1931, at the age of seventeen and a half, he joined the training cruiser *Dorsetshire* as a Cadet and subsequently as a Midshipman.

In September of that year, *Dorsetshire* joined the Atlantic Fleet assembled at Invergordon in Scotland for autumn manoeuvres which never took place. Ramsay MacDonald's government had proposed cuts in naval pay and on 15 September, urged on by agitators ashore, large numbers of ratings refused to fall in for duty. By swiftly ordering the ships back to their home ports and promising to modify the pay cuts, the Admiralty narrowly averted the worst effects of this 'mutiny'. The whole episode made a deep impression on Le Fanu who had liberal sympathies and therefore well understood the sailors' case, but was horrified and alarmed at what could be achieved by a small group of trouble-makers. For all his humanity, he remained a firm disciplinarian throughout his career.

In the gunroom of *Dorsetshire* Leffy was regarded as an amusing and congenial messmate, and there were occasional glimpses of future distinction. While he was on attachment to the destroyer *Crusader* he made an impression on Ordinary Seaman Donald Brown, one of the first two Ordinary Seamen ever to be drafted to a destroyer. Hearing a deep authoritative voice call out an order from the bridge, Brown looked up and was surprised to see that it belonged to a young Midshipman. Nearly forty years later, Brown (then a Lieutenant Commander) wrote to congratulate Sir Michael on his appointment as Admiral of the Fleet and reminded him of the incident, saying that ever since that moment he had known Le Fanu would go far. The Admiral, in a characteristic letter of thanks, replied that the success of the Ordinary Seaman experiment in *Crusader* had been entirely due to the brilliance of Brown and friend, and that, incidentally, to get from Ordinary 'O.D.' to Lieutenant-Commander was really a more terrific achievement than to get from Midshipman to Admiral of the Fleet.

As a Midshipman, Le Fanu was in the doghouse no more than most, but few can have equalled his effort one day in 1932 when he was required to take off from a carrier on a training flight in the back seat of an aircraft. While the plane was revving up on the flight deck, he decided to test his parachute—just to make sure. The resulting tangle took half an hour to clear up and young Le Fanu had 'various unmentionable indignities' heaped upon him afterwards.

Fortunately, his early experiments in navigation were more successful: as he wrote to his girl friend in Huntingdonshire: 'There was a feeling of immense satisfaction and no little surprise when, after a week at sea, we sighted land precisely where and when I had predicted.' Just as well-calculated in its way was Michael's stunt at a river fête at Godmanchester that summer, when the accomplished young sailor stuck his punt pole into deep mud, and, allowing the punt to drift on, clung to the top in a 'perfect monkey act' for what seemed a very long time, before gently subsiding into the water.

After six months as a Midshipman in HMS *York* Michael came ashore in January 1934 to take Sub-Lieutenant's courses. He worked hard, and apparently took little part in the youthful pranks of his messmates during this time. If so, there was good reason for him to be quieter than usual, for in that year Michael suffered a second family tragedy. Since his father's death, he had spent as much time as he could at home with his mother; now his brother Peter, who had gone to work as an orange-grower in South Africa (where he came to hate the way Africans were treated) caught a tropical disease while on a camping trip to the Victoria Falls and died soon afterwards. Though the Le Fanus made a point of treating even death lightly, it was a terrible blow for Michael to lose (at the age of twenty-three) the person who had perhaps been closest to him. Work was the best antidote, and Michael emerged from the courses with five 'ones' in Seamanship, Navigation, Gunnery, Torpedo and his Greenwich studies.

In March 1935, he was appointed 'sub' of the destroyer *Whitshed* on the Mediterranean station. It was a time of war in Abyssinia, now Ethiopia, and the ship was involved in the evacuation of refugees. Their plight greatly moved the young Sub-Lieutenant, whose 'wonderful touch' both with them and the ship's company was just what was needed in the emergency. By way of relaxation there were runs ashore in the South of France. The greater part of the Mediterranean Fleet was sent home for the Review to celebrate the Jubilee of King George V and Queen Mary, and *Whitshed* with three other destroyers virtually had the Riviera to themselves : they made the most of their luck. 'It was a wild time, great junketings,' Michael admitted to his wife ten years later, 'and after three weeks of Nice and Cannes were we glad of the comparative quiet of San Raphael.' But in spite of all the fun and games, it was Michael who, when the 'sub' of another destroyer in the First Flotilla got desperately behind with his studies, found time to go across and work late into the night to help him through.

In July 1936, Michael took a crucial decision about his own professional future. The appointments department at the Admiralty noted 'wants (G)' on his personal record, and after spending a year as a watchkeeping officer in HMS *Bulldog*, where he was considered by his Captain to be 'unusually promising', he joined the Long Gunnery Course at HMS *Excellent* on Whale Island in Portsmouth Harbour, in September 1937.

As anyone who has served in the Royal Navy well knows, Gunnery specialists do more than fire guns. The science of their trade is extremely complex, but it is not their brains that bring them their peculiar notoriety : they also have a special responsibility for the ceremonial side of the Navy and for parade ground drill, which does not endear them as a matter of course to the ordinary matelot or young officer under training. In the old days, especially, they were credited with more than their fair share of 'bull', and bearing in mind the practice of putting officers into shiny black gaiters on parade, Lieutenant Le Fanu (as he now was) had probably got the Gunnery picture right when he described it as 'all gas and gaiters'.

However, it was the most commonly accepted way to advancement, so Gunnery it had to be, though Le Fanu hoped he could practise it with a difference. Not long after his arrival at Whale Island he claimed to have overheard an inspecting officer saying, 'Not bad that lot, except for the extraordinary chap with red hair. Can't think how they let him in here.' 'They' knew what they were doing, in fact, for his sharp brain enabled Le Fanu to absorb the difficult technicalities of Gunnery with ease, while superficially dedicated to proving that it need not be an entirely humourless affair, confined to 'them what's keen and gets fell in previous'.

This campaign was taken a step too far in a show produced by Michael at Whale Island in 1938 to which *Excellent*'s Captain, Arthur Palliser, had invited the newly promoted Captain Lord Louis Mountbatten. All went well until the last item which was put on by a motley crew from the 'Short Air Course' and portrayed the members of the course on the parade ground at 'Whaley'. When the 'Officer-in-Charge' failed to give the order to halt, off they marched into the wings or rather, as it were, into Portsmouth Harbour.

A few moments later they returned arrayed in seaweed, old tin cans and other nautical flotsam, with Sub-Lieutenant Hopking dressed only in a pair of kippers. The howls of applause which greeted this sight prompted the misguided aviator to tear off his kippers and lob them neatly into Captain Mountbatten's lap. The curtains were at once drawn, to a great ovation, leaving only the head of another aviator showing through. The head was that of another Sub-Lieutenant, Rupert Davies, who was subsequently to achieve stardom on stage and screen. On this occasion he merely announced: 'I would like you to know that all you have seen and so obviously enjoyed was written, produced and is the entire responsibility of Lieutenant Le Fanu.'

The incident, it seems, did not affect Michael's attitude to the Fleet Air Arm which he was to champion fervently in later years, though the immediate result for him (according to his own account) was stoppage of thirty days' leave—not that Lord Mountbatten had anything to do with it. Nor was this the last time his seniors recorded their 'displeasure' at some Le Fanu ploy—he was never over-respectful of authority. Indeed, while some of his friends feared that promotion would rob him of the infectious gaiety and friendliness which were so much part of him, others thought that his unorthodox ways might destroy his promotion prospects altogether. They need not have worried on either score.

For the most part, LeF's high spirits gave no offence. Invited in 1938 to visit the Morgan household at Soberton, inland from Portsmouth, he arrived on foot after a twelve-mile walk over Portsdown Hill and made a very good impression on Prudence, the younger daughter of the family. Although she thought him rather unconventional and was awed by his obvious cleverness, she found a ready response when she asked him to play ping-pong . . . and he made her laugh. The following year Prue, who had always been athletic, felt ill while playing tennis at school, and what she thought was 'flu turned out to be polio. Three years were to elapse before she was to enter Michael's life again—this time for good.

With the obvious approach of war, Michael had decided to banish from his mind a temporary leaning towards pacifism and nagging doubts about the usefulness of a Service life. If circumstances had been different, he might perhaps have turned away permanently from the hard world of Gunnery, as he did temporarily while preparing a lecture on drama which he was required to give to fellow members of the Long Course. Michael put an immense amount of effort into this. With the backstage advice of Molly Cochrane, a friend of his sister Barbara, he succeeded in achieving what he argued was the playwright's ultimate objective, 'to hold his audience in a grip of steel'.

This had to be a passing distraction. In the autumn of 1938 he joined the staff at the anti-aircraft range at Eastney, and by the spring of 1939, a few months before the outbreak of World War Two, he was acting as 'nurse' to a batch of retired Lieutenant-Commanders being put through a Short Gunnery Course in preparation for service in armed merchant cruisers. At the end of their three weeks, each of them was required to give a five-minute talk on some gunnery topic; and Lieutenant-Commander H. B. Baker never forgot how, after he'd struggled on for the allotted time on the subject of a fire-control instrument called the 'Dumarez', Michael put a kindly hand on his shoulder and congratulated him. 'Never,' he said, 'have I heard anyone talk so convincingly about a subject of which they obviously knew so little!'

On leave that summer, Michael had to shoulder a family responsibility. 'Baby' Anthony, now twenty-one years of age and six foot three and a half inches, had become engaged to Margaret Elizabeth Joyce of Woodfield Farm in the Bedfordshire village of Renhold. Margaret never forgot how she caught sight of Michael in the distance with his sister Barbara as they strode out from Bedford to give her the once-over . . . and the way she rushed home to receive them. It was the start of a close friendship —for Michael loved to go to Renhold when he could, and to find release from tension in working with the farm hands at Woodfield.

The spell of leave in the summer of '39 also included a holiday at Uncle Tom's house in Bray where he delighted a group of young second cousins by organising picnics and helping them to dam streams. They all adored him, no one more so than four-year-old Catherine Christie, his goddaughter. Then, early in July, it was off to sea again, to join the Mediterranean Fleet as Assistant to the Fleet Gunnery Officer. Michael's job—according to his boss Geoffrey—later Admiral Sir Geoffrey—Barnard was 'to show me how to shoot down airplanes, which I couldn't do myself'. In this task LeF proved 'extremely capable' and demonstrated that he was ready for his first major wartime appointment; in December 1939 he became Gunnery Officer of one of the legendary ships of World War Two, the light cruiser HMS *Aurora*.

FOUR

The Silver Phantom

The eighth ship in the Royal Navy to bear the name *Aurora*, a cruiser of 5,220 tons, had an armament of six six-inch guns and eight four-inch dual-purpose guns mainly used for anti-aircraft defence. Commissioned in November 1937, the ship had already acquired a good reputation for Gunnery when Lieutenant Le Fanu joined her. It was not long before that reputation was further improved. However, those first few months of the war, when the ship was at sea for long periods on patrol or convoy escort duties, brought no contact with the enemy for most of the ship's company, though some of them saw action in February 1940.

Aurora was undergoing a short refit at Rosyth when news was received that the *Altmark*, supply ship of the German pocket battleship *Graf Spee* which had been sunk off the coast of South America the previous December, was making for the Norwegian coast with some three hundred British prisoners on board. *Aurora* was called on to supply a boarding party for the destroyer force under Captain Philip Vian which was ultimately to board the *Altmark*, releasing all her prisoners. This courageous exploit, and the cry 'The Navy's here!' which went up as the British sailors swarmed aboard the German ship from the destroyer *Cossack* was to prove a great inspiration as the war went on.

Michael was not among the boarding party from *Aurora*, but he had already established himself as the ship's resident bard, and he was quick to commemorate the *Altmark* episode in a ditty sung to the tune *Riding down from Bangor* and performed with great gusto to a piano accompaniment provided by the Captain of Marines. Here are samples of the fourteen verses:

Said the Lords in Whitehall,
'Goodness! Here's a go!
Cor' Chase my Aunt Fanny
All round Scapa Flow
We've no boarding parties'.
Winston said, 'Don't fuss
Take them from Aurora
They're the boys for us'

Parker, Brownrigg, Noel
Dibben, Ellum, Hill,
Higson, Talbot, Curtis,
Off to make a kill,
Harper, Davies, Lawrence,
Tyrer, full of beans
Smith and lots of sailors
And some Royal Marines.

Then the gallant Cossack
In the dead of night
Followed up the Altmark
Searchlights shining bright.
Altmark *tried to ram her*
Did her level best
But too close beside her
Cossack *came to rest.*

Toast the British Navy
Toast the battle won;
Here's a word for Hitler,
Ere this song is done.
At the next encounter
He may get a shock
For the great Aurora
May be out of dock.

In April 1940, with no warning beyond a film evening in the German Embassy in Oslo to show what had happened to those who had defied the Nazi onslaught on Poland, Hitler invaded Norway. His army over-ran the south of the country, and the

German Navy attacked Norwegian ports. The British government decided that the invaders must at all costs be dislodged from Narvik, an important northern port, and a large part of the Home Fleet was committed to the attempt. It failed, but only after a fierce struggle. For the Navy, it was one of the toughest episodes of the war.

On 18 April, *Aurora* entered the fjord on which Narvik stands, not long after a force of five destroyers under Captain Warburton-Lee had left it, badly mauled after a long, courageous fight. For some seven weeks, steam was never off *Aurora*'s main engines, and in a series of hit-and-run raids, during which the ship was under constant air attack (the near-misses provided her with plenty of fresh cod for supper!) Le Fanu and his team used their guns to devastating effect on enemy transport convoys, pill boxes and a key railway bridge. This they succeeded in destroying—or so they thought—at the first attempt; but when they returned a day or two later, it had been repaired. So *Aurora* tried again with rather more spectacular results; this time an ammunition train passing over the bridge was hit, and exploded with a flaming roar.

With the main six-inch armament pounding away at targets ashore and the four-inch guns pumping away at attacking aircraft, *Aurora*'s Gunnery Officer, one would suppose, had enough to do. But it was during operations around Narvik that Leading Seaman P. A. White was 'passed out for Petty Officer' by Lieutenant Le Fanu on the cruiser's bridge. He would be taking White through some subject or other when the call came to man the guns; after the action was over they would return to the bridge with 'Guns' saying 'Now . . . where were we?'

Michael's calmness under fire was one of the qualities which rapidly made him into 'a bit of a hero figure among the ship's company'. Once, when the ship was very close inshore, the gun crew on the four-inch gun deck saw 'Guns' walking along the starboard waist when a bullet fired by a sniper ashore struck upper works just ahead of him and embedded itself in a piece of wood. Michael inspected it and removed it carefully with a penknife, complaining merely about the spoilt paintwork.

Even the bombardment had its lighter moments. On a hill

near Narvik, the Germans had erected a flagpole upon which fluttered the Nazi flag. This was a great source of irritation to the destroyers patrolling the entrance of the fjord, and they spent some considerable time trying to knock it down before finally giving up in disgust. Naturally this was a challenge to *Aurora*'s marksmanship. 'Do something about it,' said the Captain—L. H. K. Hamilton (according to *Aurora* folk-lore) 'and a bottle of whisky if you hit it!' LeF climbed to the ship's Gunnery Director, made various sighting adjustments using the right gun of 'A' turret and finally ordered 'Shoot!' A puff of snow as the shell landed—and no flagpole. *Aurora* men still remember the cheer that went up.

In fact, it was no tactical success, for next morning, after the brief arctic night, there were three new flagpoles up on the hill, but such good shooting had raised *Aurora*'s already high morale during this exhausting time of almost constant bombardment. Over and over again *Aurora* had to speed to the aid of the destroyers on submarine patrol outside the fjord, and eventually, early in May, she herself was hit. A bomb from a Heinkel 111 —one of a stick of several—ripped open 'B' turret 'like a sardine tin', and killed eight of the Royal Marines who manned it. Coming down to the wardroom from the Director, Michael looked a deeply shaken man. But, like the ship herself, he had to fight on, even though only smoke shells were left to be fired at the enemy bombers. It was indeed a weary *Aurora* that reached Portsmouth—her home port—on 15 May.

The three months it took to patch her up were far from idle for the Gunnery Officer—the damage was in 'his part of ship' and he wasn't the man to leave the dockyard 'mateys' just to get on with it. But there was time to get home to Bedford to see D'or. She was in her element, cycling round the town in her battered old raincoat collecting National Savings, and getting the ladies from the bridge club to lend a hand with the threshing on the farm out at Renhold. When the war came, she had decided to keep a pig in the garden at home, and filled the house with members of the BBC Symphony Orchestra, who had been evacuated to Bedford from London, among them the principal clarinettist, Frederick ('Jack') Thurston. When Michael went to a concert at Bedford Corn Exchange during his leave, it was Jack who got the orchestra to break off their tuning-up to play *A Life on the Ocean Wave* as he entered the hall. When he went back to sea, Michael was always eager for news of his mother, and grateful to those who kept him fed with information about her.

In the late summer of 1940, the threat of invasion was very real, and *Aurora*'s next job was on anti-invasion patrol down the east coast. With enemy reconnaissance aircraft constantly flying over, the job of the lookout assumed great importance. To encourage these lads, LeF originated the idea of giving them a chit to be exchanged for 'Nutty' (naval parlance for chocolate) for anyone who made a brilliant 'spot'; it is alleged that this so entered into the minds of the lookouts that one of them, sighting an aircraft low in the sky, shouted out, 'Bar of Nutty Up Two-O sir!' One very successful young lookout was Sam Scott, and the story goes that his messmates used to pull his leg about the vast quantities of chocolate he acquired; so one day Sam went to LeF and said, 'Sir, I am a man now, and I don't want any more nutty!' In due course the able Sam was rewarded in more dignified form, with a Mention in Despatches. But the 'bar of nutty' trick was to remain a permanent part of the Le Fanu repertoire; in later years many a senior officer or civil servant at the Ministry of Defence who had done a good piece of work was only too pleased to find a bar of fruit and nut plonked down on his desk.

In September 1940, while *Aurora* was based at Sheerness in Kent—a situation which gave her ship's company a grandstand view of the Battle of Britain—she acquired a new captain— W. G. ('Bill') Agnew, later Sir William Agnew. He lost no time in stepping up the pace of drills and practices on board in preparation for whatever might lie ahead; there was no time to rest on the laurels acquired in past achievements (*Aurora* had collected a number of honours for the Norwegian campaign, among them a Mention in Despatches for Lieutenant Le Fanu). Like other young lieutenants in the ship, such as C. H. S. Wise (with whom Michael is said to have shared a single No. 1 uniform), D. McEwan and G. F. C. Ellum, all of whom did well in their subsequent careers, Le Fanu was single-mindedly devoted to the efficiency of his department. In his case, so much so that

Arthur Green, *Aurora*'s padre, thought he would never find time to be fond of anything or anyone except his guns. He could show anyone in his department how to do their job : when the Ramming Number in one of the six-inch turrets was having difficulty in a drill, LeF came down and helped him to improve. In the autumn while the ship was carrying out northern patrols from Scapa Flow, Le Fanu chose to 'dip out' on leave to prove that he and his team could change the four-inch gun barrels without dockyard assistance—he was the first Gunnery Officer in the Navy to do so.

Not many, either, would have relaxed after such a feat, as Michael Le Fanu did, by inviting a group of Hostilities Only Ratings to drink a bottle of beer in his cabin and read *Hamlet* aloud. In similar style, on watch at sea, he would have long conversations with the Navigator's Yeoman, R. L. Holloway, DSM, who had brought Shakespeare and Omar Khayyám to the bridge to while away the long hours of the middle watch somewhere off Iceland.

Though he could be very much the severe Gunnery Officer and sometimes terrify the wits out of some of the younger lads on board at first, Michael showed in many ways his concern for other people's problems, whatever their rank. Realising the boredom of long watches in a gun turret while the ship was on patrol, he ran quizzes over the intercom system from the bridge; or in an effort to improve the elocution of those who had to communicate by voice, he would organise poetry reading competitions. And whatever the ship was doing, especially in action, he took care that someone was detailed to give a running commentary to those who had no view of what was happening. He organised with Sub-Lieutenant E. J. Offord (later awarded the DSC) a boxing tournament for the ship's twenty-five boys under training and provided 'nutty chits' for the winners, though as their Divisional Officer he took a very firm line with them. If their kit was not up to standard, he would order them to report to his cabin in the dog watches in, say, complete tropical rig and then tell them to report back in two minutes dressed for PT. If any were caught smoking—forbidden for them in those days—he would offer 'My punishment or Commander's Report' : most opted for the 'Le Fanu touch', which in this case consisted of the appropriate number of whacks where it hurt—but at least it was over quickly, as was the spell on top of 'A' turret in freezing temperatures which was the price of falling asleep on watch.

Neither at this period nor later did LeF often get really angry and when he did, it was apt to show itself in silence rather than a flood of words. In the *Aurora* days, just because it was expected of Gunnery Officers, he was known on occasion to fling his cap down on deck and jump on it in apparent rage—but he always took care it was his second-best.

After some months of routine patrols, *Aurora* joined the newly formed Force 'A', off Spitzbergen and Bear Island. At the beginning of August 1941, she was ordered to head east and carry out a daring raid on the shipping and oil storage tanks at Hammerfest in the extreme north of Norway. As the ship, wearing (according to Kenneth Smith, a Signalman at that time) the Nazi flag, neared the enemy coast, the Captain spoke on the tannoy to the ship's company. He told them their job was to go in and cause as much damage as possible until the ship was sunk: he doubted if any of them would survive the day.

'Guns' Le Fanu spoke next. It was, he said, the second of August, his twenty-eighth birthday: there was a squadron of dive bombers near Hammerfest, and he wanted at least twenty-eight of them shot down as a birthday present. No doubt the guns' crews would have done their utmost to 'lash him up', as the naval saying goes; but a shadowing Focke-Wulf got a clear picture of *Aurora's* intentions too soon, and the ship's orders were countermanded at the last moment.

After returning to Spitzbergen, where *Aurora* was involved in the evacuation of the Russian mining community and the Norwegian population in anticipation of the threat of a German invasion, Michael was put in charge of a working party ashore whose job was to remove all vital equipment from the Russian coal mines, and while engaged in this work he came across a large coloured photograph of Stalin which he took back to the ship and placed on the wardroom bulkhead in a position of honour next to a picture of Margot Fonteyn. This new acquisition was much admired, especially by Captain Agnew when he came down that evening for his glass of sherry. However, some officers, among them the Commander, would not have 'that man in our wardroom' and ordered its removal. Next evening, when the Captain came down, he looked all round the wardroom and asked, 'Where's Uncle Joe?' Michael explained that by request he had removed the photograph to his cabin. 'What utter nonsense,' said the Captain. 'Bring him back at once.' And there Uncle Joe was to remain, through *Aurora*'s toughest days.

Aurora had the job of transferring some of the Spitzbergen Russians to the ship which was to take them home, and Michael was impressed when he saw the Chaplain waving them each over the side with what he thought was the Russian word for 'Goodbye'. Unfortunately someone had been pulling his leg and taught him the Russian for 'I love you' which, according to Michael, surprised the Russians but seemed to please them too. Fortunately the British force was able to complete its work at Spitzbergen without enemy attack; for although it was stated on the BBC news that the operations were accomplished with 'unceasing protection by aircraft of the Fleet Air Arm', Michael and his friends knew very well that the only British aircraft present was a small shipborne amphibian Walrus, maximum speed 110 mph.

Early in September, *Aurora* with the cruiser *Nigeria* was sent to raid enemy shipping in another part of the Norwegian coast— Mageroy Sound. There was low cloud, mist and driving rain— ideal weather conditions in which to avoid spotting by aircraft, but awkward from a manoeuvring point of view, with *Aurora* following close astern of the flagship *Nigeria*.

Suddenly, at about 1 am on the morning of 7 September, ships loomed out of the mist to port and starboard of the squadron. The one to starboard was quickly identified as the cruiser *Bremse* which, after an exchange of broadsides, disappeared into the murk. To port there were seen to be two ships, a trawler followed by a large merchant ship. But there was no time to consider them, for, from the direction of *Bremse*'s disappearance there came a destroyer, heading straight for *Aurora* at full speed. Her wheel hard over, she just managed to cross the cruiser's bows, but then had to run the gauntlet of her port side guns. Hit by pom-poms and a salvo of four-inch, she turned, apparently preparing to fire torpedoes, and was caught by the six-inch from the after turret of *Aurora*.

One of the gunlayers, James Quinn, wrote to Michael when he became First Sea Lord and reminded him of that 'great night' —when the enemy was so close the guns were 'at three or four degrees of depression'. Both the German destroyer and the *Bremse*, which returned to the fray, were lost, as the German High Command later admitted. *Aurora* had come through a searching test with flying colours—a night action in poor visibility against more than one enemy. If her gunnery drill had not been impeccable, the result might have been very different.

Writing home to Bedford when the ship returned to harbour in mid-September, Michael was only allowed by the censor to say that he had 'just returned from a long excursion' and that he had had his first night's sleep out of his working clothes for a month. But in *Aurora* Michael was perhaps as happy as he was ever to be in his professional life : 'I hope we shall get a week or so clear of excursions but am dubious, as Service is the *Aurora*'s watchword and we get browned off for any odd jobs that are loafing. However I prefer to have a darned good reputation and plenty to do. I feel thoroughly overworked and underpaid but wouldn't change the job for anything.'

A much more sustained trial of strength was now in store for the ship. Desperately concerned about the plight of our army in North Africa and the need to stop Italian supplies crossing the Mediterranean to Libya, the Prime Minister, Winston Churchill, had written to the First Sea Lord asking him to 'consider the sending of a flotilla and if possible a cruiser or two to Malta as soon as possible'. In the early hours of 11 October, *Aurora*'s padre deciphered a signal ordering her to proceed from Scapa without delay, in company with her sister ship *Penelope*, to the Mediterranean; and at 0730, the two ships passed through the boom. A few days later, at Gibraltar, they picked up the destroyers *Lance* and *Lively* to complete the famous Force 'K'— created to cause maximum havoc among Mussolini's Africa-bound shipping.

Owing to the extreme vulnerability of Malta to air attack, no large units of the Fleet had been stationed there for some time, and the ships of Force 'K' were warmly welcomed as they steamed into Valletta Harbour. At that time there was something of a lull in the air bombardment, and the ships' companies were able to relax a little in a climate which was a very welcome change from the one they had endured on Arctic patrols. But for 'Big Bill Agnew', Senior Officer of the Force, and his Gunnery Officer, who was now also Squadron Gunnery Officer, this was a time of intensive planning. They knew they would be called upon to raid Italian convoys, and in conjunction with the other ships evolved a special fighting routine for the Force which laid down that the ships should remain as far as possible in line ahead, that they should give priority to the destruction of *escort* ships at every stage, and that only three signals should be made : 'Enemy in sight bearing . . .', 'Speed twenty knots' and *'Lively* to pick up survivors'. Having established this routine and practised it, the force then sat tight and waited for the sighting reports which would send them out in pursuit of the enemy.

It so happened in those first Malta weeks that alarms always seemed to occur on Saturday afternoons, just as the lads were contemplating a weekend run ashore. This earned them the title of 'Saturday night sailors' among the RAF on the island, who did not entirely regret the absence of competition at Saturday night dances. Nor had Force 'K' a great deal to show by way of consolation when they returned from the first two of their 'club runs', as they became known. So when a sighting report was received from an RAF Maryland in mid-afternoon on Saturday 8 November, no undue excitement was felt, merely some irritation at missing yet another Saturday night run ashore. But when the Force left harbour at 1730 and steered north-east at 28 knots, hopefully to make contact with an enemy convoy, this time they were bound for action.

All was peaceful until after midnight, though the ships had been at Night Action Stations since 2100; and *Aurora*'s Captain announced his intention of turning back if nothing had been seen by 0100. Suddenly at 0040 a lookout broke the tense silence : 'Bearing red three-oh, darkened vessels !' Steering almost due south, some seven miles distant, there were several large merchant ships escorted by four destroyers. Reducing to 20 knots, Captain Agnew led his force around the stern of the convoy in order to place the convoy up-moon and attack from its starboard quarter.

Seventeen tense minutes elapsed between the sighting and the firing of the first salvo at one of the escorting destroyers, but the approach of Force 'K' had either not been noticed or was ignored by the convoy and its escorts. At the moment fire was opened, another group of ships appeared, but although there was a possibility that these might have been eight-inch cruisers, *Aurora* continued to engage her first escort target (as planned) until it was clear the destroyer was no longer a threat. *Lance* and *Lively* concentrated on the new group of ships, which proved to be more merchant ships escorted by destroyers, and turned them away, while *Aurora* and *Penelope* continued to deal with the main body. Steaming up the starboard side of the convoy at a range of between two thousand and four thousand yards, they simply picked off the merchantmen one by one.

By six minutes past two there were no new targets left and Force 'K' headed back to Malta at 25 knots. They were attacked after dawn by torpedo-carrying aircraft, but reached Malta to a tumultuous welcome at 1305 on 9 November, with no damage or casualties. The 'Saturday night sailors' had proved their worth, and were congratulated on all sides, not least by the Prime Minister, who cabled the news to President Roosevelt, signing himself, as he loved to do, 'Former Naval Person'.

From a Gunnery point of view, it had clearly been a triumph : of seventeen targets engaged with *Aurora*'s six-inch guns, twelve were hit with the first broadside, and 'Bill' Agnew, in his report, singled out Lieutenant Michael Le Fanu for special mention. 'This officer', he wrote, 'is outstanding. His keenness, energy and organising ability have proved themselves again and again, not only in matters concerning HMS *Aurora* but in the gunnery efficiency of the Force as a whole. I consider that the success of the action was in large part due to him personally—I recommend Lieutenant Le Fanu for immediate promotion in addition to any decoration which may be bestowed on him'.

C-in-C Mediterranean, Admiral Cunningham, did not concur in the proposal that Le Fanu, and two other officers, should be promoted—but three months later Michael was awarded the Distinguished Service Cross. The ship herself earned a special nickname in the Italian Press. From her habit of materialising suddenly out of the mists of early dawn, she became known as 'The Silver Phantom'. The name stuck and provided the title for an excellent book about her, written by members of her ship's company.

Through November and into December 1941, the club runs continued, and even when they did not make contact with the enemy, Force 'K' had the desired effect, for news of its leaving Grand Harbour was sufficient to send convoys back into port, and for some while supplies to enemy land forces in North Africa were stopped.

Encouraged by this, the Admiralty sent a further two cruisers and two destroyers (Force 'B') to join Force 'K', and for a time all continued successfully. But on 17 December came news that a large enemy convoy was nearing North Africa and at 1815 that day, Force 'K', together with the destroyers *Kandahar* and *Havock* and the cruiser *Neptune* (whose Captain, as senior officer, assumed command) sailed to intercept it before it could reach Tripoli. This time luck ran out for Force 'K'. The ships, battling at high speed against a heavy sea, ran into an uncharted minefield. *Neptune* was lost, and *Kandahar*, *Penelope* and *Aurora* were badly damaged. With an eighteen degree list *Aurora* managed to stagger back to Malta, arriving just in time to experience her first German air raid: the Luftwaffe had returned in force to Sicily.

Aurora now found herself shored up in No. 5 dry dock in Malta Dockyard for three months, a sitting target for the enemy aircraft which raided the island almost incessantly: on 29 December there were no less than seventy-three alerts. As the dockyard workers took cover in their rock-cave air raid shelters each time an alert sounded, it seemed that *Aurora*'s repairs would be indefinitely protracted. However, it soon became clear that by no means all raids were aimed at the dockyard—often they were directed at airfields some four or five miles away. What was required was a more selective warning system and Michael was the prime mover in setting one up. He established an observation post at the top of the tower in the Governor's Palace at Valetta, manned by himself and another watch-keeping Lieutenant. From there, in the good visibility normally experienced in Malta, it was possible to see the raiding aircraft almost as soon as they took off from Siciliy; and when they were between twenty and thirty miles away it was apparent in which direction they were heading.

Only if they were making for the dockyard would a warning be sounded there; it gave everyone about five minutes to find shelter. Everyone, that is, except those required on board. Among these, the duty crews of the four-inch guns and the close range weapons put up a vigorous resistance to raiding aircraft, though at first the firing dislodged the big timber supports which held the ship upright, and special metal brackets had to be welded on the ship's side to hold them in place. If he was in the ship at the time, LeF would announce on receipt of a warning from the tower, 'Port (or Starboard) watch will go to routine repel aircraft positions in about five minutes, you lucky people!' And many were the bars of nutty which exchanged hands when the shooting was up to the mark.

Opportunities for a touch of Le Fanu initiative abounded in these circumstances.

During the blitz on Malta, sailors from *Aurora* on a 'run ashore' either had to catch the last dockyard launch which left Valletta at 2300 or face a three or four mile walk around the head of Marsa creek to reach the ship in her dry dock.

One night, Michael, together with the Captain's Secretary, Roy Quinton, and the Senior Engineer, Lieutenant Ellum, was among a party of some two hundred sailors who were on board the last launch when a Red Alert was sounded; the boat was halfway across Grand Harbour and the crew, obeying their instructions, at once made for the nearest cave shelter and dis-appeared inside, leaving their passengers in the launch.

After a minute or two, Michael decided to take charge. With Ellum to look after the engines and himself at the wheel, he set off all round French and Dockyard Creeks, dropping off sailors at their respective ships and finally came to *Aurora*'s dry dock, where the boat was secured and *Aurora*'s party turned in for the night.

When the 'all clear' sounded and the Maltese crew emerged to find no boat, there was a tremendous row and the Flag Officer, Malta ordered *Aurora*'s Captain to investigate and if necessary take disciplinary action. Agnew decided that a diplomatic 'logging' would suffice to smooth ruffled feelings and sent for his Secretary to type the time-honoured words : 'Had occasion this day to admonish Lieut. Le Fanu . . . etc.' A 'logging' can either be recorded and filed in a ship, or (if the case is serious enough) it can be forwarded to the Admiralty where it becomes a permanent black mark in an officer's record. On this occasion when Quinton took the logging to the Captain for signature together with a copy of King's Regulations and Admiralty Instructions to ask whether the logging was to be forwarded to the Admiralty, the Captain laughed and Quinton, for the first and only time, had the book literally thrown at him.

Partly through her own efforts in self defence, *Aurora* survived her Maltese ordeal. But one day in March, during a particularly savage and well-planned raid in which dive-bombers and JU 88's attacked the harbour simultaneously from all angles, two five-hundred pound bombs hit the side of *Aurora*'s dock, covering her with huge lumps of rock. The water rushed in before the final rivets had been fixed.

Divers managed to fill the holes temporarily with wooden wedges and bungs, bolts and rubber washers, and two days later, at dusk, the ship sailed, with a number of Merchant Navy passengers whose ships had been sunk.

At ten o'clock the following morning, as *Aurora* was clearing Cape Bon, a strong force of torpedo bombers appeared on either bow. Although it was considered revolutionary at the time, Michael decided to use the ship's main six-inch armament against the aircraft, employing time fuses; this was so effective that the bombers on the port bow were unable to attack as planned and the torpedo tracks from those on the starboard bow were safely combed.

On 5 April, *Aurora* reached the Mersey and a few days later Lieutenant Le Fanu left the ship. On his form S206, on which an officer's qualities are graded confidentially by his Captain on a scale from one to nine, Captain Agnew had awarded him 'nines' on every count, an almost unheard-of assessment. And this recognition of merit, which gave him an additional two years' seniority as a Lieutenant, set him on a course of spectacularly early promotions.

However, exhausted by his Malta experience, Michael's only idea at the moment was to get home for a spell of leave at Bedford. There he unwound by driving a tractor and working as a labourer on the Renhold farm—but first he took his bicycle with him on a train to Oxford, where Prudence Morgan was living in lodgings with her mother. There she could be near Professor Girdlestone who had treated her for two years in the Wingfield Morris Hospital after she had contracted polio in the summer of 1939. Ostensibly, Michael had come to bring news of Prue's brother David, also a Lieutenant in the Navy, who had been wounded in the destroyer *Lance* and was in hospital in Malta; but after seeing Prue, he stayed three days, and Mrs Morgan—who in due course was to play Granny 'Mor' to Mrs Le Fanu's Granny 'D'or'—thought it worth while, with her customary regard for the conventions, to tell their Headington landlady that Michael was 'a cousin'.

On this Oxford visit, Michael also saw again his young goddaughter Catherine. With her sister Jane, she was a little mystified by the new coloured ribbon which had appeared on her godfather's reefer—his DSC had been gazetted in February 1942—so Michael wrote a little verse to clarify matters.

> 'That ribbon on your manly breast,
> Its meaning please explain'.
> He said, 'It means Devoted Slave
> Of Catherine (and of Jane).'

FIVE

Scapa Services

After the rigours of life under bombardment in Malta, the prospect of comparative relaxation during a six months' appointment as Whale Island's Senior Instructor was a pleasant one to Michael.

He joined HMS *Excellent* on 1 June, 1942, his RNVR pupils being the first of the war to take a Long Gunnery Course. He encountered an *Aurora* shipmate almost immediately. Signalman Kenneth Smith was a newly appointed Sub-Lieutenant, and one evening took a shower before dinner. Out of the next cubicle marched Michael. 'My God, Smith,' he exclaimed, 'what are you doing here?' They were, of course, both stark naked, but Michael's power of instant recall was, as always, equal to the occasion.

His first encounter with the twelve young officers shows how he trained his powers of memory. He asked them all their surnames, then, pointing to each officer in turn, repeated his name, after which there was never a mistake when talking to any of them. The young Lieutenant-Commander with the DSC ribbon soon became popular with his victims, all of whom had been on Atlantic escort duty and were therefore intolerant of parade-ground formalities. Michael's irreverence in these matters matched their own, and he was thus able to reconcile them, in commonsense fashion, to the more tiresome aspects of life at 'Whaley'. He admitted to one of his students that when he had been on his own Long Gunnery Course just before the war, he had frequently attended the last parade of the day wearing civilian clothes under his uniform so as to make a quick dash away to town. Nevertheless, within this lighthearted framework, all his pupils were aware of the relentless standards of their teacher in guiding them to technical efficiency. In later years, Michael was astonished to hear that his pupils considered him 'a tiger—a nice tiger, but none the less a tiger'.

It was during this time that Michael was less concerned with dashing off to meet friends in London than with paying as many visits as possible to Meon Place at Soberton, where Rear-Admiral Vaughan Morgan and his family offered hospitality to a number of young officers. The attraction (though at the time the Morgans did not realise it) was that Prue had sufficiently recovered from polio to return home from Oxford. Indeed, she was a working girl, able to drive her converted Austin Seven to and from her new job as secretary to the Bishop of Portsmouth. Michael, meanwhile, had acquired a powerful scarlet motor-bicycle, which on one occasion conveniently transported D'or on the pillion seat from Havant to Soberton to meet Prue and her mother. On this journey, even the fearless D'or was somewhat apprehensive. They were careering along on a damp, autumn afternoon, when she shouted out, 'What speed are we doing, Michael?' The reply came back, 'Your age'. D'or was sixty-three.

The two future mothers-in-law now met for the first time. Despite the fact that their characters contrasted in almost every way, each had a profound respect, both then and thereafter, for the qualities of the other. Prue's mother, who had been brought up in her father's rigidly conventional London and Derbyshire households, enjoyed society life, rode to hounds, and, while still a young woman, had the responsibility of running her father's homes during the absence of her invalid mother. She was elegant, capable, loyal to tradition and formality and a generous hostess, though unaware of the awe she inspired in young people, with her standards of correctness and her downright, black-and-white views on life. In any argument, Prue's mother had only to say, 'But it's a medical fact!' to silence all further discussion.

Into this happy, though formal, atmosphere, Michael introduced his easy-going, warm-hearted mother, with her brusque, direct approach, her ready wit and the engaging Australian accent she retained from her childhood. It speaks eloquently of their mutual powers of adjustment and respect that two such contrasting characters, with little in common but their basic values, should have developed a loyal and friendly relationship.

This formal, 'true blue' household must have intrigued, but certainly did not awe a personality as extroverted as Michael's. Nevertheless, having on one occasion brought a copy of the *New Statesman* to Meon Place, even he shortly afterwards decided that it might be politic to remove it from the grand piano! Although Michael won her devotion, and very soon announced that he would like to call her Molly, he caused his future mother-in-law many an anxious moment at that time, not least on the occasion of Prue's twenty-first birthday party on 20 December, 1942. All obstacles of rationing and lack of petrol had been overcome by the capable Mrs Morgan. She had even acquired enough guests, and dinner at eight was anticipated with pleasure by the house guests as they awaited the arrival of several officers from Whale Island.

By 7.35 pm, the country bus had come and gone, and no door-bell rang. Consternation, and visions of a ruined dinner were only dispelled a quarter of an hour later, when Michael wandered in with his mates, having wheeled them in for a strengthening tot *en route* at the Falcon. However, his easy charm and lively wit were able to disarm even the most correct of hostesses, and nobody could be cross with him for long. His enjoyment of his visits to Meon Place was revealed by his one-word, acrostic tele-grams—one of them, after the birthday party, reading: 'Con-tentment—Costly Officers Now Tremulously Expecting Next Trip Meonwards, Eating Near Telephone'.

In January 1943, the 'visits Meonwards' ended for a time. With an outstanding report on his work as a Course Instructor, and the now customary recommendation for accelerated pro-motion, Michael left Whale Island for remote Scapa Flow in the Orkneys, base of the Home Fleet, where he was to be Assistant to the Fleet Gunnery Officer. Apart from being the Home Fleet Base, Scapa Flow was used at that time for 'working up' ships from destroyers upwards, and a highly complicated programme of training, including practice 'shoots' had to be laid on.

This 'appalling jigsaw' was Michael's responsibility, under the Fleet Gunnery Officer, who frankly admitted that he had never before done a staff job, and was only persuaded to accept it on being told that he would have a 'competent youngster' to do the difficult sums. Michael very soon injected an atmosphere of gaiety into the routine by producing a brochure for newcomers entitled 'Scapa Services. You ask for it, we supply it'. Between them, LeF and another Lieutenant-Commander, Bill Parry, were confident of coping with any crisis. The telephone rang constantly, and LeF would announce 'Scapa Services here', dealing with all the gunnery queries himself and passing on other requests, such as harbour routine or playing fields to 'our Mr Parry'.

Informal and unconventional though the style was, the organisation was formidably efficient, and only very infrequently did a ship enter harbour 'with the moan pennant close-up' determined to raise hell with the Commander-in-Chief over inadequate facilities. On these occasions, Michael would say, 'Shall I go and fix him, boss?' and act as trouble-shooter. An hour later, all was invariably well.

The late Admiral Sir David Gregory, who was on the Home Fleet staff at this time, was deeply impressed by Michael. He saw him as 'magnanimous, straight, witty, enormously effective in all that he did, beloved by everyone, kind, thoughtful of others, quick, gay. He had all the great and good attributes that a man should have, and in huge measure'. Among the good attributes of one born to command, decisiveness must rank high. This Michael certainly possessed. Soon after he joined the Home Fleet, the C-in-C, Sir John Tovey, was entertaining King George VI to dinner in the Flagship, HMS *King George V*. The King had met and spoken to many of the officers on board, and was dining in the Admiral's cabin, with a background of light music from the Royal Marine band, when suddenly there was a terrible commotion. A strapping Canadian RNVR officer who had not been introduced to the King, and as a result had forgotten his normally teetotal habits, was about to stagger into the Admiral's cabin and remedy the omission himself. One senior officer was seen to peer out of a cabin door and mutter 'disgraceful', but did nothing. Fortunately, Michael suddenly appeared, summed up the situation at once and got the man into a locked cabin with a Royal Marine sentry outside, before anyone had time to realise what had happened. 'Quite right, quite right', muttered the senior officer, withdrawing smartly into his quarters.

In May 1943, HMS *Duke of York* became Flagship of the Home Fleet and Admiral Sir Bruce Fraser was appointed C-in-C, a change of management which introduced Michael to the man he came to admire above all others. For his part, Admiral Fraser quickly came to appreciate Michael's qualities and potential, and from that time they became life-long friends.

During these months, a mild correspondence shuttled between Scapa Flow and Soberton, revealing facets of Michael's character to an intrigued and amused, though, as yet, heart-whole bishop's secretary. His energy was boundless, and when not manning 'Scapa Services', he would walk for miles over the barren moorlands, where the goal was usually a remote farmhouse which provided boxes of fresh eggs to take back to his friends. He was an enlivening companion, clearly, in the staff office or wardroom. But he did not then, nor in later life, suffer fools gladly. He wrote later on that year, in connection with mislaid mail : 'I wonder if you are like me in this respect—in the ordinary way I am reasonably tolerant about the annoyances of this life—I battle on with a modicum of *sang froid*, but just occasionally, there occurs some patently avoidable nuisance which really riles me. In these circumstances, though I keep my temper, I uncoil a fair section of genial sarcasm on the party who is knowingly and deliberately responsible.'

In July, Michael was granted two weeks' summer leave, and arrived on his motor-bike at Meon Place for a weekend, which circumstances were to extend by many days. He wrote later that it was during the previous September that he was aware of 'Eros's encircling movement, and I suppose a less peculiar suitor would have started batting strongly. But I think I preferred to be sure—and it wasn't until I went away in January that I realised there could be no doubt. All very unfair, as I gave myself about ten months, and then popped the question to an astonished spinster.' He had, during these months, considered the problems of marrying a disabled partner, and came to the conclusion that, in fact, there was no problem. This characteristic courage, determination and optimism never left him in future years. Meanwhile, for all his extroverted confidence and relaxed manner in any company, Michael was emotionally reserved to the point of shyness. His marriage masterplan was about to be launched, the one complication being that the accomplice in the masterplan was serenely unaware of the plot.

He appeared at Meon Place on a grey, wet Saturday afternoon, not conducive to courting on a country walk even in normal circumstances; add to this the ingredient of a young girl living in the isolated, wartime Meon Valley, tied at weekends to the house through lack of petrol, with music as her pleasure and hobby. Suddenly, this Brontë-like setting was lit up by the arrival of a casual, red-haired Irishman, breezing in full of gaiety and wit, who soon had his audience creased up with laughter as each Irish story grew taller than the last. That evening Prue and Michael sat together listening to gramophone records. As Michael recalled, 'With *Eine Kleine Nachtmusik* I decided to take the plunge there and then, risking all the complications arising from rushed fences.' Some time later, he rose and switched off Beethoven's *Seventh Symphony*, and, to Prue's astonishment, suggested that it would be a good idea to get married. Her reply was often to be quoted years afterwards: 'My dear Michael, I don't think I know you.'

Very opportunely for the pair of them, Prue's employer was laid low with shingles at the time, which resulted in 'few tasks outstanding' for the somewhat distrait secretary, so the next few lunch-breaks could happily last for several hours in the warm, July sunshine. Each day, the delighted housekeeper watched the young man disappear on his motor-bike in a cloud of dust down the bishop's drive.

Four days, and many hours of talk later, Meon Place heard of the engagement of Michael and Prue, and all the inhabitants, naval lodgers, relations and staff celebrated in peacetime fashion. No one was more amazed than Prue's normally shrewd mother, who had assumed that Michael's attentions were directed towards her elder daughter. 'For the first time in her life, your mother has been tricked,' was Michael's amused comment.

For the next five months, a copious correspondence flowed daily to and from Scapa Flow, revealing more aspects of Michael's character : his mental and physical energy, his sense of the ridiculous and derision of pomposity, his views on the Christian faith, which intellectual honesty, at that time, did not allow him to share with Prue. He tossed aside her fears that marriage to a disabled partner would impede his career. He christened her useless leg 'Ermyntrude' and asserted light-heartedly, 'This is the first time I've thought of Ermyntrude for ages, in fact since about 10 July—though, of course, I was conscious of her until 21 July. Yet I don't boggle at all—not in the very least. Extraordinary, because to the uninstructed she would seem formidable—the idea of young bridegroom wheeling blushing bride about in an armchair (semi bath variety) would seem queer or odd—yet in fact it is quite natural.' He also recalled his reactions at Oxford, during their first meeting after she became disabled : their visiting a hotel where steep steps leading to the dining-room proved an awkward hazard. With his usual calm, practical approach to problems, there was no personal embarrassment, only the thought, 'Poor old Prue, she is in a pickle.'

The wedding took place in Soberton Church on 18 December, 1943, after Michael's arrival from Scapa only two days earlier. Rosemary Minnis, one of the Wrens in the choir, was deeply moved as Prue came up the aisle with her father, looking very lovely but, of course, supporting herself on elbow crutches. 'When her bridegroom joined her, she handed her crutches to her bridesmaid, and the bridegroom supported her all through the service.' Similar help would always be necessary in the years ahead, but in all other ways the mutual encouragement and support was finely balanced during twenty-seven years of an exceptionally happy marriage. Entirely without self-pity, Prue was on her wedding day, as Michael remembered later, 'confident, gay, beautiful, serene—a real shining light'; and so it was to be in the future, 'top of the Eiffel Tower one day, launching a ship the next', driving a car, running a house, bringing up three children.

After the reception for a hundred guests, when Mrs Morgan's resourcefulness and D'or's convenient friendship with the family of the Dewar distillers brought a plentiful oasis in the dry boredom of wartime rationing, they rattled off to the Anchor Hotel at Liphook in the old Austin Seven. It was here, on Boxing Day, that through the radio came the riveting news of the sinking of the German battleship *Scharnhorst* by units of the Home Fleet, led by Admiral Sir Bruce Fraser in HMS *Duke of York* (his subsequent title, Lord Fraser of North Cape, commemorated this action).

Michael had missed it all, and his ill-concealed disappointment was more than apparent to his apologetic bride. His fellow 'office boy' Bill Parry was left behind, too, minding the shop at Scapa during Michael's absence on leave. When they both finally returned to *Duke of York*, they were presented with cardboard medals adorned on one side with a picture of a rat in full flight and on the other with the words 'Shipmates ashore Dec. 26 1943'. The ribbon was made of yellow bunting and on it, instead of the oak leaves symbolising 'Mention in Despatches', there was a little white feather. It was the only dud medal that Michael ever received.

SIX

HMS *Howe*

Towards the end of that same year, 1943, the Navy's newest battleship, HMS *Howe*, had been taken in hand at Devonport Dockyard for alterations to her anti-aircraft armament and radar and for modifications to make her more habitable in hot climates. The great ship—forty-five thousand tons, with ten fourteen-inch guns, sixteen 5.25's and large numbers of close-range weapons, was destined for service in the Far East.

Scarcely had Michael returned north to 'Scapa Services' before he was on his way south again—appointed, at the age of thirty, Gunnery Officer of a First Line Battleship —the newest and most advanced in the Fleet. Quite apart from having to master a vast amount of equipment of unparalleled complexity, he would have to weld into a fighting team large numbers of RNVR officers and 'Hostilities Only' ratings, all of them relatively new to the ways of the Navy, let alone to the workings of a battleship. The appointment was of course an honour, but Michael had little time to think about that; besides, while *Howe* was in Devonport, Prue and he could live together ashore, first in 'digs' in Plymouth and later as paying guests at Yelverton on the edge of Dartmoor.

Michael had a few weeks to familiarise himself with the mysteries of *Howe* and to supervise the gunnery improvements before the arrival of his new commanding officer, Captain (later Admiral Sir) Henry McCall. Soon after joining the ship, the Captain went into the wardroom, where he was somewhat taken aback by the red-haired Lieutenant-Commander who was the first to greet him. 'I was a member of Benbow term in 1927, sir, and you were our Term Officer.'

'Good heavens,' replied the Captain, 'are you Michael Le Fanu, our Gunnery Officer?' Memories returned of the little lad in the rear rank of the seventy-strong Benbows, 'quite the smallest and quite the most red-headed boy in the whole of Dartmouth'.

And the memory perhaps flashed again across the Captain's mind a few days later. He had invited Michael and Prue to dinner with him in the Admiral's Quarters where he was living. These were situated down a long flight of stairs from the quarter-deck, and *Howe*'s quarterdeck was many steep steps below the rim of the dry-dock in which the ship was accommodated at that time. After the Captain and Michael had met their respective wives in pitch darkness on the dock-edge, where they arrived in a baby Austin driven by Prue, the Captain was astonished to see Michael pick Prue up bodily and carry her without pausing, down all those awkward steps, depositing her in a chair in the Admiral's day-cabin. It was quite a feat, even for a strong man.

Despite his lively, buoyant manner, Michael at this time suffered another personal tragedy. On 3 March, 1944 his youngest brother, Anthony, his junior by five years, and a Sergeant in the Army (he had refused a commission) was killed at Anzio during the invasion of Italy. Michael had long been something of a father to him, as he was to prove henceforth to his two sons; and Anthony's death brought great grief in Bedford—to his wife of three years, Margaret, and to his mother. Much as D'or disliked those who adopted 'an obituary voice' when speaking to her of Anthony and although she discussed the subject of death with apparent nonchalance, she readily accepted an invitation from Michael and Prue to join them in the West Country; and a few weeks after Michael sailed, she invited Prue to stay with her at Bedford for fourteen days.

Prue remained for eighteen months. She found the house in Bradgate Road attractively casual and unconventional; open-hearted herself, she was in tune with D'or's expansive hospitality, summed up in the invitation to 'come right in' offered to anyone who appeared at the door. There, Prue's taste for music was well nourished, for with Frederick Thurston, and announcer Peter Fettes among the people billeted on D'or, tickets to BBC concerts in the Corn Exchange were readily available. Life in Bedford held many other interests too : D'or could help Prue obey Michael's parting injunction to learn bridge (a game he played very well); and there were highly enjoyable visits to the races at Newmarket, where D'or usually managed to win, after a careful inspection of the horses in the paddock, 'pince-nez' on nose.

But war-work at the Central Savings Office in Bedford occupied much of Prue's time, while D'or was engaged, perhaps, on her 'egg round'—which involved collecting some ten dozen eggs a week from the countryside. These D'or had undertaken to deliver to neighbours week by week, ostensibly for cash, although her generosity resulted in a constant deficit in the final reckoning. This was remedied by recourse to an old copper-lustre jug engraved 'Jane Amlett', one of a row hanging on the Welsh dresser and which contained convenient cash to square the egg account or befriend any rogue who called at the door with a hard-luck story. Whatever she may have lost personally on the eggs, the nation benefited from D'or's financial efforts in another direction, for she collected National Savings at a faster rate than anyone else in Bedford. For Michael it was a great relief to know that D'or and Prue were together and thus happily employed. Constantly busy though he was in *Howe*, the arrival of a letter from Bedford was the greatest joy of his life.

Howe left Plymouth early in May 1944 for six weeks' intensive working-up at Scapa Flow, which gave Michael the chance of testing as a customer the 'Scapa Services' organisation he himself had put into shape. *Howe*'s own gunnery organisation was already in good order, and he was delighted to have as his 'second "G" ' Lieutenant (later Admiral Sir Andrew) Lewis. They had first met at Michael's wedding, where Andrew had been an usher, and their work together in *Howe* rapidly confirmed Michael's good opinion of this 'superb citizen' who 'kept him up to his work' and was 'a tower of strength'. But the inspiration came from Michael. Everyone from the Captain down was aware of the 'electric current running through him'—and he commanded instant attention from every occupant of the Gunnery Office whenever, as a prelude to outlining future gunnery tactics, or criticising some aspect of past performance, he banged loudly on his desk with a paperweight and declared in ringing tones, 'Gentlemen, I have a statement to make!'

After about a month at Scapa, the day came for *Howe*'s first long-range battle practice, with the target for the fourteen-inch guns practically out of sight. It was a tense moment for Michael, but as he stood on the upper bridge with the Captain, he appeared to radiate confidence; a confidence well founded—for when the ship returned to harbour, Captain McCall went to call on the C-in-C, Sir Bruce Fraser, and had the satisfaction of hearing the Admiral's Flag Captain (who had witnessed the shoot) say to the Admiral: 'I hope that we never sail again to meet the enemy without having *Howe* with us.'

This was good though not surprising news for Admiral Fraser, who had already marked *Howe*'s young Gunnery Officer for stardom and had determined that Le Fanu should play a part in the Royal Navy's return under Fraser's command to the Far East. As for Michael himself, he made an encouraging 'statement' about the shoot to Lieutenant R. B. Meston, who was responsible for the accuracy of the fourteen-inch guns and what is more, remembered every detail of their performance at a *Howe* reunion more than twenty years later.

In mid-June, with no time allowed for foreign service leave, *Howe* left Scapa en route for the Eastern Fleet's base at Trincomalee in Ceylon (now Sri Lanka) via Algiers, Port Said, Suez, Aden and Colombo. The censor allowed Michael to tell Prue in one of his many closely-typed air-letters that it was 'ever so hot (can you have possibly guessed this dark secret?)'—a problem for Michael, whose complexion never would stand up to exposure to the sun. 'Roughly speaking,' he wrote, 'the sun stinks!' A sad state of affairs which drove him, when working on deck, to wear a long-sleeved shirt, stockings rolled up over the knees, a hand-kerchief round his neck and 'dark goggles too—I need only a Solar Bowler to look quite the bearer of the w. man's burden!' But it was pleasantly cool in 'Seaview Villas' (Michael's name for the Gunnery Office, newly moved to the upper deck) and there were congenially cool visions of the Russian landscape to be gleaned in Dostoevsky's *The Idiot* which Michael was reading over breakfast and tea, having previously devoured all of Tolstoy.

LeF's literary interests expressed themselves in a flow of quotations from Shakespeare and other authors whose lines added unusual interest to the 'Remarks on Gunnery' which he produced under the title *Steam and Shoot*. He was often congratulated on the aptness of the words chosen—congratulations which sometimes raised a private smile in M. Le Fanu, for he was not above tampering with the words of the Immortal Bard to suit his purposes, or putting a new saying into the mouth of Dr Johnson. One such effort was thought particularly fitting after an aeroplane's wireless had failed during a gunnery practice : 'No, sir; to say that the art of flight would be a man's highest felicity is to postulate an absurdity. For though he may soar like a bird, yet if he cannot communicate with his fellows he is no better than a poet without the power of calligraphy.' One genuine quotation which specially pleased Michael himself came from Walt Whitman—it seemed relevant both to *Howe*'s fourteen-inch broadside and to the notorious noisiness of Gunnery Officers : 'I sound my barbaric yawp over the roofs of the world.'

LeF had an attitude verging on the Puritan towards distractions from the work in hand—though it did not detract a scrap from his popularity. His tendency to thwart 'Jack's' interest in preparing his 'tiddly' uniform for the next run ashore by mounting another gunnery practice was referred thus in a biblical-style narrative of *Howe*'s voyage : 'Then false prophets arose in the land which knew not the great God Tiddly, and drew many after them, and their names are known to this day. And their names are Steam and Shoot and Lefanoo. And Lefanoo was armed with a Sharp Dagger, and he wielded mighty weapons of thunder and lightning.'

A shrewd parody of Michael's 'Remarks on Gunnery' was produced by the Chaplain, the Rev. W. G. Sandey, after 'Lefanoo' had left the ship. 'It is not my habit to rush into print,' ran the introductory paragraph, 'but here are some bromides on the shoot yesterday. "We get tired of Cliches, but call the same things bromides and we get away with it" (Bernard Shaw). "Utter the same inanity often enough and it becomes something very wise" (Thomas Aquinas). Now we've got our usual quotations in, let's get a clue on the Gunnery . . . *Fourteen-inch* : as good as I have seen from any ship, and I have had a long experience of examining results. The very first salvo was a pippin. There's no other word for it. I've sent across a photo of this (touched up on board) to the C-in-C—"Ceteris pariter, sed non se advertunt" (Ovid). In other words, other gunnery officers are as good as I am, but it pays to advertise.'

Michael's authentic style was revealed at its best in an exchange between *Howe* and the aircraft carrier *Indomitable*, which occurred while both ships were in harbour at Trincomalee. It began with the accidental discharge during maintenance of live rounds from one of *Indomitable*'s pom-poms. They sped, alas, towards *Howe*, followed immediately by a signal which read, 'Regret two rounds of pom-pom fired in error in direction of *Howe* during test at 1510 today', and shortly afterwards by *Indomitable*'s Gunnery Officer, T. J. MacFarlan, who had come to discover if any damage or casualties had been caused. It was with some relief that he learned the only damage had been to the 'Medical Guard' flag being flown by *Howe* at the time of the incident—though, as a Scotsman, MacFarlan was abashed to think he had been responsible for shooting down a flag which bears the cross of St Andrew. But hostilities were not yet over.

That evening, the tattered St Andrew's flag arrived on board *Indomitable* addressed to MacFarlan and accompanied by the following poem:

Dear Mac,

> *Your marksmanship has made*
> *Us enviously sigh.*
> *But could you, when you fire again,*
> *Please aim a little high?*
> *We do not mind the sudden crash,*
> *The showers of shot and shell—*
> *Our months at Scapa Flow have taught*
> *Us all that war is hell.*
>
> *But look! the tattered rag enclosed*
> *Is all that's left to see*
> *Of what was once a banner proud—*
> *The Flag of M.D.G.*

(*Above*): D'or in Bedford

(*Centre*): Michael's father with
Anthony

(*Below*): 'Quite the smallest and most
redheaded boy in the whole of
Dartmouth'

Midshipman Le Fanu

(*Above*): Michael's Training Cruiser
Dorsetshire

1 May 1934: Michael was promoted to
sub-lieutenant on HMS *Whitshed*

HMS *Excellent:* according to Michael,
'all gas and gaiters'

(*Opposite*): Three ships of Force 'K':
Aurora, Penelope, and *Lance*

1 June 1942: Lieutenant-Commander
Le Fanu. 'Them what's keen and gets
fell in previous'

(*Above*): Meon Place, from the terrace.   Soberton Church, 18 December 1943

(*Above*): HMS *Howe*: in 1943, at the age of 30, Michael was appointed her Gunnery Officer

USS *Indianapolis*: Michael joined he British Pacific Fleet Liaison Office January, 1945

An Andrew's cross (et tu, Mac F!)
Beneath whose blue and white
Ten Thousand medicos have kept
Their watch by day and night—
Pray keep it as a souvenir
Of your efficient flak.
(N.B. A Yeoman bids me add
'We want a new one back'.)

Enough, Whale Island's proud of you,
And so am I, Mac F;
But choose another target ship
Another time,
> *Yours,*
> *LeF.*

For several days *Indomitable* was left to lick her wounds, but then came what she thought was a chance to retaliate. *Indomitable* signalled to *Howe* : 'One of my aircraft-handling party was struck painlessly on the buttock by a fragment of shell during Serial 5. Suggest this cancels my pom-pom assault.' But LeF was more than equal to that one. A few minutes later *Howe*'s reply read : 'Your 0950. I am astonished as I am sorry, my line of fire being 120 degrees from you. Please convey my regrets to the rating and ask him to turn the other cheek.'

It seems it was always thus in those *Howe* days, whether it was a case of organising the crossing the line ceremony or the ship's broadcasting service, a job he accomplished, or so he wrote to Prue, 'by means of 95% decentralisation (the way I run my "G" work as much as is possible) and the rest commonsense and boloney'. He was perfectly well aware that he could talk the ship's four Commanders (Executive, Engineer, Paymaster and Principal Medical Officer) into doing what he wanted by playing the 'deferential young gunnery officer', and bringing into play what LeF described as his 'main, if not only, good point—my ability to "sell" the stuff'. Captain McCall regarded Michael's many talents as a great boon to the ship, particularly during the four-month period *Howe* had to spend in the heat of Trincomalee from August to November 1944 while decisions were

65

taken at a level far above Gunnery Officers and even battleship Captains about the future course of the war, and about the Royal Navy's part in it.

On 22 August, a fortnight after *Howe* reached Trincomalee, Admiral Sir Bruce Fraser became C-in-C Eastern Fleet, and took an early opportunity to meet *Howe*'s officers. Michael 'retired rather to a corner, not wanting to steal any thunder and having seen plenty of Bruce in the past—however I was lugged out and had a long conversation with the old man'. What the censor did not allow Michael to reveal in his letters home was anything Fraser may have told him about the ultimate purpose of this great buildup of ships in Eastern waters.

Since the tragic loss of Force Z—the battleships *Prince of Wales* and *Repulse*—in the South China sea in December 1941, almost three years had elapsed since any major British units had operated east of Singapore. During those three years the Navy's resources had been more than fully stretched in other theatres of war. But now it was possible to think of sending a British fleet into action in the Pacific against the Japanese alongside the Americans who had borne (with the significant but small-scale aid of the Australian and New Zealand Navies) the entire brunt of the war at sea in the Pacific. The British government considered it politically vital that the Royal Navy should be in at the kill in the Japanese war in some force, particularly as so many former British territories were involved.

As John Winton relates in his book *The Forgotten Fleet*, there were many Americans in high places who did not share this view, and for much of 1944 there was considerable doubt as to the role a British Fleet might play in the Pacific—if indeed it would be required at all. However in September 1944, at the second Quebec conference, Winston Churchill offered the British Fleet to President Roosevelt—and 'no sooner was it offered than accepted'. Huge problems remained, not least that of supplying the Fleet over colossal distances—but the commitment had been made, and by VJ Day in August 1945 the British Pacific Fleet was to consist of more than six hundred ships and upwards of a quarter of a million men.

On 22 November, 1944, Sir Bruce Fraser hoisted his Flag in

Howe as C-in-C BPF, and soon afterwards the ship sailed for Sydney, where he was to set up his headquarters.

As Andrew Lewis recalled, the move came as a great relief for everyone after 'those trying and inactive months in temperatures consistently over 90 degrees—when the ship's company slept on deck to escape the intolerable heat of a steel box with no air-conditioning'. No longer would Michael have to type his letters home sitting in his cabin with 'a pillow over his chair to make the typing easier and nothing on except a small towel draped tastefully across the lap and a wrist-watch'. But there were con-solations in Ceylon: a pleasant spell of leave in the hills, for instance—the preparations for which taxed Michael considerably, or so he claimed. 'When it comes to organising one or two simple things affecting the private life of M Le F, not only do I get a sort of woolly feeling in the head but I make a far worse job of it than I do of organising the complete lives of one thousand officers and men.'

Michael realised, too, that there was the chance of an early promotion to look forward to, though if it did not come through, he had firmly decided that 'My dear wife will become my pro-fession and the Navy a mere sideline necessary to bring in spondulicks until retiring age is reached'. Not that there was much chance of that happening, as Michael well knew—and success mattered to him, as he honestly admitted. 'I suppose,' he wrote, 'that if someone sacked me from this steamer and told me to go back to a shore job in England I would be as sick as mud and the re-union would have a taste of ashes.'

In the last weeks of December Michael found himself vividly re-living the sensations of twelve months before—'the expectation of leave—the travel south—the meeting—the wedding', but could not linger over letters home once the ship had arrived in Australian waters and all the young officers found themselves fêted on all sides, as the Australians gave an overwhelming wel-come to the British Fleet.

Michael made the most of Australia together with his sociable friend Andrew Lewis. He gave a tremendously successful chil-dren's party on board ('I am now persona grata in a dozen ex-pensive homes!'), and there were visits to the races, cocktail parties, dinner parties, endless hospitality. Yet on Christmas Day he wrote two long air-letters to Prue—'all the time I am thinking how much *you* would enjoy the party, so you see I am only receiving these citizens Strength One, poor dears. Dash your whiskerettos, you villain of the day, why can't you be by my side at this moment?' And for professional reasons too, Michael soon grew tired of the social round—the ship's company were having a well-deserved ball, but he knew it would be bad for all concerned if it went on too long.

However, when on 1 January, 1945 Michael's vastly accelerated promotion to Commander came through, he himself gave a champagne party for a hundred and twenty people ('in the highest traditions of the "G" of this concern') and the whole round of parties started again. But by mid-January, the 'Battle of Sydney' was over; Michael knew he was to leave the ship for a new, vitally important job 'which is quite tricky and quite foreign to my talents and training' and was feeling very sad about moving on. 'It is hateful to leave a job which you like and in which you are well liked.' That 'Guns' really *was* well liked was made abundantly clear when the time came for him to leave the ship, as R. B. Meston vividly recalled :

'It was in the Philippine Islands, Leyte Gulf, in January 1945. The time—just before 2100, when the Captain broadcast to the ship's company that Commander Le Fanu would be leaving the ship at 2100. Throughout the darkened ship, men moved aft slowly but surely, carrying with them such utensils as pots, pans and mess kettles; some with drums, others with bugles, until by 2100, the gangway was blotted out by scores of men wishing to bid him farewell; Commander Le Fanu was about to join the American Flagship as Liaison Officer for the British Pacific Fleet. After saying goodbye to the Captain, Michael LeF came on deck and worked his way aft with some difficulty; it was dark, and by now the men were creating a well-meant musical farewell at the top of the gangway. He shook the hands of the men nearest to him, and just before he made his way, by the light of a torch, down the gangway and into his boat, he turned round—and in a voice deep with emotion said : "Gentlemen, for once I have no statement to make." '

SEVEN

Limey Rhymes

By the beginning of 1945, after more than three years' hard fighting, the American Fleet had won control of the Pacific, and defeat for the Japanese—though no one could say how long it might take—was but a matter of time.

The huge armada, alternately under the command of Vice-Admiral W. F. ('Bull') Halsey and Rear-Admiral Raymond A. Spruance and known alternately as the Third and Fifth Fleet, was by this time 'the largest, most powerful, most flexible and self-sufficient weapon naval history had ever seen'. Inevitably, the Royal Navy, entering the Pacific war at this late stage, was a poor relation for the first time in its history—and a great deal depended on the quality of the Liaison Officers appointed by Admiral Fraser to serve with the American Fleet, above all on the man who would represent the British with the Fleet Com-manders. Michael Le Fanu, his third thick stripe barely sewn on, but well-endowed with brains, diplomacy and bonhomie, seemed just right for the job.

On 23 January, 1945, at Ulithi in the Caroline Islands, he joined *Indianapolis*, the 9,800-ton cruiser which served as Admiral Spruance's flagship; for four months he saw no English-men, and very few thereafter until the fleet moved into Japanese waters. Charged with advising the Americans on the potentialities of the British Fleet, and giving the British some idea of what they might expect in the conduct of joint operations, Michael's job was both responsible and (in spite of the unfailing friendliness of his hosts) lonely. 'The way they fling me out into the cold world with soft words and then leave me to rot is a fair corker' he wrote, commenting on the apparent lack of response to his reports from British Pacific Fleet HQ in Sydney. As a matter of fact his reports were brief and somewhat infrequent. 'I only write,' he confessed, 'when I have something to say', and it was only during dull patches that he felt 'hells bells, I must write a report about something'.

But whatever Le Fanu did write was read with close attention —and not only by the British. His impressions of life and methods in the US Navy were considered by the American Chief of Staff to show 'very acute observation' and were influential in the post-war shaping of the Royal Navy. Michael was being less than just to himself when he wrote that his reporting technique was 'to give an account of operations and then discuss higher policy in an elevated tone of voice as it were. This gives the thing a Churchillian air and saves me from delving into details of American ideas and gadgets.' But gadgets were of less importance in the Le Fanu canon than people, and most of his time was spent away from his desk promoting Anglo-US relations in the highly personal—and highly successful—Le Fanu manner.

Ever since the famous 'Order 99' of July 1914, the ships of the US Navy had been officially 'dry', whatever ingenious ways (such as the issue of bourbon by flight surgeons to naval pilots on the orders of Admiral Halsey) were found to modify that state of affairs. Officers and men of the Royal Navy, of course, have always been accustomed to the idea of alcoholic refreshment, whether it took the form (as it did until 1970) of a daily tot of rum for ratings, or a duty-free bar for the officers in the ward-room. As Michael repeatedly had to explain to his new American friends, this did not mean that all British naval officers were permanently drunk; but it did mean that Liaison Officers felt acutely the absence of a reviving draught enjoyed in the sociable atmosphere of a British wardroom.

In the *Indianopolis* there was no wardroom life as Michael had known it. The wardroom—the Admiral's day cabin, in the case of his staff—was used for meals, after which people tended to retire to their 'rooms' until required again for duty; and meal-times were decidedly formal by British standards—officers nor-mally occupied the same places according to their rank, with the same neighbours on either side ('a dreadful prospect if they are nice, and if they are dreary, quite appalling'.) This was not the most receptive setting for Michael's brand of humour, but he decided that the best way to promote good relations was to induce a certain amount of 'letting down of the hair'; and although he felt that 'clowning here is rather like putting on slap-stick at the Athenaeum', he embarked without delay on his self-appointed task of cheering everyone up. Privately he felt it a strain to 'come down to supper at six o'clock after a tiresome day with suicide planes and be expected to be the jolly Englishman, when I would have given a lot to have had something under my belt', but he very soon gained a reputation with all ranks as the best of good fellows, which did just what was required for the image of the Royal Navy.

The style was established very soon. 'Diffident charm' and 'a slightly exaggerated English accent' (to use Michael's own phrases) helped break the ice; but the Englishness was soon abandoned, except for a Union Jack on the door of his cabin to declare it 'British territory'.

Not long after Michael joined *Indianapolis* the Chief of Staff informed him that Admiral Spruance had been made a Compan-ion of the Bath and asked when he (Michael) was going to invest him with the Order. Michael explained that in the British forces, junior officers were not encouraged to invest people with Orders —but this did not satisfy the Chief of Staff, so Michael decided he would have to do something about it. 'That evening after supper I rose to my feet, and after dilating on what an honour-able Order the Admiral had been awarded, I whipped out from under the table a large ribbon of red bunting with a tin bath tub attached to it. This I hung round the Admiral's neck. Merci-fully this was considered to be very droll, and a few days later the Admiral riposted by making a short speech in which he said he was frightened that my shoulder boards and brass hat might get rusty and presented me with an American hat and insignia. I welcomed the opening and wore American uniform from there on in.'

It was not only in the wearing of American uniform that Michael participated in the life of his new ship. He volunteered to take a turn as Staff Duty Officer 'driving the American Fleet round the ocean'; and as he was perhaps less consistently employed than the American members of the staff, he worked hard in his well-studied role of 'little friend to all the world'. He spent many hours pacing up and down the quarterdeck (the fo'c'sle in a British ship) as the chosen companion of Admiral Spruance, who had a passion for walking and thinking aloud as he did so. This was a testing form of relaxation, for Spruance's thoughts were of a very high order. A quiet, ascetic man who loathed publicity, he had come to be widely regarded as 'the greatest sea-captain of the Pacific'. Michael was soon to see his qualities demonstrated in the assault on Iwo Jima which began on 19 February after weeks of air attack from the carriers of the fleet.

With no specific duties allotted to him on the flag bridge, Michael adopted a wandering brief in action, and spent much time with the enlisted men in the flag plot. Many a life story was related to him at such times, and many were the small tributes to the confidence he inspired. One day he was approached by a sailor clutching a much-thumbed paperback. 'Good morning, Commander, how are you today?' 'Fine, fine. And how are you?' 'Fine thanks. Say... have you read *Call House Madam*, sir?' 'Can't say I have.' 'I have it here, Commander, and I had to talk fast to get it for you. You won't be too long with it, will you?' Michael promised to read this account of life in a brothel, and did. 'The things one does', he wrote in a letter to Prue, 'for England!'

While the action off Iwo Jima was proceeding—the battle was bitter and tough, and it was a month before the island could be regarded as 'secure'—the British Fleet had made its way to the unhealthy and uncomfortable anchorage at Manus in the Admiralty Islands under the command of Vice-Admiral Sir Bernard Rawlings. There the ships lay waiting uneasily for further orders. Would they be assigned to some minor job, or would they be committed to the main assault, the approach to Japan itself through the chain of islands which led up to it?

On 15 March the answer came; the British Fleet was assigned to the C-in-C Pacific, Admiral Nimitz, for 'duty in operations connected with "Iceberg"'. 'Iceberg' was the code name for the invasion of Okinawa (the main island of the Ryuku archipelago) which was to prove the most costly of all Central Pacific operations. The British ships, which consisted of two battleships (*King George V* and *Howe*), four carriers, five cruisers and eleven destroyers were to bear a full share of kamikaze and other forms of air attack in their role of neutralising the Japanese airfields on the Sakishima Gunto islands, near Okinawa.

'Task Force 57', as Admiral Rawlings' fleet was called, was stationed on the extreme left of the main American battle-line, and although Rawlings had had no chance to meet Spruance before the Okinawa operations began—their knowledge of each other to a great extent depended on impressions conveyed by Michael—he had seized on the vital importance, in his role as British sea commander, of getting on good terms with his American colleagues, and Spruance soon formed the highest opinion of his qualities in action. Spruance also was deeply impressed with the way the British carriers, with their armoured flight decks, stood up to kamikaze attacks. He had special reason to appreciate this because, in the course of the preliminary bombardment of Okinawa, his flagship *Indianapolis* was 'kamikazed' on 31 March, the day before the first landing took place. Many casualties were caused—and the incident nearly won Michael a medal.

'I'd just gone from Dawn Action Stations and was having a shower, and there was a rather belated pip-pip-pip of a twenty-millimetre cannon, and I thought "ah, I know what this is, someone coming out of a cloud" and sure enough there was a bit of a bang. I didn't know whether to dash up on deck because I was frightened or come up in an English way, fully dressed and immaculate. I rather hurried, and cracked my head on the side of the shower; then I went on deck to see what was going on. A bit later in the forenoon a chum of mine, the Flag Secretary, Charles Barber, said "Hey, Mike, Purple Hearts being given out now." I said, "Oh good, I must see that." He said, "Not see it, you're getting one." Somebody had noticed my little gash from the shower, and had lined up a "Purple Heart" for me. I managed to get out of it, though.'

Undeserved though Michael's 'Purple Heart' would have been, *Indianapolis* had suffered severe damage. The aircraft had gone right through her and blown off two propellers, and Admiral Spruance had to transfer his flag to the battleship *New Mexico*. Six weeks later, on 13 May, she too was struck by a kamikaze, and this time Michael saw the aircraft approach. 'I was scared, of course—one always is scared—but it was very exciting, even though you think the thing is coming at *you*. It hit the five-inch gun deck, and after that I nearly always spent my time in action down there. They were a little bit shaken up—and on the principle that lightning never strikes twice, I thought it a very good place for me to be.'

The battle for Okinawa was long, defended as it was by a garrison of some hundred thousand men and an estimated ten thousand aircraft, of which four thousand were suicide planes. Against them were pitted more than half a million allied troops and an invasion fleet of some one thousand three hundred vessels, and it took three months—until early July—before the islands, three hundred miles from the Japanese mainland island of Kyushu, could be considered conquered. All concerned were under immense strain, which was not helped by a deplorably erratic mail delivery service. Michael helped to lighten the tension with a few lines in doggerel, to be sung to the tune of *Smoke gets in your eyes*. (NATS means Naval Air Transport Service.)

> *They asked me back at Pearl*
> *Could I trust my girl.*
> *I said 'She'll be true*
> *Letters cannot fail—*
> *NATS will bring my mail.'*
>
> *They said 'Some day you'll find*
> *Postmasters are blind;*
> *You must realise*
> *Whereso'er you sail*
> *NATS get in your mail.'*
>
> *With a laugh*
> *I cried 'I'm on the staff!*
> *Why don't be so darned absurd!'*

But today
Five years have flown away
And from my love—no word.

No matter how I've tried
Tears I cannot hide.
Let me draw the veil
O'er this tragic tale
NATS GET IN YOUR MAIL.

And there was *More about Mail* to be sung to a well known hymn tune.

From Greenland's icy mountains
To Vermont's verdant vale,
The natives, to their great surprise,
Peruse the Fifth Fleet Mail.

Per contra up at Okie
The staff in anguish cry
As once again there sidles up
An empty LCI.

My son, observe this warning
And when the world's at war,
Eschew the rolling ocean
And sweat it out on shore.

For Spruance and the majority of his staff there came relief towards the end of May. At midnight on the twenty-seventh, Admiral Halsey took over command, and the Fifth Fleet thereupon became the Third again. But there was no relief for Michael; with the two suitcases which constituted his only luggage throughout the assignment, he transferred on the twenty-sixth with the Japanese-speaking Intelligence Officer Gil Slonim to Halsey's staff, in the battleship *Missouri* ('The Mighty Mo').

The prospect of getting to know a whole new staff appalled him—a staff twice as big as Spruance's, with the result that he had to share a room. This he found a real problem. 'I absolutely crave a soupçon of privacy sometimes. Like most people who live by their wits—i.e. who can put the switch to charm, intelligent appreciation, or pseudo-man-of-action at will, I definitely must drop the façade from time to time.'

The change in the style of management also took some getting used to. Far from riding in 'some old and inexpensive craft' like Spruance, here was Halsey running around in 'a large and expensive ship with considerable fanfare'; and in place of the withdrawn, publicity-shy Spruance, here was a gutsy extrovert, a colourful, flamboyant man and a born leader, only too anxious to let the world know (through his Public Relations man, Jim Bassett) how effectively the Third Fleet, and he, Halsey, were 'clobbering those yellow bastards'. At supper the first night with the Admiral, Michael—whose convivial reputation was already known—found he had to parry 'massive shafts of wit from the top end'.

Just before Halsey's arrival, the British Fleet, after sixty-two days continuously at sea (broken only by eight days at Leyte Gulf in the Philippines) had withdrawn to Sydney for a more extended period of repair and replenishment. Michael was offered a passage, but decided he would be better employed getting to know the new boss and his staff, even though this involved such apparently unwarlike activities as playing medicine ball and deck tennis and watching endless movies—'Ninety-nine per cent of American Naval Officers never dream of missing a movie—it is the only relaxation available'.

But in mid-June, when Halsey withdrew for a spell to Leyte, he did decide to go to Sydney for a four-day meeting of Liaison Officers. It was a trip, as Michael later said, 'ostensibly to see my boss—actually to have a drink'; his British colleagues found him incredibly American and could hardly believe it when they saw him approach Admiral Fraser with a Yankee-type salute and the unheard of greeting : 'Good morning, Admiral !'

Everyone knew that the final stage of the Japanese war was now imminent. Michael rejoined Halsey's staff at Leyte on 28 June, the day the British Pacific Fleet left Sydney. Three days later Halsey sailed with the Third Fleet to attack the enemy's home islands and on 16 July, Michael in *Missouri* had the great joy of seeing the British ships join the American Fleet off the north-east coast of the Japanese home island of Honshu. 'It was,' he wrote, 'the high spot of one man's Pacific war, the end and the beginning'. After meeting Admirals Rawlings and Vian on board *Missouri* Admiral Halsey told 'Lef' how confident he felt at the prospect of working with the British. Some of that confidence was no doubt due to patient salesmanship over the previous few weeks on the part of Michael, who, now that the two fleets were together, worked hard to promote co-operation, particularly in the area where the British most needed help—that of fuel supplies.

One of the American anxieties about the presence of a British Fleet in the Pacific had been the question of keeping it replenished, and the US Commanders were officially forbidden to give any assistance, for they had enough problems in keeping massive numbers of their own ships at sea. By assembling in record time a motley collection of transports, the British had managed to set up a fleet train which functioned amazingly well by and large, but difficulties none the less remained. However, Halsey, like Spruance, was capable of turning a blind eye. One day there arrived from the British Fleet a Biblical signal which read : 'And the foolish virgin said unto the wise virgin, give us of your oil, for our lamps are gone out', and Michael devised the reply, 'Foolish —no. Wise—maybe. Virgins—no comment'.

And it was Michael who, on one of those occasions when Sir Bernard Rawlings was due to visit Halsey to discuss the next stage of operations—a trip he would normally have made by destroyer—suggested that he should come instead in his flagship, HMS *King George V*, while *Missouri* was oiling. So it happened that while Rawlings was conferring and subsequently lunching in the *Missouri*, *King George V*, on the other side of the tanker *Sabine*, contrived to haul on board about one thousand tons of American oil.

It was not long after this that Halsey visited the *King George V* and after talks with Rawlings, Michael took him to the wardroom where he was invited to consider himself an honorary member of the mess. On the way back, Michael explained what the title meant, so the next time Halsey visited the British flagship's wardroom, he marched—well briefed by Le Fanu—straight past the welcoming party and up to the bar, banged on it and demanded in a loud voice, 'Six gins please!' Fortunately for Michael, the state of total prohibition had slightly eased under the Halsey regime; for one thing Michael himself had managed to bring back a few bottles of whisky from Sydney which had found their way on board *Missouri* as 'electronic spares' (the brand was VAT 69 which the Chief of Staff insisted was the Pope's telephone number) and for another the Admiral had, in Michael's words, 'his own ideas on what was medicinal'; the 'fruit cocktails' which were served at supper in Halsey's mess were often mysteriously potent affairs.

At this stage in the war, although there was a good deal of action, with constant air strikes and bombardments of the Japanese main islands as a preliminary to the projected invasion of Japan, there was some chance of relaxation, and time for Michael to reconsider the course of his life thus far, and his plans for the future. As his letters to Prue reveal, he had no illusions about his ability to handle men—American or British; he felt that perhaps the most worthy of ambitions was 'to make everyone you meet feel good—I daresay it would be more useful than anything we could achieve in the Navy or politics or anything else. You should know, seeing as how you have rung the above-mentioned bell in all cases of which I am cognizant. If I put my mind to it, I am reasonably confident that I could do likewise . . . indeed to some extent it has been my professional stock in trade. The only people who present any problems are those I love, because you are the only people with whom I can "let down", as the Americans say. So there you are, you can look forward to thirty years with a husband who is perpetually morose and fretful because he's ever so busy spreading sweetness and light.'

At this time Michael was entertaining serious doubts about the Navy as a career. 'I cannot believe it is morally right to be no more than a hired assassin, no matter how much I talk to myself about the values of waving a flag and keeping the peace; secondly, I don't think it is a full enough existence. On the other hand as a Commander or better, one exerts quite an influence on the men under one, an influence I would not exert were I to manage a pub, take holy orders or do welfare work in a slum. In the event I daresay I shall soldier on in the Navy; but if I do, it will be to some extent through laziness and I shall always have a lingering doubt about "that one talent which is death to hide".'

As July turned to August, there was less time for personal philosophising, for in the first fortnight of that month the final defeat of Japan was achieved. At noon (local time) on 7 August Michael learned of the dropping of the first atomic bomb on Hiroshima. The full horror of the event was not yet clear, but Michael at once realised, 'It was the pay-off as far as war is concerned, and made certain what was already probable that any future war will be the end of this reputed civilisation'. Such broad issues apart, hopes at once rose for a quick end to the war, and on the tenth—the day after the second atomic bomb on Nagasaki, the Japanese opened peace negotiations. Michael thought nothing less than a complete surrender should be accepted. Meanwhile he had engineered a lunch for Sir Bernard Rawlings in the *Mighty Mo* with Admiral Halsey and had taken good care to have them filmed together afterwards against a background of White Ensigns and American flags. Michael himself was invited to appear in some of the shots 'wearing my baseball cap, which I am afraid may look rather silly'. A pleasant interlude during four days of 'hanging around off Japan and not knowing whether to hit them a crack or get ready for the hurrah party'.

On 15 August, it was all over. Peace was heralded in the American fleet with the hoisting of battle flags and long blasts on the ships' sirens. 'Then we hoisted the flag signal "Well done" to the fleet. And that was all—it was queer to think of the people in America going wild, about ten o'clock in the evening in the middle states. After lunch Admiral Halsey made a very good and deeply felt speech to the fleet. He really is a fine old boy—64 years of age, and he has been at sea practically the whole war. Now we have a vast problem on our hands—the end has come so quickly and one doubts if we are anything like ready for it. People have been pretty busy winning the war without thinking of the peace.'

Meanwhile if ever there was an event which called for celebration it was this. At about 4 pm on 16 August, the British C-in-C, Sir Bruce Fraser, came on board the *Mo* to meet Halsey with the words, 'Well, Admiral, I *have* looked forward to this', and to present him with a KBE. At Michael's suggestion, on the same day, Admiral Halsey made the time-honoured British signal to the fleet, 'Splice the Mainbrace'. Since the American ships were 'dry' the signal of course had to read 'negative groups 38.1, 38.2' etc.—the American groups of ships. However, in the meantime Michael had done a little quiet fixing with Sir Bernard Rawlings (referred to by Halsey in his autobiography as 'Bert') in *King George V*.

That same afternoon, at about 4.45, Rawlings and his staff were transferred by jackstay from a destroyer to the *Missouri*, and after Rawlings had made a prearranged broadcast to 'the fighting Third', he joined Fraser and Halsey with their staffs in the Admiral's day-cabin. 'Now Admiral,' said Rawlings to Halsey, 'I have been studying with great care your "Splice the Mainbrace" signal and I see you've exempted all the American groups except 38.0—your own group in *Missouri*'. Upon which two jars of 'Pusser's' rum were produced and, in Michael's words: 'we proceeded to splice the mainbrace aboard the good old USS *Missouri* in a big way. This really made the party go—everyone loved everybody else madly—and I glowed a stinker as they say! Later on we had a Victory dinner for Admiral Halsey (a family affair—the Limeys had left). Lots of speeches. I am quite a cynical old thing, but I have been much drawn to this team who are very closely bound and very sincere in their loyalty towards one another and towards the Admiral.'

As for Halsey himself, Michael described for Prue one incident in particular which showed him as a 'marvellous, very loveable chap'. Among the Admiral's wilder threats had been that he would ride the Emperor's white horse through the streets of Tokyo when the war was over. 'Poor man,' wrote Michael, 'he is really worried about it now; just an idle word at a press conference months and months ago and now here he is with a terrific publicity build-up about it. Two beautiful sets of spurs arrived some time ago, but the saddle and bridle that arrived today (25 August) really were something. I've never seen a more massive or luxurious bit of work. Beautiful leather with chased silver all over it, and an enormous built-in rug. We set it all up over the backs of a couple of chairs this morning. Then when the Admiral walked in, we proceeded to sing *Home on the Range*. Great laughter.' The story, as told in Halsey's autobiography, relates that he then pretended to ride but caught himself in the crotch. After letting out a yelp he said, 'Why can't I remember I'm just a poor clapped-out old bastard and keep my big mouth shut goddamit!'

The days following the surrender were busy ones for Michael —'organising a peace is quite a job and I have to try and cut the British in on all the info'. In addition, he had another report to complete. For this he got the draughtsmen's office to make a cover using the photograph of him wearing a baseball cap and standing between Admirals Halsey and Rawlings—'Fraser will laugh (I hope) but their Lordships will be furious; I shall probably be slung out!' Then on 27 August came the memorable and uncanny experience of entering the harbour of Sagami Wan near Tokyo. 'It was a lovely sunny day as we led up harbour, with Fujiyama loud and clear on our port beam. Rather an over-rated eminence I'd say. No snow and rather a dull shape. We anchored at 1330 and Fraser in the *Duke of York* was close after us.'

Thus the British presence in Japan was firmly established, and the cause was furthered when Michael and Bill Kitchell, Halsey's Flag Secretary, were together charged with making the arrangements for the surrender ceremony, fixed for 2 September on board the *Missouri*; it seemed the ideal location since President Truman of the United States was Senator for the State of Missouri. 'Hey,' Halsey had said one day, 'I hear from the President we've gotta fix this surrender. You two had better go and do it. The General (MacArthur) will be coming on board.'

'You know, it was rather amusing,' recalled Michael later, 'for one young Commander and one young Lieutenant-Commander, formerly of Du Ponts, to be told to go and fix the surrender of the Japanese Empire. So we just sat down and I said : "Well, the first thing we want is a table and some chairs." I provided the chairs which came from the *King George V*—nice wooden ones instead of these American metal ones.' The table, too, was to come from the British battleship—and Michael took good care the Press knew about it (they didn't cotton on to the fact that at the last moment the table proved to be too small and a larger

American one had to be substituted). The Press in fact proved the biggest problem. 'You know the kind of thing', Michael confided to Prue. ' "Give me all the facilities I want or I will blackguard you in the papers." ' The three hundred and twenty Press representatives arrayed in 'various natural and artificial grand-stands' outnumbered the two hundred or so people involved in the actual ceremony on the superstructure deck.

Michael greatly enjoyed it all, not least seeing a Russian reporter (the Russians had declared war on the Japanese six days before the surrender) almost knocked off his perch by an American. The arrangements he and Kitchell had made seemed to work well; Michael had a grandstand view 'only twelve feet from Uncle Doug' (MacArthur) and he relished the contrast (in the run-up to the actual ceremony, which took place at 9 am local time so as to catch the US papers) between exchanging good-humoured banter with his friends among the enlisted men, while greeting each new grand arrival as a long lost buddy.

One of these was Admiral McCain, commander of the famous Carrier Task Forces, who pleased the newly anglicised Commander Le Fanu by putting his arm around his shoulder and exclaiming, 'Mike, you old rascal, you've gone British on us again.' And there was the gratification that evening ('I detected a slight post-wedding atmosphere') of organising a party in HMS *Duke of York*, Fraser's flagship, which was a great success, with Halsey repeating to tremendous applause (after being made an hon. member of the Duke's wardroom) the 'six gins' trick he'd worked so successfully in the *King George V*.

Two days after the signing ceremony, Michael had the 'odd sensation' of attending a 'conventional matter-of-fact party' ashore at the Yokosuka Officers Club, an all-male affair which he found civilised, but which made Halsey and his staff 'really angry and upset' owing to the absence of nurses from the hospital ship—an omission rectified at a repeat performance a few days later 'with everybody rather tipsy and cutting in on everyone else'. More to Michael's liking was the party given by Sir Bruce Fraser for some of the junior officers of the American Fleet. 'What shook them was there being a party at all. Though the Americans are excellent on mass production items such as ice cream and movies, they do not make a habit of dealing with their juniors as individuals.'

As for Commander Le Fanu's own relationship with his Admiral, it was close enough for him to be able to tell Sir Bruce that, other things being equal, he would like to go home soon : but he could hardly refuse when the Admiral asked him to stay on for a while 'if he was not too tired'.

Seven days after the surrender ceremony Michael travelled through the streets of Tokyo with Jim Bassett, in a borrowed jeep. 'It was an extraordinary sensation driving along there, just two unarmed Commanders and a driver, when only a few weeks ago we were at each other's throats. Going into Tokyo we went for mile after mile and met nothing but devastation . . . except for the centre of the city, Tokyo is quite flat. I have no brief for the Japs but all the same it really shocked me—what a reflection of our civilisation. At the British Embassy we found the care-taker, a queer shrivelled old man who was delighted to see us; he wasn't at all popular during the war and his only relaxation was to take the tram once a week and go down to compare notes with his opposite number at the American Embassy. Luckily it seemed that everybody had got the word about the war being over, and though we excited a good deal of curiosity, nobody bothered us. One party of girls, great strapping wenches who could have seen us off easily, fled like the wind as we approached their door. I suppose they had been listening to Tokyo Rose!'

Tokyo Rose (the Japanese equivalent of Lord Haw Haw, the Germans' English language propaganda broadcaster) was the subject of one of the most successful of the Le Fanu doggerel verses, entitled *Oh to be in Nippon*. Two sample stanzas ran as follows :

In our country of mystery, romance and charm
Of cherry tree blossom and snows,
When dreamboats come drifting from Saipan and Guam
We preserve our inscrutable Japanese calm
For although we may fry yet we suffer no harm,
According to Rose (who is safe in the Snows)
According to Tokyo Rose.

So spend your vacation in Nippon this year
In the country of blossoms and snows
The Cabinet state there is nothing to fear
In the greater East Asia Prosperity Sphere
When you die, for the emperor pays for the bier,
According to Rose, according to Rose,
According to Tokyo Rose.

In the days following the surrender ceremony, Michael was kept extremely busy on his liaison duties and became increasingly involved in the repatriation of prisoners of war, many of them in a pathetic state of health. But he also found time—in response to numerous requests—to put together some of his best verses in a 'volume-ette' entitled *Limey Rhymes*. It was printed on board USS *South Dakota* (now the flagship) in early September and produced in a second edition in USS *New Jersey* in November, after the return of Admiral Spruance to the fleet. The little book bears the dedication : 'To my friends of the United States Navy : I have learned many things from you, not least that you have an abiding passion for souvenirs. So I have collected these doggerels that you may have a keepsake from me. For the rhymes themselves, I offer no excuse beyond saying that nearly all were written in haste, to meet a special occasion, and to be forgotten.'

Limey Rhymes, however, was not forgotten. Many a sailor in the Third/Fifth Fleet has it to this day, a reminder of the extraordinary Englishman who served with them in the last days of the Japanese war.

Now that the war was over, Michael began to feel increasingly weary of his assignment. When he rejoined Spruance's staff in the *New Jersey* on 19 September, however, he masked any reluctance he might have felt with a welcoming rhyme called *All Yours, Fifth*. Addressed to Admiral Spruance, it ended :

So welcome to the Empire and welcome to the Nips,
And their rat-infested Navy which has everything but ships,
And welcome to the dust and smell, the gnat and the mosquito
And chief of these, MacArthur's aide, the Emp'ror Hirohito.
We welcomed you sincerely for we're glad of the relief,

From Loscap, Eichelberger and the oddities of FEAF.
They are yours, with 'Bull's' white charger which unridden
   ever waits—
In the fall the Third Fleet's fancy lightly turns towards the
   States.

Life on board Spruance's flagship was not quite so stark as it
had been formerly; one or two congenial spirits managed to
secrete 'medicinal supplies' in their rooms, though Michael
grew tired of the eternal movies and American-style parties in
officers' clubs ashore with the inevitable contingent of nurses and
the fixed determination of all hands to get drunk before six
o'clock. He became involved with diplomatic comings and
goings of various kinds, and managed to organise some fascinating runs ashore for himself and sundry friends, American or
British. One of the most entertaining involved 'two arch clowns'
from the cruiser *Swiftsure*—Charles Bennett and David Jones,
Captain of Marines, who were requested to assemble 'wines and
spirits for a week (courtesy of RN)' and come aboard 'a jeep
with Rations' (courtesy of US Govt.) on 'a safari to meet our
Japanese cousins'.

'The only thing we had in common,' recalled Charles Bennett
later, 'was a sense of the ridiculous. When we stopped in villages,
Mike was a master in communicating goodwill whether English
was spoken or not; but the inn-keepers at our palatial rest-houses
were absolutely terrified. Fortunately we found the local police-
man—nicknamed "Rushing Water" for reasons I will not go into
—and he restored order. The next three days were pure farce and
we were almost sorry to start the trip back. When nearing the
port we met head-on a truck of armed US soldiery who took
up a very threatening attitude. "Leave the talking to me," said
Michael as the Colossus of a Sergeant approached. Passes were
demanded. The first pass was rejected—"never heard of the
guy"; second pass "no dice"; a third pass was offered with
deliberate care. This pass staggered the Sergeant, who waved his
men back into the truck and waved us on. I asked whose signature was on the third pass. "MacArthur," said Mike with a grin

—"no one bucks that." Asked why he had not produced this pass at once he replied, "When you hold a good hand don't lead with your main trump." I only hope that somewhere in today's Navy there is another "rogue" in the pack who will develop into another Le Fanu.'

Fun and games apart, Michael interested himself that autumn in writing a document addressed to the C-in-C British Pacific Fleet which incorporated many of his impressions of the US Navy and which was, in spite of the deceptively light tone of voice, a prophetic glimpse of the future Royal Navy. Realising that 'the Americans have all the aces' and that 'England has exhausted herself' he felt that 'all our energy should be devoted to making a Navy of the highest quality and to hell with the number of ships'. His 'What Shall We Do with the Post-war Sailor?' emphasised the many fields in which the Royal Navy needed to learn from the Americans—in such matters as ship design, organisation of watches and more civilised living facilities for ship's companies. 'The food in British ships,' wrote Michael, 'would in many cases be eyed distastefully by a performing seal.' He advocated a total revolution in lower-deck life with its hammocks and individual messing arrangements ('shamefully squalid'), in favour of bunks and cafeteria feeding, employing the advice of 'successful civilian restaurateurs'. Above all, Michael recommended rates of pay comparable with those paid for work of similar quality and quantity ashore.

'What Shall We Do with the Post-war Sailor?' incorporates recommendations by a relatively junior officer which have now come one hundred per cent to fruition in the Royal Navy; in 1974 the document was deposited at Spruance Hall in the Naval War College in Newport Rhode Island, together with other memorabilia of one who gave unique service to the cause of Anglo-American naval co-operation.

On 8 November, 1945 Admiral Spruance was relieved by Admiral Towers. As a four-star Admiral, Spruance was entitled to a farewell party of eight sideboys and Michael made the suggestion ('ever so dashing for an American ship') that the eight should in fact all be members of his staff. 'I need hardly tell you,'

Michael wrote to Prue, 'that the British Liaison Officer was one of the eight.'

After this farewell Michael had to wait with increasing impatience for several more weeks for news of his own future movements and the arrival of a relief. There was time for some serious reading, of Blake and Walt Whitman among others, and time for some depressing reflections on the way the American Press, in the immediate aftermath of war, was misrepresenting the British contribution to victory. 'They cannot get the idea that anyone had anything to do with the war except themselves. The men I talk to are fully aware that Britain bore much of the heat and burden of the day, but in the public pronouncements, even the Service people—big wigs—are so busy proving that the Air Force did the job as opposed to the Navy or vice-versa, that they quite forget to state that Russia and Britain may have had something to do with the final result. I dislike seeing so much popular goodwill being dissipated. In any case I reckon our worries should be directed at the really important things. There seems to be no urgency in the deliberations of the great, and the great are ultimately only the spokesmen of the people's will. I suppose that sometime the masses will rise and say in a loud voice : "Now look here ! Stop all this nonsense and let's set about organising world peace—otherwise we have batted." '

At last, on 3 December, Michael's relief arrived, and he was free to go home 'with the two suitcases I brought with me in January'. In due course he was to be awarded the American Legion of Merit for his work with the Third/Fifth Fleet, work which bore valuable fruit in the years ahead; and he was deeply disgusted when he was told that not long after his departure, his relief had informed the Admiralty that there was nothing for him to do—no one seemed to want him—and he asked to be recalled. Their Lordships complied.

'To think,' Michael told a friend much later, "that we actually HAD a permanent place with the afloat staff of the US Fleet which THEY wanted us to keep, and it was thrown away. What a lack of imagination. The Liaison Officer's job was to 'be there on the spot, when needed; out of sight if not wanted; unobtrusive yet helpful; eventually essential at all levels . . . not sitting in an office writing reports or issuing orders. We have thrown away something which will never be offered again.'

Perhaps the job could only be done by someone of the Le Fanu stamp. As for him, in his last letter home before setting off via the States for the UK, he said flatly, in spite of a year's exhausting endeavour, 'I have not made as much of this job as I might have.'

EIGHT

Experimental Commander

In the months after the war ended, Michael had toyed with the idea of Prue meeting him in America on his way home, but the operation had proved too complicated for various reasons, not least the cost, although this obstacle would have been the last to deter someone with Michael's easy-going approach to finance. Michael, however, was determined to travel by train across the country which was now the most powerful in the world, accepting a few of the many invitations from his American friends. This delayed his return to England until early January 1946, but Prue afterwards agreed with his 'taking the long view', for such an opportunity of visiting the country of his new friends might not be repeated. There is no doubt, too, that his good personal relations with the United States were later to prove of great importance to the Navy. In any case, there was the likelihood of a sustained period of home life immediately ahead, whatever Michael's next appointment might turn out to be.

He himself was privately eager to leave behind his Gunnery specialisation and work for Sir Bruce Fraser, perhaps in an Admiralty appointment. But events forestalled this hope, and he found himself returning reluctantly to Gunnery, but to a job which was to provide exceptional scope.

The Experimental Commander and his staff at HMS *Excellent* on Whale Island, had the task of overseeing all the new gunnery equipment being constructed or fitted in HM ships and of co-ordinating the work of the civilian intellectuals involved in thinking up new concepts in naval gunnery, both in the use of materials and of men. When an 'XP' Commander was due for relief, it was the custom to scan the list of new Gunnery promotions and pick out one of the brightest boys as his successor. But, hearing that Michael was on his way back from the States, Whale Island's Captain, William (later Admiral Sir William) Slayter, who had served as Chief of Staff, Home Fleet, and therefore knew Michael of old from the 'Scapa Services' days, decided to by-pass the New Year promotions of 1946 and appoint him to 'Whaley' as Experimental Commander.

Michael started work there on 2 February, 1946. His father-in-law had recently been appointed Admiral Superintendent of Portsmouth Dockyard, moving from Soberton into the official elegant Georgian residence near Admiralty House. As Michael and Prue at that time owned no home of their own, they decided to accept the Morgans' suggestion that they should live at the Admiral Superintendent's House, nicknamed by Michael 'Dock-yard View', which would allow them their own living quarters. This convenient arrangement, although comfortable in the highest degree, was not without tension, and Prue afterwards recalled being occasionally caught in the cross-fire of her husband's casual approach to his private life and her mother's more formal attitude as hostess in a house full of naval staff. Prue's loyalties were split as she tentatively suggested to Michael, 'When in Rome . . .'

After the strains of war and, in particular, his time in the Pacific, Michael had decided on a calculated slackening of the pace to include as many visits as possible that summer to race-meetings in the south of England. His First Lieutenant at Whale Island, knowing Michael's professional efficiency at first hand, was only mildly surprised when the 'XP' Commander walked into the office one morning in plain clothes and said, 'If the Captain wants me, tell him I am at a meeting, but, unless pressed, don't say it is Goodwood.' But taking casual days off in this way seemed incomprehensible to Mrs Morgan (or 'Lady Meon' as she had irreverently been christened by her son-in-law) and during one busy period of race-going, Prue's mother was driven to ask anxiously, 'Is Michael thinking of his career?'

In fact, of course, he was. To Michael's great relief he soon realised that, far from being involved in the square-bashing aspects of Gunnery, his 'prime task in the XP Department, and a very congenial one, was to consort with a collection of Docs and Profs who were said to be good for the Navy'—in the sense that they were engaged to devise new and more imaginative uses of materials and human resources, and to find ways of making sailors more comfortable and efficient.

Liaison with the members of the Royal Naval Personnel Research Committee which included such illustrious names as Sir Lindor Brown of the Medical Research Council and Professor le Gros Clark and Dr Weddell, both of the Anatomy Department of Oxford University, proved highly enjoyable to one of Michael's intellectual capacity, and he thoroughly appreciated the Royal Society soirées and the dinners at Oxford and Cambridge Colleges which now became part of his social round.

Dr Weddell and John Streatfeild, who was First Lieutenant in the XP Department when Michael joined, had been to the USA and studied the way the US Navy was making use of 'human engineering'. Now the Royal Navy, too, began to look scientifically at the way the human body reacts in the constricted and often hazardous environment of a fighting ship. 'We did some fascinating work,' Michael recalled later, 'under cover of a vote which was then capable of elastic treatment. The academics got some interesting tasks to do, a certain number of sailor-type bods as subjects and some odd, *very* odd bits of hardware known (in the Navy's parlance for craftily acquired contraband) as "rabbits". Those were the great days. Days of the Oxford Seat (a new and extremely comfortable seat for Gunnery operators which was not adopted by the Navy and the patent for which, according to one account, was sold by Dr Weddell to two men in an Oxford pub and later provided the basis for the seats of the Rover 2000); days of Mackworth's Clock Test and Dr Weiner's Naked Men (Weiner was testing the reactions of men working in the confined space of an ammunition magazine—work which caused one sailor to break his arm, to Weiner's great distress); days when Bessie and June, two redoubtable goats, went to their last reward in the Alverstoke tank, faithfully recorded by my photographers, on a strictly "rabbit" basis.'

One important move made by the XP Department at this time was to invite Professor Bartlett of St John's College, Cambridge to send a time and motion study team to look at the workings of a gun turret. Michael was delighted when they were able to shorten the firing time considerably, and as a result of this experiment, the Navy's first time and motion study unit was set up.

If academic help was welcome at Whale Island, interference from high Admiralty officials was not, and Michael's staff greatly relished the way he would handle any external opposition to their ideas. For example, they all felt strongly that the new six-inch gun mounting which was eventually fitted in the 'Tiger' class cruisers should have mechanised supply arrangements in the magazines and handling rooms to cope with the mounting's high rate of fire. However the Director of Naval Ordnance thought differently. So the XP Department rigged up a mock-up on a rolling platform with hand supply arrangements, put oil on the deck and invited the pundits from Bath to witness the trial and take part themselves. They were impressed; and at the subsequent meetings Michael, who had briefed himself with great thoroughness, was able to put over the department's views with irresistible cogency.

He was also admirable at supporting his staff when things went wrong. One of Tom Best's tasks when he was First Lieutenant was to run the Ship Target Trials which involved firing every sort of shell from six-inch to coastal forces weapons at ships about to be scrapped. Every effort was made to stop the target ships sinking in the fairway, or, if they were secured between buoys, from breaking away in a gale; but inevitably one ship did break away and was stranded in Bracklesham Bay. Michael had delegated responsibility for the trials to his No. 1, but he delegated none of the effects of the furious blast which came down from the Commander-in-Chief.

By far the largest new ship project in hand at this time was the completion of the 42,000-ton battleship *Vanguard* which already incorporated, Michael was glad to see, many domestic improvements similar to the ones he had advocated in 'What Shall We Do with the Post-war Sailor', and all the latest scientific developments, not least in the Gunnery Department. The acceptance trials of her eight fifteen-inch guns took Whale Island's Experimental Commander to sea in the first few months of 1946—and, incidentally, got him into trouble with a future bishop.

This arose during the 'blast' trials on 'B' turret, just forward of the bridge. John Streatfeild was seated in the turret, connected by phone with Michael who was supervising operations on the bridge with *Vanguard*'s Captain—none other than 'Bill' Agnew of the *Aurora*. The object was to discover how far aft 'B' turret could be trained without causing mortal damage. As Streatfeild remembered: 'We fired with the turret trained further and further aft until the bridge became untenable, and a semi-permanent stop was put in. To decide the position of the permanent stop, the bridge was abandoned, and we went on firing until we started to damage the ship's structure. The damaged portion turned out to be the Chapel, but the resulting havoc was forgiven by the padre, the Rev. Geoffrey Tiarks, later Bishop of Maidstone, in Christian spirit and he remained a friend of Michael's for life.'

But there resulted a small *quid pro quo* on Michael's part. Writing as the sales manager of Messrs Rabbit, Rabbit, Scrounge and Rabbit Ltd ('The Wunoff Wonders') of Warren Works, Whale Island, he agreed to supply a new offertory box for the battleship's Chapel of St Barbara, if necessary 'up to the dimensions of our "Uncle" type special dog-kennel size (suitable for cathedrals)'. Replying from 'HMS *Vanguard*, Bedlam', her Gunnery Officer Guy Western (best man at Michael's wedding, and known in the Navy as 'Aggie' Western on account of the resemblance of his name to that of the naval benefactress 'Aggie' Weston) told the sales manager that 'our Mr Tiarks' wanted an *eight-inch* model with two compartments, so as to receive notes as well as coins of the realm, clothing coupons and other salvage. 'We note,' his letter continued, 'that you propose to fit your standard "Tiffy-prufe" lock and would point out that in view of the recent visit paid to our firm by your Mr Le Fanu, and the subsequent extensive alterations that have proved necessary as a result of the visit, the lock should be of the blastproof variety and fitted with an alarm buzzer to ring in the damage control headquarters when the lock is tampered with. Another refinement would be a ring of joybells to sound when a coin is dropped in the box, but we appreciate the fact that this may have to stand over until the conclusion of the present emergency.' The offertory box was duly made in the workshop by a man 'known as "Breeder" because he makes so many rabbits' and despatched to *Vanguard* with an apposite rhyme :

There are fairies at the bottom of our proof butts,
Who are normally not seen by mortal man;
But if perchance you're dining when a sickle moon is shining
You may glimpse them, and may hear the pipes of Pan.

There are fairy lights in Mr Stacey's workshop—
You can see them glowing faintly through the murk;
And the piping so seductive makes the fairies more productive
It is, in fact, their Music While You Work.

There are fairies brazing boilers in the foundry,
There are elfin electricians by the score—
Making radios for Nobby and a frigidaire for Bobby
And a trolley bus complete for F.C.4.

A gang of gnomes is working for the Vanguard
On a tube to meet her Captain's earnest wish,
And when that job is over, they'll polish up Lamb's Rover
Then offertory boxes for the Bish.

The light Le Fanu touch was greatly appreciated at Whale Island, a place not normally renowned for humour—it was just what was needed in those years after the war, with their shortages and uncertainties. However, it was never wise to go too far with LeF; one rather lively Wren driver who misjudged the position was made to write out a hundred times, 'I must not flirt with the boss'. But it was surely easy to 'miss the pipe'—to get the message wrong—when the only meetings announced on the notice boards appeared to be race meetings, when a departmental dinner would become a 'Dîner Expérimental' with a specially designed menu, and when a panel had to be formed to implement 'Staff requirements for XP's motor cycle'.

The 'operational use' of this machine was 'to carry XP Cdr. from Petersfield to Portsmouth and return, daily, except Saturdays, Sundays, Public Holidays and Race Days'. This panel soon reported with the wit and efficiency equally prized by LeF that 'a party equipped with radar, bloodhounds and hazel twigs' had located a bicycle with suitable specifications, a 150 cc Coventry Eagle, for £30; but 'thought that the drastic experiment of actually purchasing a machine is ill-advised and a blow to traditional XP policy. A few well chosen words and a benign smile directed towards the Transport Officer should obtain a motor bike for the period required.' However Michael asked his panel to purchase the Eagle so that he could proceed

> *All licensed and legal*
> *Per Coventry Eagle*
> *(Its speed just a dignified lope)*
> *From Petersfield daily*
> *Through Cosham to Whaley*
> *And back in the evening—I hope.*

Of course, as always with Michael, the light touch masked a dedicated application to the task in hand. These tasks he accomplished with the maximum concentration, leaving time, as part of his 'slackening the pace' routine, to take a course of flying instruction at Portsmouth Airport leading to a civilian pilot's licence, in accordance with a 1946 Admiralty Order announcing that all officers of the executive branches were to be given the chance of learning to fly. There were many 'business' outings with XP colleagues and their wives to various corners of the British Isles—and many local parties too; at Whale Island they long remembered how Michael literally lifted Prue off her feet at a ball there and whirled her round the dance floor, giving the impression that she was as active as anyone else.

During the summer and autumn of 1946, Michael and Prue spent enjoyable days house-hunting, eventually deciding to buy 37 Heath Road East, Petersfield, a modest house overlooking the golf course, where the Le Fanu family were to live happily for some fourteen years. On 14 November, their first child, Mark, was born by Caesarian operation, and in view of various complications earlier in the summer the event caused universal rejoicing, not least amongst the 'Whaley' typing-pool girls. Michael always made a point of dropping in to see them from time to time, perching on the edge of a desk to drink a cup of tea, and taking Prue along for a chat whenever she happened to be there.

During this winter, Michael enjoyed reliving his time with the American Fifth Fleet, through the frequent visits of his friend, Charles Barber, Admiral Spruance's former Flag Lieutenant, who was then a Rhodes Scholar, reading Economics at Balliol College, Oxford. At Mark's christening, Charles became a godfather, and the following summer the Le Fanus and Morgans attended his wedding at Oxford. Between them, Michael and Charles arranged for Admiral Spruance to lecture at the Naval Institute during a visit to London, and in December there was the gratification of hearing that Michael had been awarded the US Legion of Merit for his work with the Third/Fifth Fleets—his phoney wound, self-inflicted in the shower-room of the *Indianapolis*, notwithstanding!

By now the house at Petersfield was ready for occupation, and the family gathered at the Superintendent's House for a farewell dinner. The exodus to Petersfield would inevitably leave a void for the devoted grandparents, and particularly for Prue's father who above all enjoyed recounting the latest dramas of his dockyard to LeF. For his part, Michael was devoted to his father-in-law, admiring his charm and schoolboy enthusiasm as well as his shrewd judgment when dealing with people and with all the post-war dockyard labour problems. As soon as the familiar phrase rang out, 'What *do* you think, my dear chap,' Michael would settle happily back for a vivid account of some 'hideous affair'!

The family were at last packed up, and when Mark was six weeks old, they moved to Petersfield in a snowstorm. There followed a happy year for the inexperienced householders. Michael had always been domesticated, and now added his skills as nursemaid if the nanny was away. He trod a delicate road with tact and matter-of-fact calm, never interfering with Prue's determination to be independent in her own field, but always there if action had to be taken in a crisis. Prue appreciated this sensitivity. 'He handled me and the situation very cleverly—and never fussed.' She now had the opportunity of becoming proficient in the kitchen, after D'Or's original cooking lessons in wartime Bedford. Michael, meanwhile, studied books on gardening, the advice from which he applied to the letter, producing rows of immaculately regimented vegetables in the hot summer of 1947, when even sweetcorn responded to his attentive encouragement.

He was never an expert carpenter or mechanic, as both his sons were to become. Willing though he was, the simple planing of a sticking bathroom door somehow seemed to result in half the door being knocked down. He became, nevertheless, an accomplished painter and decorator, even wrestling single-handed with the intricacies of papering a room for the first time, his head entirely enveloped in a white naval cap cover. He became proficient at golf, too, crossing the road on fine evenings to practise on the nearby green. He soon became a popular member of Petersfield Golf Club. They liked the way he would breeze in unexpectedly and announce himself to anyone who happened to be around as 'Michael . . . are you looking for a game?'—a style which never changed even when he became a full Admiral. In fact those who did not know his professional position would never have guessed it from the off-duty Mike; if anyone asked what he did for a living he would reply, 'Oh, I'm in the Navy.'

In February 1948, Michael was appointed Executive Officer of the Home Fleet cruiser *Superb* and the time had come to leave Whaley. There was a notable farewell 'Dîner Expérimental' on the sixteenth with a menu designed to read like a work indent. 'Crème de Bâtard au Tête Rouge'—'Red-headed Bastard Soup' —was followed by 'Poulet Rôti au Spiv Nauticale' with 'Pommes Corps de Chamel' (a reference to the so-called 'Camel Corps' at Whaley, the go-anywhere-do-anything-brigade) and 'Choufleur Lapin' (Rabbit Cauliflower). Finally there were 'Champignons Superbes'. At the foot of the indent form, in the space left for 'XP Commander's decision (if required)' someone inserted the Michael-type comment—'Corny. This needs sorting'. At the dinner itself, Michael characterised various chums in well-chosen quotations, and they were inspired to compose the following farewell verses :

> *What then are we going to do*
> *Now we have no Le Fanu?*

4—DG

Can we plot a loading cycle
Now we cannot lean on Michael?
Blind with tears; to comfort deaf,
See us mourn the loss of LeF.

We the Overdriven staff,
Choke our sobs back as we quaff
All the liquor we can stow
Hoping it will drown our woe,
That starry eyed and through a haze
We may face the empty days.

Past a sign which read 'Newmarket 130 miles' a party of sailors and fellow officers hauled Michael out of Whaley on a horse-drawn cart—it was a spectacular farewell. But Whale Island's Captain McLaughlin had the last word. On Form S206, he gave Michael an outstanding report for the 'Marked qualities of leadership which have exerted an influence far beyond his own department', faulting him only for 'a certain carelessness in his personal appearance'. He was, said Captain McLaughlin, summing up and recommending him for promotion, the possessor of 'a keen intelligence, a crisp wit, considerable literary and poetic talent and a knowledge of form (flat racing in particular)'.

NINE

The Old Super-B

Michael's appointment as Executive Officer of HMS *Superb*, 8,800 tons and flagship of Britain's attenuated post-war Home Fleet, marked the end of his service as a Gunnery specialist and provided a welcome interlude of sea-time before taking his first steps on the Whitehall ladder.

Meanwhile no one who felt the Le Fanu touch in the *Superb* ever forgot the experience, and at least one distinguished visitor went back to Whitehall declaring that her poetry-quoting Commander was bound to be First Sea Lord one day.

One of his first acts after joining the 'Super-B', as she was known in the Fleet, was to persuade the Royal Marine Band-master to make an arrangement of Stanford's sea song *The Old Superb* suitable for untutored sailors' voices. Every morning after divisions, LeF would stand on the top of 'X' turret, over-looking the quarterdeck, with an enormous pantomime-type song sheet behind him, rehearsing the ship's company in what was to be their signature tune. 'Once more, Mr Bandmaster,' he would shout, 'Quarterdeck men only in the verse, all join in the chorus ... now then ...!'

Alternately conducting and pointing to the words with his telescope, the Commander directed the assembly until he was satisfied, after which he would turn the ship's company forward and they would all march off to work singing *Superb*'s own song. It was performed, perhaps, with more enthusiasm than skill, though invariably with robust enjoyment—especially as the cruiser moved in and out of harbour and her crew could relish the look of mute astonishment on the faces of those in more serious-minded ships. In foreign ports, the song could often be heard issuing forth from bars late at night or being sung by sailors and Royal Marines on their way back to the ship—and in Casablanca, it led to trouble.

LeF had in fact forbidden the song to be sung on account of the anti-French tone of some of its words ('The French have gone to Martinique, and where they go the *Old Superb* will go'); but full of the local brew, some of the sailors forgot the instruction and a fight or two broke out. The song was performed innocuously at children's parties on board, and incidentally provided a nickname for the motor fishing vessel which acted as tender to *Superb*. The cruiser *Cleopatra* had one which of course was christened *Antony*; *Superb*'s tender, because of the reference in the song to the *Old Superb* as 'a lame duck lagging, lagging, lagging ALL the way', naturally became *Duckling*.

Nicknames were a Le Fanu speciality in *Superb*. What LeF called 'the Admiralty Joke Department' had sent the ship a large number of ratings by the name of Young. In any normal ship, they would have been referred to by their rate and their initial, but this wasn't *Superb* stuff. They all had an official nickname. Thus there was a 'Brigham' Young, a 'Nicely-Nicely' Young, a 'Sticks' Young (a Royal Marine drummer), a 'Smoker' Young (a boy seaman not allowed to smoke) a 'Stripey' Young (a young seaman whose behaviour was rather too old for his years), and two brothers, one old enough to be allowed his tot of rum and the other too young, who were known respectively as 'Gulpers' and 'Sippers' Young. These nicknames were used on the most formal occasions (indeed no one would have been greatly surprised to hear the command 'Gulpers Young, Off Caps' at the defaulters table, though there is no actual evidence of such a thing happening)—and visitors were frequently astonished to hear on the ship's broadcast system some such pipe as 'Squareface Young lay aft to the quarterdeck'.

There were some eight hundred men in *Superb* and the new Commander soon appeared to know all their surnames, and many of their Christian names too—nor did he ever seem to forget them. The story of Captain Neil MacEacharn's first meeting with LeF when he joined *Superb* as an Able Seaman direct

rom HMS *Crossbow*, gives, among other things, a hint of
Michael's powers of recollection. After reporting to the Regulat-
ng Office, MacEacharn glanced at the notice boards before
etting off to meet his Divisional Officer, and on the way was
topped by the Commander, carrying a telescope and smiling
cheerfully.

'Why are you wearing a *Crossbow* cap tally?' he asked.
MacEacharn replied that he had only just joined from *Crossbow*
and would shortly be putting up a *Superb* tally. After a few
moments of conversation about the new AB's previous career,
he Commander asked his name. 'MacEacharn, sir,' was the
eply. 'Mac-what?' MacEacharn repeated his name several
imes, after which LeF got it right. But the interview was not
quite over. 'What is my name?' asked the Commander. Frantic-
ally racking his brains, the lad fortunately remembered the
signature he had seen at the foot of daily orders on the notice
board and replied in the best French accent he could muster,
'Lee Fanew, sir.' LeF smiled, thought for a moment, and then
left the new addition to *Superb*'s crew with the words, 'Next
time we meet we shall both be able to pronounce each other's
names.'

Twenty years later, as First Sea Lord, Michael greeted
MacEacharn with the words: 'I pronounce your name
Makeékarn, how do you pronounce mine?'

Perhaps it was only a cursory glance at the notice board which
had given MacEacharn his clue to the Commander's name; if he
had studied it longer, he could not have failed to be struck by
the extraordinary style in which the Commander's orders were
written. If Gunnery practice was to be part of the day's routine,
the orders might be headed by Prospero's words from *The
Tempest*: 'Be not afeard, the isle is full of noises . . .', or by a
passage from Ernest Bramah's *Kai Lung* stories: 'Kites in the
form of aggressive dragons floated about every point likely to
incur assault, and other protective measures were not lacking,
while the almost continuous discharge of propitiatory crackers
could be heard.'

Prominent on the shelves of the Commander's Office was an

Oxford Dictionary of Quotations, liberally scribbled on by LeF and Peter Kimm, the Sub-Lieutenant who acted as his assistant, in their search for lines appropriate to the day's activities. They did not hesitate to alter these to suit their own purposes. Thus Walter de la Mare's *The Traveller* became *Middle Watch Blues:* 'Is there anybody there, said the Sentry, knocking at the Lobby door . . .'

Kimm often employed his talents as a cartoonist to embellish the orders, especially when some poorly executed task provided an opening. Once, during Home Fleet manoeuvres, *Superb*'s attempt at mooring was a disaster; this gave Kimm a chance to go to town with fouled cables and confused mermaids, and prompted a footnote in daily orders from 'Our Man Stanley' (a fictional reporter named after the American newspaper man who found Dr Livingstone). It read:

WELL MOORED, MEN. Our man Stanley reports from Sick Bay: 'Covered Moor-Ship operations as directed. Now slowly recovering. Here are vital statistics: Shackles dropped on toes—twelve times. Fingers nipped by wire—14 times. Flat on face—28 times. Bawled out—50 times (approximately). Caught foot in bollard strap, sprained ankle, no sympathy. Would appreciate next assignment being somewhere gentlemanly, such as Quarterdeck.'

It is frustrating for a ship's company to be kept in ignorance of what is happening while their ship is carrying out a series of apparently inexplicable manoeuvres and LeF always tried to anticipate this feeling in daily orders. An example read:

RUNNING AROUND IN CIRCLES. This is precisely what we shall be doing for the next couple of days. We drop a buoy in the middle of the ocean, steam off a couple of miles, then dash madly round it hoping that it's watching. Then off we stalk again, and round again, and so on and so on and so on, until the buoy sinks or the Chief Quartermaster gets giddy, whichever is the earlier. The object of this complicated caper is to collect data on the ship's manoeuvrability, and the real

work is done by a Brains Trust of crafty Constructors herein-
after to be known as the Legs XI. They stand in the most
hideously exposed positions fore and aft looking through things
and making Constructive noises. When we make a particularly
fast pass at the buoy, the ship will heel over more than some-
what, so look out for your fannies and your crockery.

If LeF was adept at producing the right word at the right time, his actions were no less effective. Due to pay a visit to Copenhagen, the ship had been engaged in exercises in bad weather and was not looking as smart as the Commander thought she should. He was particularly unhappy about the appearance of the foremast and decided it should be painted during the dog watches of the Sunday immediately before the arrival in Denmark.

The ship was rolling heavily and several of the young boys in the Foretop Division were clearly frightened of going aloft. Just as the Petty Officer in charge was wondering how to get the job finished, the Commander arrived on the scene. 'Give me a pot-and-one' (a pot of paint and one paint brush). Without more ado he went up the mast dressed in No. 5 uniform and a raincoat and for the next two hours, with one other volunteer, he painted the radar platform while the boy seamen worked below them, struck from time to time on the head by small splashes of grey paint from aloft.

The visit to Copenhagen was only one of many occasions when *Superb*, under LeF's direction, organised a children's party of never-to-be-forgotten splendour—the result of meticulous preparation and extremely detailed Orders.

Duckling *will be used for embarkation. A proportion of about*
one Pirate to every dozen children is desirable . . . the motor
dinghy, crewed by Popeye and Olive Oyl (Or Near Offer)
will provide entertainment during embarkation and dis-
embarkation . . . the whole operation must be conducted with
great tact and firmness and it is important that the pirates
and boats' crews should not overdo the skylarking at this stage.
The First Lieutenant will be O.C. Clowns (what again?): the

*job of the Clowns and Pirates is to jolly the children around,
relieve congestion and generally do their stuff; Tea
schedule . . . the whole of this manoeuvre is very tricky as well
as very crafty and requires close attention to detail . . . in ports
where it is practicable, all available fireworks will be loosed off
in one hit as soon as range is clear . . . the inducement to make
the children leave will probably be in the form of a 'pirate
landing'.*

Gothenburg as well as Copenhagen witnessed an extraordinary
spectacle along these lines in the summer of 1949, as did a
number of home ports in Scotland and England.

Home visits—for example to Eastbourne and Dover—provided a chance for Prue to come and stay locally for a few days;
with Michael at sea again, the house in Petersfield had been let,
and she was once again living with her parents in 'Dockyard
View', as Michael called it. He was away when their second
child, Victoria, was born—in October 1948, at St Mary's Hospital in Portsmouth; in fact, like every other sailor's wife, Prue
saw Michael very little during the eighteen months he was in
Superb except during leave periods—and they only managed one
short holiday away together in the summer of 1948.

Michael had suggested that Prue should book them into a
hotel in the Cotswolds—and without consulting the map as closely
as she might have done, Prue decided on Malmesbury in Wiltshire, which is not exactly Cotswold country. When not best
pleased, Michael usually resorted to a stony silence, and it was a
very silent Michael who arrived at that Malmesbury hotel; however, he cheered up when he saw that a great deal of vigorous
walking could be done on the Wiltshire downs.

Physical exercise formed a large part of the *Superb* scheme of
life at this time; more than one visitor to the ship as she lay in
Chatham Dockyard found the Commander absent, leading his
men at a brisk jog round St Mary's Island—which became, on
one memorable occasion, the scene of the XIV(A) Olympiad.
The *XIV* Olympiad was being held in Britain and so *Superb*
must go one better. The affair opened with the least likely looking
sailor charging into the arena with the Olympic flame (a large

piece of oily cotton waste) held high, and ended with presentations by 'Midshipman HRH Hamlet, Prince of Denmark', in which role a very young Ordinary Seaman was so convincing that many people were uncertain whether the whole affair was a leg-pull or not. His arrival in an imposing car and his deferential reception by the Captain created such nagging doubts in the minds of the winners that they came up to take their awards with great solemnity, just in case the young chap *did* turn out to be a prince of the blood.

Dressing up was a favourite LeF pastime, especially if it led to deflating the pompous. A cruiser came into Chatham while *Superb* was refitting and the officers invited themselves for a drink by making the cheeky signal, 'WMP', indicating acceptance of an invitation 'With Much Pleasure'. *Superb* replied that they would all be welcome, and when the visitors arrived they nonchalantly accepted drinks served by a ginger-haired Steward and a singularly obsequious Wardroom Attendant—LeF and the Major of Marines respectively—who did not reveal their true identities until they were sure of causing their guests the maximum embarrassment.

But Michael never would cause embarrassment to those who might be seriously hurt by it. He might lash out, in a general kind of way, at 'Ordinary Seaman Solid' in daily orders; but he showed genuine respect for the work of others, whatever their job. Senior ratings were impressed by his ability to talk with real knowledge about their particular expertise—'dockyard mateys' liked the way he would 'have a go' himself at whatever they were doing, whether it was electric welding, drilling, riveting, caulking or the pneumatic cutting of steel plate. Once he created a memorable impression by climbing, for a bet, 210 feet up to the top of a 120-ton crane. Dockyard men are not given to great admiration for naval officers as a rule, but to the men who worked on the *Superb* at Chatham, this one was 'great'.

To the ship's company he was 'Mad Michael'—an epithet bestowed largely in admiration but partly in bewilderment; and it has to be recorded that not all LeF's superiors approved of his style. Michael knew this perfectly well. He took the calculated risk of shocking his senior officers, aware that his unusual approach drew the maximum loyalty and efficiency from the men. Among those who understood and accepted this was Admiral Sir William Slayter, who arrived as Flag Officer Second Cruiser Squadron in May 1949, bringing with him, as Flag Lieutenant, Michael's brother-in-law David Morgan. The family atmosphere of the Admiral's lively mess or "cuddy" was long to be remembered. His red hair and dry wit matched Michael's, and they renewed with pleasure their earlier acquaintance.

At this time, every *Superb* officer, almost without exception, was a keen golfer, and Lieutenant, now Commander Anthony Boyall, recalls the careful arrangements, during various Replenishment at Sea trials, to ensure that the *Superb* entered only such ports as possessed conveniently-placed golf courses. Recreation, yes; inefficiency, no. One evening, Boyall left his return to the ship, after a game of golf, dangerously near the time of sailing. He caught the last picket boat, slipped on board to change, he hoped unnoticed, and was taken to one side by Michael with the words : 'I have secured your quarter-deck for sea, Tony'. Never has he forgotten this rebuke, more effective than any amount of ranting.

At the end of June 1949, Michael was promoted Captain at the age of thirty-five, the youngest in the Navy since Beatty, though it was decided he should remain as a 'four-ring Commander' in *Superb* for a few weeks longer. General rejoicing greeted the news, and Peter Kimm echoed the LeF practice in daily orders of giving 'a big hallo' to anyone who had done well by producing for the notice board a half-page picture of the Commander in shirt sleeves sewing on his fourth ring in the manner of a rating sewing on a new badge or stripe—with a caption which read, 'A very big hallo'.

Kimm was one of many people who found the Le Fanu blend of fun, enthusiasm and efficiency irresistibly infectious. Peter became virtually a disciple—and therein lay one of the dangers of Michael's magnetic style of leadership : it was often imitated but was essentially inimitable, as Michael himself was very well aware, warning others to 'do as I say, not as I do'. Dangerous or not, most people succumbed at first encounter to the Le Fanu charm, whether it was the party of public school cadets visiting *Superb* for whom an appendix was added to daily orders in Classical Greek (and who delighted LeF by spotting a grammatical error) or the Chatham taxi driver who asked a naval passenger which ship in the dockyard he wanted. When told, the driver commented, '*Superb* ... Yes ... Commander Le Fanu. Lovely man!'

TEN

The Navy's Youngest Captain

After Michael's promotion at the end of June 1949, *Superb* became that rare thing in the Royal or any other Navy, a ship with two Captains. It was thought good for Michael to spend a few more weeks—until the summer leave period—as Executive Officer of a sea-going ship, so the *Superb* added briefly to her other distinctions that of having a four-ring Commander.

But on 18 August, Michael departed, the richer for a silver telescope and a personal report in which Captain, Alan Scott-Moncrieff, awarded him the highest possible marks in every category and expressed the confident hope that he would 'reach the highest ranks of the Service, and the sooner the better, because I know he has the welfare of the Service very much at heart.'

True though this was, Michael had the welfare of the Le Fanus young and old very much at heart too, and as soon as he was away from *Superb*, he switched his mind to family matters. Prue and the young Mark and Victoria (nicknamed 'Toy' by her brother who found her name impossible to pronounce) had to be moved back from 'Dockyard View' to Petersfield; then Michael took Prue and D'or off to Ireland to spend a few weeks at *Ballymorris* in Bray. The house had been inherited in 1942 by Michael's Uncle Harry, whose distinguished career in the Australian Church made it unlikely that he or his children would ever return permanently to Ireland—so he passed *Ballymorris* on to Michael, who in his turn also decided he would have little use for it. Although this 1949 holiday was a great success, with Michael striding purposefully all over the Wicklow Mountains while the rest of the party picnicked quietly on the lower slopes, he made up his mind to sell the house to his cousin William. From part of the proceeds he realised a long standing ambition— to finance a trip by D'or to visit her sister in New York and her brothers in British Columbia.

After the Irish holiday, Michael's new appointment placed him firmly on the Whitehall ladder. In mid-September he joined the Third Sea Lord and Controller of the Navy, Sir Michael Denny, as Naval Assistant, a job Michael was quickly describing to his friends as Vice-Controller! It was an admirable apprenticeship for his own four-year spell as Controller in the 1960s and brought him closely into touch with plans for the future shape of the Navy, for the Controller's department—responsible as it is for the Navy's hardware—is a vast one covering development and the construction of new ships in every detail from drawing board to commissioning.

The immediate post-war period was a particularly difficult one for the Royal Navy. Massive scrappings and sales of ships had followed the end of hostilities, while many others had been placed in reserve. Apart from being drastically reduced in numbers, the Fleet had yet to assume a pattern geared to the shape of things to come—a shape which was changing very fast for a number of reasons.

First, there was the arrival of the nuclear age. After Hiroshima and Nagasaki, a series of atomic bombs were tested against a fleet of ships at Bikini Atoll in July 1946, with results which demonstrated the need for an entirely new approach to the disposition of fleets at sea, and to the size, shape and strength of new ships. Second, the growing underwater fleet being developed by the Soviet Union constituted a threat which had to be met by new and faster anti-submarine vessels. Third, the new generation of aircraft and the development of missiles rendered old concepts of ship-borne defence useless and called urgently for the development of guided weapons. Speed, and the instant availability of power, became even more vital in ship propulsion systems.

While the everlasting cry for economy was heard from Westminster, and both the post-war Labour government and the Conservative government which succeeded it in 1951 instituted comprehensive Defence Reviews, much experimental work went forward at this time—on gas-turbine propulsion, on the use of the 'Snort' (Snorkel) breathing apparatus which allowed the submarine *Alliance* to carry out in 1948 a three thousand-mile voyage continuously submerged, on the strengthening of ship's hulls and the development of guided weapons with new types of ships to carry them, to quote just a few examples.

All these areas of experiment would have a great influence on the Navy in which Michael Le Fanu was destined for high command, and his mind was of a calibre to master both strategic implications and technical details. Already, too, as Commander of *Superb,* he had shown his flair for human relations with people outside as well as inside the Service, and this was a vital consideration in a department which had to deal constantly with shipbuilders, scientists and the many thousand civilians employed in the Admiralty offices at Bath in Somerset.

As the Navy's youngest Captain and one who was new to the ways of Whitehall, even the irrepressible Michael had to feel his way a little at this stage. Off duty he stayed in 'digs' during the week in Kensington, as paying guest of a sister of Guy Western, his best man—a situation naturally disliked by Prue, who avoided boredom at Petersfield by becoming part-time secretary to two local farmers when not dreaming up an excuse for a jaunt to London. Michael worked long hours but many an evening he spent with an old friend from the *Aurora* days, her former Chaplain, the Rev. Arthur Green, helping him to run a men's club at St Bartholomew's Church off Lavender Hill in Battersea. Here Michael's exuberant style of leadership (no doubt somewhat under restraint in Whitehall) could find expression as he organised 'Paint Ship' parties at the club, whose members soon succumbed to the Le Fanu charm as surely as the men of the 'Old Super-B'—especially after word got around that one lunchtime he had met in Trafalgar Square a bricklayer who was a member of the club and, after exercising his powers of instant recognition, had taken him for a pint, to meet some of his 'mates from the Admiralty'.

Apart from leave periods, there was only one substantial break in two years of work at the Battersea club. 'Sorry chaps,' he said one evening. 'See you in three weeks'—which was all they ever knew at St Bartholomew's about Michael's visit to Washington as Flag Captain to the First Sea Lord. Michael's old friend Admiral Sir Bruce Fraser was currently in the Navy's top job, and when called on to go with the other Chiefs of Staff on a visit to the United States, had 'borrowed' Michael from the Third Sea Lord to accompany him. These were consultations of considerable importance about the setting up of a Command structure following the signature of the North Atlantic Treaty in April 1949 and the inauguration of the North Atlantic Treaty Organisation; but Michael's role as Flag Captain was chiefly a social one—no easy task in a get-together involving representatives of twelve nations, but one for which he was well suited, particularly as he had already formed such good personal relations in the most important of those countries, the United States.

He proved his social worth very quickly by being, according to Admiral Fraser, 'the life and soul' of the trip across the Atlantic in the *Queen Mary*. One evening he had organised a 'Bingo' for the Navy and Army contingents (including the Army Chief of Staff, Gen. Sir William Slim) when he suddenly noticed a young African in beautiful robes sitting by himself. After consulting 'the boss' Michael at once invited the African to join the party. That was how Dr Busia, future Prime Minister of Ghana, came to be introduced to the mysterious delights of bingo. The Navy's team (including Dr Busia) managed to win, and Dr Busia subsequently wrote a letter to the First Sea Lord which revealed how much the friendly invitation had meant to him.

But however well developed Michael's diplomatic talents were at this stage of his career, he was still liable to slip up in sartorial matters. When the *Queen Mary* was about to berth at Pier 90, New York, he left the immaculate No. 5 uniform he was to wear at a dockside reception hanging on the sprinkler guard in his cabin while, dressed in an old jacket and his naval raincoat, he had gone on to the 'flying bridge' to watch the ship come alongside. Unfortunately as she turned to starboard from the river, the *Queen* nudged the knuckle of the pier with an impact which was sufficient to break the sprinkler glass and deluge Michael's jacket (and his cabin) with not overclean water. It was only thanks to the skill of the *Queen Mary*'s valet service that he got to that reception properly dressed and on time.

Later during the visit, LeF went so far as to win support for Admiral Fraser's nomination as a presidential candidate. They were travelling in a train and had gone to the bar for some refreshment, wearing uniform. A reporter who'd been watching their arrival from the other end of the bar and who was 'a bit over the odds' sidled up to LeF (obviously the young assistant) and asked, 'Say, fella, who's your boss?' 'Haven't you heard?' replied Mike. 'He's got the nomination!' 'Jeez . . . what's his platform?' 'He's the Republo-coat . . . and I say Fraser for President!' Upon which the reporter filled everyone's glass, and raised his own with the resounding cry, 'Fraser for President, Fraser for President!'

The social flair seemed to work in all circumstances and at all levels. Back in London, Michael once again met his god-daughter Catherine Christie, now thirteen years of age, at a party given by her parents. 'Do you know the most important duty of a god-father?' he asked. 'He has to be the first man to take his god-daughter out to dinner.' So out they went—to a Chinese restaurant—a great and never-to-be-forgotten event for Catherine, for whom Michael was always, according to her future husband, the hero *'sans peur et sans reproche'*. As a small girl of six during the war, she had decorated her godfather's bedroom with flowers when he came to stay with the family in the country, and had lovingly presented him with a bottle of green ink.

Whatever the pressures of life in Whitehall, Michael always seemed to find time for gestures that would give pleasure to other people, even if they were only remotely connected with him. One day in 1950 he heard that his brother Anthony's mother-in-law at Renhold near Bedford was dangerously ill and that she had expressed a desire to see him in uniform. Quite unheralded, he turned up a week before she died, dressed in full regalia. Then, this time wearing a dark suit and bowler, he suddenly appeared in the village church for the funeral, having organised a quick leave of absence from an exercise in the North Sea.

It was with such personal gestures that Michael secured a

niche for himself in so many hearts; throughout his career he managed to write to everyone who wrote to him—almost always a handwritten letter, almost always containing some personal reference which raised the reply out of the routine. One lifelong correspondent was Peter Kimm, from the *Superb* days. While Michael was Naval Assistant to the Controller, Peter wrote to tell him of his new appointment to the Boys' Training Establishment, HMS *Ganges* at Shotley in Suffolk, and of his intentions to change a few things in Le Fanu fashion. In a long, tactful reply Michael tried to discourage him.

'Don't,' he wrote, 'try to reorganise the place in the first few weeks, or take all your Division to a blue cinema in Ipswich to broaden their minds. Equally you should pay no attention to the advice of Le Fanu. It has always been my habit to play things my own way. Sometimes, I realise it might be better, considered *obj*ectively, for me to pursue more "pusser" (orthodox) methods, but I know that *subj*ectively I am no good at being pusser and would not be successful at it. Similarly I have seen a few serious-minded characters trying to be droll à la Le Fanu—and failing dismally. And furthermore, confusing the hell out of their sailors. If they had stuck to their own line, all would have been well.

'For the record, I think that the prime secret of my success (it is idle to deny that I have been successful in the small field of naval matters) is that, through no merit of my own, I am extremely sensitive to other personalities and can handle anyone from Admirals to OD's (Ordinary Seamen): i.e. I quickly and unconsciously assess what sort of thing they would like to hear —then I say it! This savours of sycophancy and expediency— and indeed I am guilty of both in a large degree. However I kid myself that doubtful means are often justified by a worthy end.

'I can tell you this because I want you to know how firmly I believe in being yourself ... it would not worry me to see you develop more facets of your character which roughly correspond with the best facets of my own. On the other hand, I have some dreary qualities which you could do without—and you have some sterling attributes which I lack ... as an obvious example of this, you have doubtless observed that I am totally irreligious. This is

my loss, I daresay, but I am too lazy, too cynical and in a roundabout way too honest to climb on a bandwaggon in which I have
no confidence. On the other hand I admire those who are
happily aboard said bandwaggon, provided they don't try and
haul me on too!'

A letter quoted at some length, since it reveals much about
LeF in his late thirties, and helps to explain some of the
comments Sir Michael Denny wrote about him when he left the
job of Naval Assistant to the Controller in September 1951.
'He has a wide knowledge of all branches of the naval service
and is blessed with a receptive and original brain which misses
nothing; is very observant and has a happy knack of acquiring
Service information, generally from other than "the usual
channels"; a quick worker who finds time for many outside
interests; has established for himself a position of regard and
respect vis-à-vis US Navy Officers, both those who are his contemporaries and those who hold the highest appointments in that
Service; happily married to a partially disabled wife, his domestic
life is a model of guts, determination, harmony and originality
which well reflects his character.'

Throughout Michael's job with the Controller, his domestic
life (absent as he was for five days a week in London) was under
the kind of strain so many Service people have to experience, but
towards the end of his time as Naval Assistant, a particular
drama had a happy ending. Prue was expecting a third child,
and all was well until in June 1951 she set off with Michael on
holiday to Southwold in Suffolk. There she became unexpectedly
ill and had to be rushed to hospital in Norwich, where she spent
some weeks before, to the great relief of all, Hugh arrived on 23
July. Still unable to travel by car, Prue and the baby eventually
travelled home by ambulance to Petersfield; it was just as well
that the other two children, Mark and Toy, had been trained
to be highly independent from a very early age, for Prue, at this
time in particular, was unable to do a great deal for them. As
a matter of fact Toy was already a capable mother's help, and
when Prue decided that a little touch of feminine embellishment
would improve her morale, Toy, aged three, astonished her
cousin Catherine by marching into the chemist, delivering a long

and complicated message, and emerging with several shades of nail varnish for her mother to choose from.

Fortunately, Michael's next job, as Captain (D) Third Training Flotilla, based at Londonderry, was an accompanied appointment, and by October Prue was well enough to fly over with the children ('a huge success' according to Michael) and establish herself in part of a large old house with a pleasant view over the River Foyle. From there she was able to watch Michael drive his own ship for the first time in his life and negotiate the sharp 'dog-leg' bend in the River Foyle below their windows. On 31 October he took a frigate in and out of Derry in the dark. 'The performance', commented Michael, 'was undistinguished, but nothing was bent.'

His Navigating Officer, Tim Hall, had been warned before the arrival of the new Captain (D) that Michael had had no previous seagoing command, and that he must expect to do most of the manoeuvring at any rate for a time. However, as Hall later remembered, 'LeF took shiphandling in the narrow waters of the River Foyle in his stride, and after a month or two said to me, "Can I take off my L-plates yet, Tim?" ' Tim was happy to 'grant him a licence', impressed by the complete lack of self-importance and grandeur in his new commanding officer, qualities which were further displayed as Christmas approached. All the ships in the squadron received small, inexpensive children's Christmas cards signed 'Michael and Prue Le Fanu'; at least one Wardroom Mess Secretary thought they were from the Le Fanu children, and sent a child's Christmas card in reply.

Happy though their circumstances were at this time, Prue's run of bad luck was not over, for she slipped in the bathroom and broke a leg. But in due course they continued to explore the Donegal countryside during Michael's breaks from duty, enjoying family picnics on the isolated sandy beaches as well as the generous hospitality of many Irish families. The freedom from dreary British rationing was still a novelty when travelling over the border. On one trip, more butter than was strictly permitted by the Customs found its way into the Le Fanu car. Prue was somewhat conscience-stricken but, quite unmoved, Michael ordered her to sit tight : 'They will never order you to get out when they see your sticks!'

Throughout 1952, Michael, with his Third Training Squadron, contributed to the work of the Joint Anti-Submarine school in developing new techniques in one of the most vital areas of the Royal Navy's work. His recall to London in December 1952 for 'special duties with the Deputy Chief of the Naval Staff and the Ministry of Defence' came all too soon for the family who had greatly relished their taste of Irish life; Prue's first reaction, when she heard the news, was to say : 'You go— we'll stay here!' In due course however the journey took place, Michael going by sea with the car while Prue and the children flew from Belfast.

Thick fog delayed the flight and for hours they hung about the crowded airport; after eventually taking off, the aircraft was diverted from fogbound Heathrow to Blackbushe. There, finally, at dead of night, a hired car crawled in dim visibility the thirty miles to Petersfield. For once Michael's equilibrium was shaken by the thought of his whole family flying somewhere overhead as the ferry crossed the murky Irish sea. He sent off a ship-to-shore cable for news, as his father-in-law was due to meet the plane at Heathrow. Confusion followed, but a network of phone calls eventually established everybody's whereabouts and the nightmare journey ended safely, Mark still faithfully clutching the parcel of Londonderry sirloin he had been entrusted with some fifteen hours earlier!

Michael's new job was highly confidential, and the details have remained secret. In general terms it was concerned with the production of a report on the defence of the country in the event of atomic attack, and was chiefly important in his career because it established him for the first time in a tri-service setting. These nine months at the Ministry of Defence called on his ability to form sound judgments in a very difficult field. He was considered to be 'the major contributor to the report of the military members of the staff', and made an impression as 'a naval officer with a wide view of the requirements not only of his own Service, but of the general defence of the country'.

With such experience behind him, Michael's next appointment

—to the Imperial Defence College—seemed logical. He spent most of 1954 there, working, according to Prue, 'three hours a day'. A delightful time for the family, for Michael was home at Petersfield every day by early evening and there were jolly family excursions and holidays. Almost the only long absence was when he went on a visit to West Berlin, where, apart from matters of business, he indulged in his lifelong habit of collecting *Hamlets*. Arousing a good deal of suspicion, he made his way one evening alone into the Russian sector of the city, where he had heard the play was being performed. At last he managed to find the small theatre concerned, only to discover there was no performance that night. So back he went the next evening and another (German) *Hamlet* went into the bag. What had he made of East Berlin? asked his family when he got back. 'Seedy and tumbledown,' was the reply; 'rather like Dublin.'

ELEVEN

HMS *Ganges*

Arguably the most feudal of all the Navy's institutions was—until it closed in 1976—HMS *Ganges*, the training establishment for new entrants, situated on the Suffolk coast at the junction of the rivers Stour and Orwell. Generations of young lads, separated for the first time from home and parents, made their first acquaintance with the Navy in this place. Many of them hated it, and most found it hard at first to come to terms with Naval routine.

In the mid-fifties, *Ganges* was still a training establishment for 'Boy' entrants, and there was very little cushioning for them. The seasoned Chief and Petty Officer instructors were not given to mollycoddling, and the officers, above all the Captain, often seemed remote and unapproachable, while it appeared to be the primary concern of many officers that a boy should salute them correctly. Exceptions, of course, existed, but to at least one Seaman Boy of that period, his Captain appeared to be 'a Victorian character who put in routine appearances at Divisions or bobbed past at Saturday morning rounds' accompanied by a Commander known as 'Horrible Horace'! The treatment the boys received, he later decided, would probably have been little different had the year been 1914.

It was into this strange, closed world, part public school, part penitentiary, that Michael was consigned after his year at the Imperial Defence College. From serving his own apprenticeship in the higher strategies of defence, he now found himself in charge of a thousand or so teenagers adjusting with varying degrees of success, to their first taste of the Navy.

He could have played the country gentleman, integrating into the life of the County (as was traditionally expected of the Captains of HMS *Ganges*) and coasted through his duties as Commanding Officer. But this would not have been characteristic. In spite of advising Peter Kimm, as a young *Ganges* Divisional Officer, 'not to upset the applecart', Michael had meanwhile decided that he himself would turn the establishment inside out in order to direct the vision of officers and ship's company away from what he called (referring to the deadly formalities of kit inspection) 'the boys' socks attitude'.

No doubt remembering, too, his own first unhappy steps up the hill at Dartmouth, and for the rest making the imaginative leap necessary to put himself in another fellow's shoes, he set out to bridge the gulf which existed between staff and boys by getting to know personally as many of his charges as was possible. From the moment of his arrival at Shotley on New Year's Eve 1954, he threw himself into this self-appointed task, and was to become so absorbed in the life of the establishment that he rarely took a day off, even when Prue occasionally tried to lure him away to the attractions of Newmarket races.

Prue, meanwhile, was naturally happy at the thought of being with Michael for two years, but, at the age of thirty-three, not so happy at the daunting prospect of being the wife of the Captain of so vast an establishment. The Commanding Officer's house, Erwarton Hall, was a beautiful Tudor mansion some two miles from the *Ganges*. Surrounded by peaceful gardens and countryside, it was full of the atmosphere of the past centuries and reputedly haunted by the ghost of Anne Boleyn. Here, Prue knew she would be expected to play the role of gracious hostess, which appealed to her far less than the freedom of private life at Petersfield. But faced with the inevitable, she adapted (rather grudgingly, she afterwards admitted to the family), to the life of isolated grandeur, and, in fact, enjoyed the flow of official guests, whose duty it was—especially, it appeared, during the summer months!—to come and inspect HMS *Ganges*, perched, so conveniently, on this attractive and unspoilt promontory of Suffolk.

For Prue the most enjoyed and relaxed time of the week was Monday morning, when she regularly visited several house-bound old people in Shotley village, in particular Mrs Mower, a saintly person, who had been bedridden for many years and had lived in Suffolk all her life. From her flowed vivid stories of sailing traffic on the River Stour, and of happy, frugal times in the days of horse-drawn traffic. Her devoted husband and visiting family used to join in the memories, and one of Toy's best friends at the village school was Mrs Mower's granddaughter, Barbara.

Although Michael, in the words of a subordinate, had decided to 'revolutionise the treatment of young boys coming into the Navy', he in no way stood the place on its head. He was always fundamentally firm on discipline; firm enough, even at home, to send Toy indoors for the duration of an Erwarton Hall children's party when he overheard her claiming, in a misguided moment, 'first go' on the overhead swingboat, because she was 'the Captain's daughter'.

He allowed no slackness with the boys, either, although instead of merely acknowledging the salute of a passer-by, he would stop and have a word, and having discovered where he came from, would seize on some shared piece of local knowledge to establish closer contact. One lad from Blackpool, who had spent most of his time planning how he could buy himself out of the Navy, got chatting with the Captain about Stanley Matthews. The memory of home brought a tear to his eye, but the conversation, he remembered, helped him 'in the change from mother's apron strings to independence'. He remembered, too, how Prue Le Fanu, in her wheelchair, always had a friendly word for the boys: 'Not a lot, but to young lads away from home, it was a lifeline.'

The new style soon made itself felt. On the day after Michael arrived, a Gunnery Instructor, complete with boots and gaiters, was attempting to referee a trainees' inter-mess rugby match. He knew very little about the rules, and was surrounded by thirty boys all arguing about a decision that had been made. The GI was busy consulting his rule book when a civilian walked on to the pitch to see if he could help. He appeared to know what he was talking about, so the GI was only too pleased to offer him the whistle and allow him to take over the game.

Soon after, the Instructor's Divisional Officer wandered over to see how the game was progressing. He was surprised to see the GI on the touchline and asked who was refereeing the game. Reply : 'That civvy offered to do it, so I let him.' The Divisional Officer did a 'double-take' and informed the GI that the 'civvy' was none other than the new Captain. Result : one speechless GI.

LeF often decided to abandon the badges of rank and wear his own rather disreputable brand of civilian clothes, if he thought this would break down barriers. Thus attired, he would spend hours walking round the 'Annexe'—where new arrivals spent the first part of their time at *Ganges* being kitted out and generally indoctrinated. 'Shore leave' was not allowed during this period, which was apt to produce feelings of uncertainty in most new recruits and positive misery in some, and Michael made a habit of sitting on the boys' beds to chat over their problems with them. He even went so far as to credit them with some sensitivity (a quality apt to be despised in military training establishments) and told them not to take too much notice of the constant 'f . . . ing' used in every sentence by the Instructors—they would get used to it.

'The kindness of the man was obvious', one lad recalled in later life, 'particularly when every senior rating and officer seemed to exist solely to bring about your discomfort, and a very strong desire to be at home with dear old mum was never far away.' The boys were naturally won over by LeF's apparent ability to talk to them as equals (he would begin his addresses with the words 'Now men . . .') and they would certainly have supported his pet theory (had they known about it) that 'there are no bad boys, only bad parents'. This view he would make clear to any doting parent who expressed worries about 'little Willy's' progress after attending divisions on Sunday morning.

LeF's touch with visiting families was just as sure as it was with the boys themselves. When he wrote inviting a number of parents to attend a confirmation service during the week, he apologised for the inconvenience by explaining 'these clerical folk are a bit rushed on Sundays'; and after the service, at a small party organised for them, the visitors were somewhat surprised when the Captain, bearing a large teapot, appeared at their table and proceeded to fill their cups. But as he did so, LeF leant over the shoulder of one boy and said quietly, 'You'd better tell your father it's not like this every day!'

Games were always an important part of life at *Ganges*, and LeF, as the rugby incident suggests, played a full part in them. He introduced baseball to the establishment as well as the more traditional British games, of which golf was probably his own favourite. The story goes that one day he was chatting to two of the boys—Danny Leighton and Melville Reynolds—out in the sports field and discovered that Danny had quite a reasonable handicap. The following week, Danny was invited to play the Captain on a local course. Some time afterwards, Danny and Melville were sitting in the mess when the Captain walked in and said, 'Thank you for the game, Leighton. Here is a book of Golfing Rules for you, and I would like you to pay particular attention to rule 1(A).' As soon as the Captain had left, Danny opened the book : there were the printed rules 1, 2, 3 and so on. Rule 1(A) was inserted in manuscript. It read, 'When playing golf against your Captain, always let him *win*!'

Bowls was another game at *Ganges,* and much interest attached to the derbies played twice a year between the officers of the establishment and the Shotley village team. In spite of Drake's example, bowls is not a game at which the average naval officer excels, but LeF revealed a talent for it which saved the home team from humiliating defeat when the first match was played one year at *Ganges*. It was therefore a great disappointment when it was found that the Captain had a previous engagement on the evening of the return match, to be held at the Rose in Shotley.

The setting at the village pub on a warm summer's evening was idyllic, with the bowling green surrounded by yew trees and a barrel of beer on hand : to complete the picture, sitting on a bench beneath the trees was an ancient village rustic, attired in Panama hat. Eventually the old man rose unsteadily to his feet and doddered across the green to captain the village team. As he did so, the Roman Catholic Chaplain from *Ganges* whispered to a fellow member of the *Ganges* team : 'Who's that funny old bugger? I've seen him somewhere before.' It was not until after the game, some two hours later, that the *Ganges* men realised the true identity of their opponent and the nature of their Captain's previous engagement : for this match, as the tenant of Erwarton Hall, and therefore a Shotley villager, he had joined the village team !

A good deal more slippery than Shotley village green was the area of parquet flooring in each mess hut at HMS *Ganges*—the 'mess square' as it was known. Tradition required that a very high polish should be imparted to this area just before Captain's rounds, but there can have been few Captains who tested the polish as Michael did on one occasion. He took a run at each square, and those messes where he was not able to reach the opposite side in a single slide were 'given a re-scrub' (i.e. told to do it again). There is no evidence that Michael took a polisher in hand himself to show how this particular job should be done, but in other ways he often led by example. 'Going over the mast' was to many people a terrifying prospect, so every now and then the 'Mast Class' would find a ginger-haired fellow in sports gear going over it with them.

Once, walking into the gym long after the last PT class of the day had been dismissed, LeF found three rather miserable boys still there. Why? They couldn't climb a rope. Flinging off his monkey jacket, Michael went up the rope himself and stayed with the boys till they had mastered it too.

In such ways was solidarity built up at *Ganges* in the Le Fanu days. And the Captain had just as imaginative a touch with his officers as he had with the trainees. One former submariner who had joined the staff found the rules a little irksome after the free-and-easy ways of submarines—particularly the one which decreed that the wardroom bar remained closed until 1230 at lunchtime. So together with one or two fellow officers, he had formed the habit of finding some reason to visit the Pier Head, only a stone's throw from the Bristol Arms at around 1130.

One morning they heard that the Captain was walking in that area with his 'Doggy' (the unattractive name given to the Boy Seaman who acted as Captain's messenger) so they decided to delay their visit to the Bristol Arms until the coast was clear. When they did arrive, they were informed by the landlord that the Captain had been in at 1130, had a pint for himself and a half pint for his 'Doggy' and then, ten minutes later, had walked out remarking: 'I'd better not have the other half or I'll keep your regular customers away.' The gesture was more effective than any number of lectures would have been; as was the gentle but pointed comment LeF wrote on the report of one departing dental surgeon who was new to the ways of the Navy. He had conducted himself, said the Captain, 'entirely to my satisfaction; albeit occasionally to my surprise'.

The informality of LeF's manner seemed only to heighten respect for him. One young officer, invited with his wife to dinner at Erwarton Hall, had left the invitation card in his office when he went home to dress, and as a result mistook the time of the invitation. When they arrived a few minutes after 1930, the surprised Steward told them they were early—the invitation was for 2000. 'In that case,' said the young guests, 'we'll go away and come back at the proper time.' But before they could leave, the Captain appeared in his underpants, ushered the early arrivals into the sitting room and entertained them happily until Prue came in. Then he disappeared to finish dressing.

LeF brought a light touch to matters of discipline whenever he thought it would be effective. At the end of the summer term in 1956, all the officers, instructors, and boys were mustered in the gymnasium for a few end-of-term words from the Captain. These usually consisted of rather pompous injunctions about how to behave on leave without disgracing the uniform, and consequently went in one ear and out of the other. But this occasion was rather different, as Tony McCrum, Commander at the time, recalled:

'There they all were in the gymnasium, fallen in, stood at ease, waiting for the top brass to walk solemnly down the central gangway, when a figure in seaman's uniform appeared, rushing in all adrift, very scruffy. He darted past the officers and instructors, and jumped on the stage. Instructors rushed forward, Divisional Officers shouted, until they suddenly recognised the Captain and everyone hooted with laughter. He took off his cap and out fell the illegal fags—all the corniest jokes in the ship's concert party book were pulled, but it had the effect that everyone remembered what he had to say when he turned on the one serious bit about behaviour on leave.'

It was the time of rock 'n' roll riots, and there had been a certain amount of trouble 'ashore'. There was also a tendency for lads who found things difficult, to break out of the establishment and make a get-away after dark. Some of them came back after a night in the cold, others were missing for several days—and one made it all the way to Aden in a merchant ship.

Under the Naval Discipline Act, these boys were guilty of desertion and as a result, the Punishment Return of *Ganges* showed a high incidence of this particular offence—which led to a letter to LeF from the Second Sea Lord asking for an explanation. Michael pinned a minute sheet to this letter and sent it round to heads of department and Divisional Officers. The Commander began by commenting that he thought the Lords Commissioners should have greater worries than small boys high-tailing it across fields—and, as the minute circulated, the remarks grew more and more dismissive, ending with a page from the senior C of E Chaplain detailing his views on the Chaplain of the Fleet. Some time later the Captain was asked at a meeting what he had replied to the Second Sea Lord. 'Oh!' was the reply, 'I just bundled all the minutes into an envelope and sent it off to him.'

Whenever possible, Michael tried to take the heat out of disciplinary problems, realising that he was dealing with boys and not mature men, and his matter-of-fact approach was very refreshing. One night some communion wine was stolen from naval stores, and many hands were raised in horror at what was regarded as 'this sacrilege'. 'Nonsense,' was Michael's reaction. 'It's not holy until it's been blessed. I just want to find out who did it.'

LeF's independent attitude was well illustrated in another episode of *Ganges* days, which came about as a result of events on the other side of the world in the River Yangtse in 1949. The story, headline news at the time, may now need re-telling.

Civil war was raging in China, and the Chinese Nationalists were retreating before the Communist advance, which was nearing the city of Nanking, where, by agreement with the Nationalist government, a British warship was stationed to assist in the protection of British nationals. In April 1949 the destroyer *Consort* was due to be relieved by the frigate *Amethyst* in this task, but *Amethyst*'s passage up the Yangtse was threatened by the presence of Communists on one bank of the river, who refused to guarantee safe conduct to the ship. However as *Consort* was desperately short of supplies, it was decided to attempt the passage.

Sixty miles south of Nanking, *Amethyst* was attacked by Communist batteries : her gyro compass, lighting and gunnery control systems were put out of action and her Captain fatally wounded. The ship grounded on a sandbank known as Rose Island, and there she had to remain for three months, in spite of attempts to rescue her by *Consort* and by the cruiser *London* sailing up river from Shanghai. However an RAF Sunderland managed to deliver medical supplies and an RAF doctor (*Amethyst*'s doctor had been killed) to the stricken frigate, many of whose surviving crew had managed to get ashore and eventually reached Shanghai. Lieutenant-Commander J. S. Kerans, Assistant Naval Attaché at Nanking, had been ordered to take command of the ship and of the sixty RN and Chinese ratings who remained on board together with three of *Amethyst*'s officers.

After three months of fruitless negotiation with the Communist leaders for the release of the ship (the Communists had now captured Nanking and, lower down river, were now in possession of both banks) Kerans decided to break out. Although the ship's effective armament was reduced to one oerlikon and one four-inch, and fuel supplies were low, all hands were unanimous in supporting him. Under cover of darkness on the night of 30 July, *Amethyst* contrived to make the one hundred and fifty-mile passage to Woosung at full speed, returning Communist fire as she went, and before dawn on 31 July Kerans was able to make the famous signal to his Commander-in-Chief : 'Have rejoined the Fleet South of Woosung. No damage or casualties. God save the King!'

This heroic exploit was an obvious subject for a film. In due course, Herbert Wilcox persuaded the Admiralty to lend *Amethyst* from the Reserve Fleet for the purpose, and the River

Orwell, flowing to its wide estuary through the flat Suffolk countryside, was cast as the River Yangtse. As a result, *Ganges*, with Michael at its head, was drafted into show business for several memorable weeks.

Tony McCrum joined the establishment as its new Commander during the filming and thought 'he had joined a madhouse rather than an HM ship. Normally highly disciplined young boys were whooping round the place dressed as Communist guerrillas or hobbling around as gallant and wounded British sailors. One got the impression that the film producer was really Mike Le Fanu rather than Wilcox and certainly he played a major role in organising the naval side of it and making sure the loaned frigate did its stuff realistically.'

It was just the sort of skylark Michael enjoyed, especially as it provided a welcome break from routine for everyone at *Ganges*. One day Michael Marsh, son of a wardroom gardener, was down by the pier dressed in his oldest clothes, when the Captain's car drew up beside him. 'Doing anything in particular?' asked Michael as he got out of the car. 'No sir,' said the astonished lad. 'Come on then', said Michael, and they set off in the Captain's boat for the *Amethyst*, lying offshore. 'I'm not really dressed properly,' said the boy. 'Never mind,' said Michael, 'I'm in the scruff myself.' Which meant (if Marsh's memory served him well) a red jersey and a pair of old trousers.

It is not clear if this was the occasion when Michael felt obliged to take over the ship.

As the frigate lay in the 'Yangtse' it was necessary to simulate the splashes from Communist gunfire, and for this purpose HMS *Vernon*, the Navy's Torpedo School at Portsmouth, had provided a number of underwater charges, set to explode at varying depths and at varying distances from the ship, which in due course had to receive a 'direct hit' on 'X' four-inch turret aft.

'Unfortunately', wrote John Kerans, who had been engaged as technical adviser by Wilcox, 'there were a number of re-takes, and, as the tide turned, a number of *Vernon*'s charges drifted towards the ship's side and blew the frames below the waterline.' As the water flooded into the ship's empty fuel tanks, a heavy list of 15 degrees to starboard developed which brought about 'a rapid movement of camera crews who abandoned their equipment like rats leaving a sinking ship.'

All this was reported to Michael while he was having dinner one night, and not liking the possibility that one of HM ships might actually sink on his own doorstep, Michael at once signalled the Admiralty : 'Have assumed command HMS *Amethyst*.' Who leaked the story to the Press is not clear, but Fleet Street was rapidly extended in the direction of *Ganges*, and one paper announced that *Amethyst* had struck a German mine—hardly likely in the mid-fifties in the approaches to one of Britain's busier ports. Herbert Wilcox, however, could hardly object to such a spread of advance publicity for his forthcoming film; and as for *Amethyst*, with the help of the local fire brigade she was 'counter-flooded' and brought on an even keel, patched up and pumped out.

Before their Lordships had had time to do very much except tell the Captain of *Ganges* that he couldn't assume command of anything without their knowledge, they received Michael's signal. 'Have relinquished command HMS *Amethyst*.' It made a story Michael loved telling, with perhaps just a suspicion of extra colour as he described the distinguished film stars diving over the side and swimming for their lives and *Amethyst* settling in about six feet of muddy estuary. The right lessons were clearly learnt from the incident by the men from *Vernon*, for the final run down the 'Yangtse', which could only be 'shot' once, went without a hitch.

The making of *Yangtse Incident* was of course a quite exceptional episode in the life of *Ganges*, where the regular round of classes and drills soon reverted to normal—except that the Le Fanu touch continued to humanise things whenever possible. Terence Wyss, who had won a Seamanship prize and was due to receive it at divisions one day, was unfortunately rushed to hospital to have a cyst removed : but his disappointment vanished when he saw the Captain coming through the ward to present him with the certificate personally. 'Shall I sign it Michael or Captain M. Le Fanu?' he asked Terence, who opted naturally for 'Michael' and never forgot the encounter.

Michael Marsh, the gardener's lad, who had to have a kidney

Prue and Michael with Mark, born
14 November 1946

(*Above*): The 'Old Super-B'—HMS
Superb

Erwarton Hall, near Ipswich, Suffo[...]

The Le Fanus lived here when Mich[...]
was Captain of HMS *Ganges*

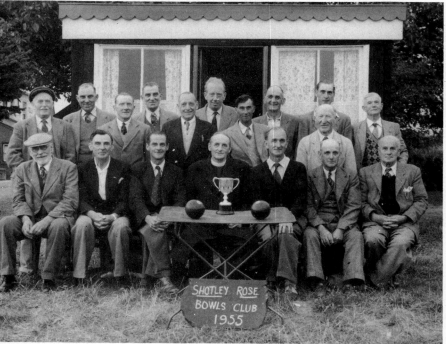

(*Above*): During a visit to HMS *Ganges*, Prince Philip chats to a young trainee

Michael as a member of the Shotley village bowls team

Farewell to the Le Fanus: thirteen
hundred boys sing carols outside
Erwarton Hall

HMS *Eagle*: together with *Ark Royal*
she was part of Carrier Strike
Group Two—the core of the British
component of the NATO strike fleet

(*Above*): Walking was always a
favourite relaxation of Michael's

With Hugh on board *Water Violet*
during a family canal expedition

Commander-in-Chief, Middle East

(*Above*): The Middle East C-in-C shows the flag

Admiral on horseback: the Middle E[...]
C-in-C with High Commissioner
Sir Humphrey Trevelyan

operation, wondered what was happening when he saw the Captain's car draw up outside his ward, and Prue being helped out by her husband. He was astonished when he discovered they had come to see him. Michael Le Fanu remained in touch with Michael Marsh for the rest of his life. When he himself became ill with leukaemia, Marsh was among the friends LeF informed in a circular letter of his decision to resign. And when Admiral of the Fleet Sir Michael Le Fanu died, Michael Marsh received tickets for the memorial service at Westminister Abbey.

Such was the affection Michael and Prue inspired at *Ganges* that when it became known the Captain was nearing the end of his appointment, the boys thought of a gesture that would make their feelings clear. At the end of the autumn term, one evening just before Christmas 1956, they decided to walk the two miles from *Ganges* to Erwarton Hall. Traffic was halted as, by the light of flares and torches, a total of some thirteen hundred boys (together with their officers and instructors who had been invited to join in) headed for the big house where they poured through the front gates unannounced and sang carols to Michael and Prue for a full half hour.

It was tribute to one whose 'natural concern for all', as a *Ganges* boy later put it, 'made it a sure thing that there was nothing you would not do for him. He was a born leader, a man's man, he had style—and terrific compassion.'

TWELVE

Carrier Captain

Halfway through Michael's time as Captain of HMS *Ganges*, Vice-Admiral Sir Frederic Parham, as Commander-in-Chief, The Nore, recommended that his next appointment should be in command of an aircraft carrier, the most coveted seagoing appointment for a Captain, and one which, in addition, would give Michael the experience of air operations which so far he lacked. In accordance with this recommendation (it was in any case the logical next step in Michael's progression to Flag Rank) he assumed command of HMS *Eagle* on 18 February, 1957.

Eagle had unfortunately acquired a reputation as an unhappy ship, and Michael took her over at a very unpropitious moment. On the way back after the Suez operations, the ship had suffered a disastrous fire and as a result was undergoing a refit in Devonport dockyard. If ever a ship needed a fresh start, it was *Eagle* at this time, and it was very soon apparent that he would provide it.

When Charles Denman, the Captain's Secretary, went to Plymouth station to meet the new boss, he felt the impact at once. 'Are you my Secretary?' asked Michael, as he jumped off the train and, scarcely waiting for a reply, added, 'You poor bastard! Get my bicycle out of the luggage van will you?' Next morning Denman, almost as new to the ship as Michael, was momentarily stumped (though he didn't show it) when the Captain said, 'Tell Arthur to come and see me!' To have asked 'Who's Arthur?' would have been fatal. Rapidly scanning the list of officers, the Secretary noticed that the Commander had the initial 'A' and forthwith summoned him. It proved the correct guess, and thus Charles Denman made the first move towards a fruitful professional collaboration and a close friendship. In the future, Charles Denman was to serve as Secretary to Michael in several of his appointments, including his two years as First Sea Lord, and much was to depend on the intuitive rapport which grew up between the two men.

In *Eagle* Denman watched for the first time the Le Fanu style of leadership in action. A priority was to create 'confidence in the management,' and to this end Michael set out at once to see as much of the ship and to meet as many of his men as he could— an object he achieved by what he called 'potholing'. This consisted of diving down any open hatch and pursuing the ladders vertically down through the various decks, pausing en route to talk to anyone who was around, whether sailor or dockyard worker. The knowledge that the Captain might suddenly turn up at any moment in the least likely places had the double effect of stimulating effort and creating a feeling that 'the management' cared about what was going on down below.

At last the refit was over, leaving *Eagle* with the prospect of a very hurried work-up for an important exercise in northern waters. Together with *Ark Royal*, she was to fulfil her main role as part of 'Carrier Strike Group Two', the core of the British component of the NATO strike fleet. Michael took the first opportunity to 'clear lower deck', and behind closed doors in the upper hangar he began by saying that what he had to tell the ship's company was secret. Their complicity thus assured, he went on to outline the challenge ahead. The Captain told the men that his message contained 'naught for your comfort' and promised them nothing but hard work. But he made them feel that they could, within a matter of weeks, easily rival the efficiency of *Ark Royal*, and thus prove themselves worthy members of the Royal Navy's highest élite.

Watching from *Ark Royal*, Captain (later Admiral Sir Frank) Hopkins felt that *Eagle* had 'changed almost overnight'; within six weeks of leaving the dockyard, Michael was ready to embark *Eagle*'s squadrons. Although he had gained a civilian pilot's licence, he was a little worried about the fact that he was not a naval aviator, and yet might very well have to take life-or-death decisions affecting flying men. He knew that aircrews tended to distrust a carrier Captain who was not himself an airman, and that he might therefore have an uphill struggle to win their confidence. In the event they came to accept and trust him completely after a very short time.

Michael made a good start by going down to the Royal Naval Station at Culdrose in Cornwall to inspect the squadrons at work, after which he asked if they could all be brought together so that he could introduce himself and say a few words. Indeed the words *were* few, but in the opinion of Captain Desmond Vincent-Jones, then in command at Culdrose, they were 'among the most effective he had ever heard uttered to sailors'.

'You and I,' Michael began, 'are going to spend the next year or so serving together in a large vessel called *Eagle* and I'm sure we'll get on well together. There is only one thing I want from you men, and that is good manners. Good manners . . . got it? I do not want "Would you please very kindly pass the salt, please?" Neither do I want "Pass the f . . . ing salt". I just want "Pass the salt please".' End of speech.

The squadron men, who had expected the usual longwinded spiel about 'pulling together', 'bands of brothers' and 'every sailor an ambassador' were most pleasantly surprised and impressed. Incidentally, later that evening, Captain Vincent-Jones was equally impressed when his overnight guest discussed the niceties of French cooking with his wife, displaying a remarkable degree of knowledge—and Lef's 'bread and butter' letter, received a few days later, contained not bread, but a recipe for making *croissants à la Française*.

With the squadrons on board, the pace of life in *Eagle* accelerated. Brian Kennedy, the padre, found it extremely hard to conduct a Sunday morning service on the quarterdeck (situated aft, below the flight deck) with the thump of aircraft 'landing on' above his head, and the roar of an attendant helicopter hovering close on the port quarter—but was resigned to such things. He was, however, less pleased when he found that offices and passages were being scrubbed out as usual on Sundays—that, in fact, the routine being worked in every department was the same as on any other day of the week. So the padre wrote a lengthy memo to the Captain, pointing out that a day of comparative rest was essential for the ship's company if at all possible; the Captain might perhaps recall that in Russia, after the Revolution when Sunday was abolished, another day of rest had to be instituted, for production declined alarmingly. To the Chaplain's great surprise, Lef published this memo in full, together with his reply, which was to the effect that heads of departments were to see that no inessential work was done on Sundays, but ended with the punch line : 'However, I am sure the Almighty realises that we have a problem!'

On the way north to join the NATO exercise 'Strike Back', *Eagle* put into Rosyth, where the ship was stricken, as was the flagship *Ark Royal*, with a heavy bout of Asian 'flu—indeed most of the ship's company went down with it. This made things in no way easier for *Eagle's* Captain. When the Admiral signalled to enquire his state of readiness for sea, he replied, '2500 disgruntled seamen, 250 resigned officers, but anything you can fly, we can flu better'.

The job of Carrier Strike Group Two, with their American colleagues in Strike Group One, was to support the northern flank of the NATO line in Europe with air cover and to 'attack' targets in that area—a task which took the ships well to the north of the Arctic Circle in appalling weather conditions. Asian 'flu or not, the exercise had to go on, and both *Eagle* and *Ark* succeeded in operating their aircraft round the clock as long as they were required to do so.

In these trying circumstances, everyone on board was under a strain, and the Captain's sense of humour had to survive some severe tests. Once, during night flying, when the destroyer *Cavendish* was acting as aircrew rescue guardship, she made a signal to *Eagle* saying she would have to break off, in order to pass across to the big ship an emergency appendicitis case. Flying was stopped and a rendezvous arranged. However, shortly afterwards, when the two ships should have been virtually alongside each other, there was no sign of *Cavendish*. Michael was pacing up and down the bridge, far from pleased, and was in no way mollified when a red-faced Navigating Officer approached him to confess that they had been steaming on a reciprocal bearing (in the diametrically opposite direction) for the past ten minutes.

What the Captain said to the 'pilot' is not recorded; but to *Cavendish* he signalled: 'We have had an anatomical evening. You have lost an appendix, we have made a balls.' Not the kind of admission a carrier Captain likes making to a destroyer.

LeF's former Navigating Officer in the Third Training Flotilla, Tim Hall, had now graduated to his own command, the frigate HMS *Salisbury*—and found himself in company with *Eagle* during this series of exercises. No problems here. When the ships came in sight of each other, Tim was summoned to the radio telephone, over which came Michael's voice, saying how good it was to be working again with an old friend—thus creating a valuable upsurge of morale in *Salisbury*. This good state of affairs was improved further when he visited *Salisbury* to dine with Tim. Hearing that she had on board some junior seamen newly out of *Ganges,* Michael said, 'Let's go down and see them on the messdeck'—where Tim Hall was astonished to find that LeF remembered all the lads by name, only hesitating briefly over one. No wonder *Salisbury*'s junior seamen appeared to regard LeF as 'next to God, if not God himself'.

He had no ambitions to replace the Almighty: the secular arm was sufficient for him, and he was content to leave things spiritual to those whom they concerned. His view of the proper relationship between temporal and spiritual powers was revealed in his brief telephone exchanges with *Eagle*'s Chaplain, who, among his other tasks, ran the wardroom library. Always avid for new reading matter Michael phoned the Chaplain almost every day with a laconic 'Church? State. Books!'

Michael's personality was such that people seemed almost to enjoy appearing before the Head of State as defaulters. 'Next time I'll throw the book at you, Smith,' was a favourite form of warning to a first offender. If the offence was repeated, the Captain would say: 'You know what to expect, Smith?' 'Yessir.' 'The book, Smith!' And the man would go off as if he'd been promoted, though no doubt the euphoria evaporated when he discovered the contents of 'the book'.

LeF also injected a personal touch into the routine business of 'Captain's Rounds'. On the back of some formal personal cards, inscribed 'Captain M. Le Fanu, RN, HMS *Eagle*,' he wrote the words 'Big Brother is watching you'—and these cards he would deposit in the pockets of coats or in sailors' caps which might be left 'sculling' around the messdecks. Often such visiting cards were not discovered until days later, with unnerving effect. The sailors relished the idea of having such a 'character' for a Captain, particularly as he was professionally impeccable : but it paid to be alert at all times, for there was no knowing when 'Big Brother' would strike again.

Once, after going ashore by the quarterdeck gangway wearing civilian clothes, Michael decided to return on board via the forward gangway, normally used by the ship's company. Each sailor was issued with a 'Station Card' which had to be surrendered to the Quartermaster or Corporal of the Gangway when going ashore and claimed again when returning to the ship. Great indeed was the bafflement produced when a tall gingerhaired fellow (Michael had not long been on command) announced, 'Le Fanu, M. Station card please !' They never forgot the Captain's face after that.

As for Michael, he knew not only the names but something about the personal background of most of the two thousand seven hundred people under his command, taking particular care as always with the youngest and greenest. The first time *Eagle* went to sea, there were a number of young sailors on board, and he took the trouble to go down and reassure them, saying that he well remembered his own seasickness when he first went to sea. The Captain also took a great interest in the midshipmen under training in the ship—young men at a stage in their careers when encouragement from above is much needed, and is by no means always forthcoming. Nor was it a case of 'out of sight out of mind' where *Eagle*'s men were concerned. Some years later, when Peter Langley Smith, who had been the popular commander of *Eagle*, was killed in a helicopter crash, it was Michael, then Controller of the Navy, who organised a fund for his family, though such singling out of a Service casualty was not looked upon kindly by the authorities. Subsequently an official 'dependants' fund' was set up.

There seems little doubt that LeF's flair for leadership never showed itself more fully than during his days as Captain first of

HMS *Ganges* and then of HMS *Eagle*. The majority of his friends agree that, for all his remarkable achievements in high office, he was at his best when commanding people and not bits of paper, and that if Britain had been at war, the man who was such a superb carrier Captain (at a particularly trying time for *Eagle*, with all the traumas of a refit and recommissioning) would undoubtedy have displayed the kind of leadership in action associated with such men as Cunningham and Mountbatten. As things were, he was allowed just under a year in *Eagle* before being appointed once again to Whitehall, this time as an Acting Rear Admiral, at the age of forty-four.

LeF's departure from *Eagle* was greatly regretted by all on board; by the sailors for whom the pipe 'clear lower deck' to hear the latest 'buzz' never afterwards had quite the same connotations of wit and brevity; and by the officers, a group of whom gave him a dinner ashore to mark his promotion, and devised a skilful limerick which admirably expressed the *Eagle* brand of 'good manners':

> *The language of Captain Le Fanu*
> *Scarcely ever would deafen you;*
> *But its varied content*
> *Left no doubt what was meant*
> *Without adding 'CK' to F and U.*

THIRTEEN

Director-General

After *Eagle* there was time for leave before once again embarking on the Whitehall routine. Andrew Lewis, now serving on the staff of SHAPE in Paris, invited Prue and Michael to his rented farmhouse near Versailles, where in bitter February snow and winds, they enjoyed a holiday during which the pair of them made it to the top of the Eiffel tower as well as seeing most of the other sights of the French capital, including, as a contrast to all the culture, a strip-tease show at 'La Tomate'. Michael also found time to chat with Andrew about his new job, which offered a most interesting prospect.

In 1957 a special committee under Sir Barclay Nihill had considered the way the material requirements of the Navy were organised, and had recommended the re-grouping of the eighteen departments reporting to the Controller under Directors-General, a grade new to the Admiralty : it was a process which inevitably became known as 'Nihilism'. There were now to be three major departments—the Ship Department (whose new Director-General was regarded as *primus inter pares* of the three departmental heads), the Weapons Department and the Aircraft Department. Each department was to have a number of divisions—in the case of the Weapons Department, there were five : based on the former directorates of Naval Ordnance, Naval Ordnance Inspection, Underwater Weapons, Radio Equipment and the Compass Department. This was the empire which Michael had to set up when he took over in March 1958 as Director-General Weapons Designate, in the rank of Acting Rear-Admiral.

Obviously such a major change of organisation created immense problems, both technical and human—and many differing points of view had to be reconciled if things were to run smoothly. From the outset, Michael decided to make haste slowly —by changing as little as possible in the existing set-up. He was perfectly well aware of the arguments raging all round him, which approached him most closely in the persons of his Civil Assistant, Harry Driffield, and his Technical Assistant, Commander Brian Tippett.

Between themselves they discussed with great heat the rival merits of dividing the department according to 'subjects' (the existing state of affairs) or of making a more fundamental reorganisation to bring research, design, development, production and inspection together (the 'functional' split). They also each considered themselves (probably with justice) overworked. And they fondly imagined that LeF knew nothing of their plots and stratagems. Only later did they discover that he was engaged in drafting a little dialogue entitled :

> *The Impossible we fix at once—*
> *Le Fanu takes a little longer.*

This is an abbreviated version :

B *This is a mess, the whole dear delightful Wep Dep. It needs sorting.*

H *What do you think I've been trying to do for the last eighteen months?*

B *You've tried, Harry, you've tried. But I see this with a fresh salty mind. I'm going to tell the boss he's got to reorganise. Apart from anything else, I'm overworked.*

H *Me too. What have you in mind?*

B *Well, we want a Common Services Division to handle all the awkward customers. The head of it can get all those goons out of my hair, and he can stand, or even sit, and listen to the vilification of all those stuffy Captains in the other divisions.*

H *You have a point, but how are you going to put it over?*

B *I'll just march in there and tell him.*

H *No, no, dear boy. You'll never sell him the idea thataway. What you must do is put over a different plan. He'll slap it*

*down. Then, if you play it right, he'll come through with
your original idea, only by then it will be his.*

B *You crafty old civil servant you.*

H *Let's see, then. You go in and say you want a Deputy DGW
to do his work (and ours). That'll make him good and mad.*

B *. . . then just mention what a problem the Common Services
are . . .*

H *That's the idea. I'll sit beside you and look statesmanlike
but not commit myself.*

B *Whacko. How long do you think it'll be before he's selling
our ideas as his?*

H *About a fortnight. Say three weeks, allowing for Christmas.*

Three weeks later.

B and H (in unison) *There you are, what did I tell you?*

By means of this dialogue, LeF skilfully let his assistants know
that he knew what they were up to, and at the same time subtly
flattered them by giving them the credit for a change of course.
But keeping a finger on the pulse of his department at all levels
was very much a Le Fanu priority; he accomplished it, as always,
by unconventional means. He made a point of getting around as
many of the offices as he could, frequently appearing (before he
became well known) incognito, so as to collect uninhibited
comments and criticism. In the many workshops which came
under his control he would, in the words of a senior adviser,
'creep around as if he were an ordinary-idle!-worker, and would
casually chat up the man on the bench to get his views, which
were seldom those of the management'.

Most of those Michael met in this way were quite unaware of
any ulterior motive, and indeed very often his motives were
exactly what they appeared to be : to encourage progress, to show
interest in everybody's work, and to make each person feel
necessary. For instance, he got to know all his drivers personally
and made a point of visiting the garage from time to time, with
the result that he acquired among them 'a body of men who
would have followed him over a cliff'.

Few opportunities for a friendly gesture were missed : LeF was going round a trials ship one day (it could have been either HMS *Cumberland* or HMS *Girdle Ness*, for the same story is told about both ships . . . maybe it happened twice !), led by the bugler in front sounding a 'G', followed by the Master at Arms, the Commander, staff officers and heads of departments, and accompanied by the Captain. Suddenly Michael noticed a sign reading 'Ship's Laundry'. 'Let's go in here,' he said. Inside he found a lone seaman ironing his 'smalls' and asked, 'Do you press trousers?' In the meantime the Petty Officer in charge had been sent for, and when he arrived, found a Rear-Admiral in the middle of the laundry minus his trousers, which were in the process of being pressed.

The knack of making others feel they mattered worked as well in an Admiralty Department as it had in a ship. It must have taken extraordinary ability to establish not only polite but cordial relations with another Rear-Admiral senior to himself who was serving as Director of one of his divisions; and in a wider context, Michael very soon started to achieve a feeling of contact with all his workers through personal newsletters circulated throughout the Department. In the first of these written almost throughout in his own hand, he finished up with a competition to devise a suitable horoscope for the vesting day of the Weapons Department. When the entries poured in by the hundred, Michael's Civil Assistant sorted them and painstakingly prepared an analysis of their relative merit before presenting them to the Director-General on the closing date for entries. 'Goodness,' he said, 'you don't expect me to read them all do you? Now let's see, the prize-winners must include a typist, a naval officer, a draughtsman . . . a representative selection. And I will give them each a luncheon as a prize.'

A subsequent newsletter announced the 'Vesting Day Competition Result' with the comment : 'An enormous entry. Sorry my purse and digestion can't manage a prize for all. Winners listed below will be consulted about the consumption of prizes, probably in October.' And the newsletter also included an item which read : 'The Surface Division, on which the burden of looking after me has largely fallen, and to which I am most grateful, will be relieved to hear that I am slowly acquiring a small personal staff. Later on some clerical aid will be forthcoming. All of which leads me to reflect that :

> *Director-General high sounding title*
> *visions of smart bowler hat*
> *whaleboned foundation garment*
> *personal motor car*
> *obsequious secretaries bowing and scraping*
> *issue directives*
> *administer do not execute*
> *work to be done not by the chief*
> *but by highly disorganised indians*
>
> *facing the facts*
> *does anyone know of a part of an office in Somerset*
> *and a share just a share of a typist*
> *and a cupboard or shelf in a cupboard*
> *for stowing the sugar*
>
> *(Advertisement)*

There was also *Random Harvest—a few more ears from the corn-bin* which gave some down-to-earth definitions of Whitehall phrases, in the following manner :

When I say . . .	*What I mean is . . .*
Of course I'm not trying to Empire-build	I *am* trying to Empire-build
Responsibilities must be clearly defined . . . but	I may have to take the can back . . . but
Appropriate liaison must be maintained at all levels.	. . . I may *not*.
Although your proposal has much to commend it, it is not perhaps in all the circumstances wholly appropriate at this time.	I'm senior to you *or* Look ! I can write a 21-word sentence.
Of course this talk is absolutely off the record.	I've got a concealed microphone in this room.

I don't think we can take this conversation much further until I have consulted my colleagues. I've got a concealed microphone in this room, but I've just realised it's not working.

The notion that Michael himself took a somewhat disenchanted view of high-sounding jargon and formality naturally endeared him to the troops. In 1959 he went to visit the Underwater Weapons Launching Establishment at Poole in Dorset, where great preparations were made to receive him. He toured the establishment, chatting with everyone he met, had luncheon and when the time came to depart, expressed his appreciation of a most enjoyable visit. But it was his parting shot that was remembered and quoted. Just as he was about to enter the car to be driven to the station, he shook hands with the reception party and was overheard to remark under his breath, 'I must remember to be pompous!' In fact, he never did, even as Admiralissimo; and he seized every opportunity to puncture pomposity in others.

While he was Director-General Weapons, Michael went to visit his old friend and best man Guy Western who had retired as a Captain and was living by the sea in West Sussex. From time to time, Guy—himself a man of no false pretensions—would go down and give a hand in the icecream kiosk on the beach at West Wittering. Naturally during the course of his visit, Michael said he would come and help too. Alas for the serving Captain RN who, all unawares, came up to the kiosk and asked for two choc bars. Recognising Guy, the customer exclaimed in horror, 'You can't do that as a retired Captain RN.' 'Quite right,' said Michael quickly, handing over the two choc bars, 'you need a serving Admiral to look after you!'

Promotion to full Rear-Admiral in fact came in July 1958, by which time the 'Wep Dep' was beginning to function as Michael wanted. That August there was a family holiday down at Bridport, Dorset, in a caravan parked on land belonging to John Streatfeild, now also retired from the Navy, and a farmer. With that extraordinary facility for changing gear which was one of his characteristics throughout life, Michael dropped entirely for a couple of weeks the cares of his office and entered into the children's problems. Whether young Hugh was using the right kind of bait seemed to be the greatest of his worries—that, and making sure that Prue's disability did not prevent her from taking a full share in the fun. On journeys official and unofficial, colleagues, friends, and members of the family alike were by now accustomed to the command, 'Get Prue's spanners out of the boot!'

It was back to work much too soon, certainly for Prue and the rest of the family, who found that Michael was only able to make passing calls at home on the almost incessant round of travelling required by his work. Petersfield in Hampshire was one corner of what came to be known as 'the deadly triangle'. The second was London, where the Controller (to whom Michael was responsible) had his office; and in the third corner was Bath in Somerset, where much of his Department was based. Apart from these main centres of activity, Michael also frequently had to visit Slough in Buckinghamshire, Portsdown (near Portsmouth) and Portland, as well as many other establishments up and down the country.

An indication of his state of perpetual motion was given in a letter to Andrew Lewis of mid-October 1958, when they were trying to arrange a foursome to see *My Fair Lady*. 'Looking at my diary, I see I am in Bath on 29/10, London 30 and 31. Home for weekend, then London 3/11, 4 and 5/11 might be London or Bath. Spending 6/11 at Aberporth where I believe they have some G.W. (Guided Weapons). In the train night of 5/11 and 6/11.' The letter went on to say that much as Michael and Prue would like it, it would not be possible to have the Lewises to spend a weekend at Petersfield, for Michael's sister Barbara was very ill (with cancer) at Dorchester, and it was necessary to have D'or staying at Petersfield: most Sundays there was an expedition to Dorchester.

Apart from family worries and the administrative problems of creating and running his own new department, Michael also had something of a running fight with the Ship Department, whose headquarters were 'on the other hill' at Bath. The perpetual question was whether weapon systems should be designed to fit into the ships or the ships should be designed around the weapons. With several important new types of ship in various stages of design and construction, these differences were wide-ranging.

A White Paper of 1957 had announced sweeping changes in all three Services over the next five years: changes which were further defined for the Navy in the Admiralty document 'The Way Ahead' published in August 1958. This proposed many reductions in the Service—the closure of many home and overseas shore bases and further paring of the Reserve Fleet. But this gloomy appearance was offset by the increasingly rapid development of a new kind of Navy—smaller, perhaps, in numbers of men and ships, but much better suited to the likely pattern of any future conflict. Battleships, it was now finally admitted, had had their day in the nuclear age; the aircraft carrier, at a time when missile-firing nuclear submarines were not yet a reality, was still the Navy's capital ship.

The fourth and last of the 'Hermes' class of light fleet carriers joined the Fleet in 1959—a year when Britain's first nuclear submarine, *Dreadnought*, was nearing completion at Barrow-in-Furness. In response to the need to cope with 'brush-fire' wars, the light fleet carrier *Bulwark* was being converted in 1958 to a new role as a commando carrier. Two new classes of frigate, the 'Tribals' and 'Leanders' were coming off the slipways; in March 1959, the first of the important 'County' class of 5,000-ton guided-missile destroyers was laid down at the Birkenhead yard of Cammell Laird, as the result of the successful tests of the 'Seaslug' ship to air guided weapons. Among many other projects, some still at the drawing board stage, was a new kind of assault ship, of which the first to be launched was to be the 12,000-ton *Fearless*.

The load on those responsible for the development of what amounted almost to a new Fleet was immense. In Michael's case it was leavened throughout with humour. He had been involved in a discussion about the role of the Flag Lieutenant to the Board of Admiralty, who had to arrange appropriate welcoming parties for VIP's at London Airport or other places. Subsequently Michael circulated a minute which read: 'The following offering (composed during the consideration of Vote 8.111.B) should be chanted slowly and sorrowfully to the tune of *Trees.*' This moving song, you will recollect, concerned a character who thought that he would never see a poem lovely as a tree upon whose bosom snow had lain, etc. He concluded, reasonably enough, that poems were made by fools like he but only God could make a tree.

> *I pray that I may never be*
> *Sent off again to LAP*
> *In No. 5's without a sword.*
> *The Flag Lieutenant to the Board*
> *Sends me to Tilbury in sleet*
> *Or Blackbushe in the blazing heat.*
> *Upon my bosom snow has lain—*
> *Don't tell me to go off again.*
> *But if you do I'll only go*
> *For four-star Admirals and below—*
> *They can be met by fools like me*
> *But only God meets M of B.* (Earl Mountbatten
>   of Burma).

And the apparently endless moves called for in the course of the setting up of the new Weapons Department were another source of inspiration to the Le Fanu muse:

The Unhappy Wanderer

> *In the far Western Desert a number of gents*
> *Like Bedouin Arabs are folding their tents*
> *And seeking cases of neighbouring sheikhs*
> *Who will probably house them for several weeks.*

> *Come bring me my T square, my slide rule, my pen—*
> *The powers in Whitehall are at it again.*
> *Their faith can't move mountains—instead they move us*
> *On mystery tours in an Admiralty bus.*

> *O'er the sand of the desert, in yashmak or veil,*
> *The Bedouin ladies are hitting the trail.*
> *(The proper procedure for stating complaints*
> *May be found in Arabian Office Acquaints).*

Come bring me my carbons, my dockets, my comb,
I am off to another impermanent home,
And Allah the Merciful only can tell
If it's Warminster, Ensleigh or Empire Hotel.

So saddle my camel and crank up my heap,
The way may be weary, the hills may be steep,
The goal may be far and the road may be gritty
But at least there's a satisfied Nihill committee.

These Le Fanu effusions were eagerly awaited, and snapped up as collector's pieces by anyone who could get hold of them. But woe betide anyone who mistook good humour for tolerance of inefficiency or of anyone who did not realise quite clearly who was boss. Michael expected results, not excuses, and could come down with great weight on those who did not co-operate. On one occasion he happened to overhear his Technical Assistant complaining to a colleague that a Divisional Director (senior to him of course) had not done what had been requested on a file. Michael interrupted the conversation and demanded the file, which was reluctantly handed over by a very embarrassed TA. After which Michael minuted the file back to the Director concerned, 'Do as I say' and initialled it 'M Le F, for TA to DGW'.

Even in that case, the reprimand was neatly turned. But if there is one story which sums up Le Fanu, Director-General, more sharply than any other, it is perhaps the one told of his encounter with an engine driver at Carmarthen Station, on the way back from one of his visits to Aberporth. Michael was in uniform, and, while waiting for his own train, took a stroll down the platform. In a siding at the end was a small shunting engine, and its driver, complete with peaked cap, was leaning contentedly on the edge of his cab in the evening sunshine. Michael immediately went up to the fence, and, leaning on it in an exactly similar pose to that of the engine driver, looked him in the eyes and said, 'Swop?'

A pity, perhaps, that such an exchange could not have been arranged, for towards the end of January 1960 Michael, no doubt as a result of the many different strains of his job, suffered what turned out to be a mild heart attack while walking down

Regent Street. He came home to Petersfield that evening looking far from well, and next morning was reluctantly persuaded to abandon his proposed programme for that day and seek medical advice. It was apparent to his doctor that he must go immediately by ambulance to the Royal Naval Hospital, Haslar, where he spent nearly a month of enforced rest, on a stringent slimming diet, even allowing himself to be taught basket-making to pass the boring weeks of inactivity, while attempting to banish from his mind the underlying worries about his future in the Navy.

Prue retained indelible memories of his sudden departure to hospital, and of the remarkable resilience of young children. Some hours after the ambulance had gone, Toy dashed in from school, followed by Hugh and a school-friend who flung themselves on the floor to prepare for battles with fort and toy soldiers. Choosing her words with care, to lessen the shock, Prue explained that their father was not very well and had gone to hospital. Toy pondered this news in silence for several moments, then asked anxiously, 'Who will change the water in my goldfish's bowl, then?' while Hugh sat back on his heels, thinking out this unexpected event. He then said cheerfully, 'Come on, Duncan, you can be the Germans today.'

Discharged from hospital for a further month at home, Michael was not an easy patient. The washing out of the goldfish bowl could not keep him occupied for long; nor did 'Painting by Numbers', which he took up at this time, to prevent him champing round 'like a caged lion'. It was finally decided, much to the delight of the family, to hire a television for the first time, in an effort to keep their father still. It effectively kept the whole family still for many hours. Soon, a few holes on the golf course provided an outlet, and in March Michael was recovered enough to drive off with Prue for a walking holiday in Dovedale. He did the walking, starting from point A, while Prue drove round to find him at point B. But it was an anxious time for him, with the ever-present fear that his Naval career, so full of high promise until now, might be at an end.

The fears happily proved groundless. The doctors passed him fit; and the Controller recommended him no less enthusiastically for the Vice-Admiral's list, after his recovery than he had done six months before . . . with a rating of ninety-eight per cent.

However, it was thought that a period of 'light duty' was called for. On 1 April, 1960, Michael was appointed for 'Temporary Duty with the Controller'. The duty however was as far from light as can be imagined : he was asked to produce a report outlining the best way to organise a 'Polaris' programme in the United Kingdom.

Following the explosion of Russia's first hydrogen bomb in 1954, the Americans decided to develop a new submarine ballistic missile system, and the new weapon, at first called 'Jupiter' and subsequently 'Polaris' was successfully tested in 1958. During his tenure of office, as First Sea Lord, Lord Mountbatten had kept a very close watch on these developments and had made up his mind at that stage that Britain too must ultimately be equipped with this or a similar deterrent weapon. America had already built a considerable fleet of Polaris submarines before the Nassau agreement was reached in 1963 allowing for the construction of a British Fleet of these vessels, which would ultimately take over the nuclear deterrent role from the Royal Air Force.

By 1960 such an agreement was little more than a gleam in the eye of Britain's Chief of the Defence Staff : but that office was now held by Lord Mountbatten, who had in no way lost sight of his determination to get 'Polaris' for the Royal Navy. The report undertaken by Michael at the request of the then Controller of the Navy, Sir Peter Reid, would provide essential ammunition when the tough talking had to start.

At least, while he was preparing this report, Michael was able to shut himself off from the constant round of decision-making of the previous two years. He lived at home, working leisurely hours in London in an atmosphere far removed from the racket of the Weapons Department triangle. He confessed one evening that so engrossed had he been in reading a novel that morning on Petersfield Station that he looked up to see his train disappearing in the distance. He decided that he might as well go on reading as another train was sure to turn up eventually.

Michael spent most of this period thinking—and to very good effect, for when the British Polaris programme did eventually get going, it was on the basis of what he had written. Special project teams were to be set up, to cut through red tape : many a sacred cow was to be sacrificed. The Chief Polaris Executive, when appointed, would need to have powers which would cut across many an empire in the Admiralty and the Ministry of Aviation, and he would have to be able to exercise direct control over shipyard progress.

The beginnings of Britain's Polaris programme were to coincide with Michael's time as Controller of the Navy. The building task took nine years, and throughout he watched attentively as each successive stage was punctually completed. Much of the success, of course, was due to others. But he had the satisfaction of knowing that the initial blueprint had been his, and that in all essential details it was on target.

In June 1960, Michael was appointed Companion of the Bath, a tribute to his pioneering work as Director-General Weapons, and in July there came a sea appointment as Flag Officer Second-in-Command, Far East Fleet, which was a welcome relief from the intricate infighting of the last two years.

This new job also gave Michael a chance, after his illness, to recover the brilliant flair he had shown as a Captain and junior Rear-Admiral. In those days it had been clear to everyone who met him that here was a future First Sea Lord. To most people, there was still no doubt that he was destined for the top. The clarity of vision, the wit and humanity were still as much in evidence, though perhaps that warning shot across the bows had slowed him just perceptibly.

FOURTEEN

The Chinese Admiral

Leaving Prue at home watching the Open Golf Championships on television, Michael left on 7 July, 1960 to take up his duties as Flag Officer Second-in-Command, Far East Fleet. Not long after his arrival, he went to call on the Prime Minister of Singapore, and this occasion gave rise to the well-known Lee Fan Yew incident mentioned in the Preface and a new nickname: 'The Chinese Admiral'.

In those days Britain still maintained a powerful presence in the Far East, and Michael exercised command at sea over a sizeable array of ships, for whose training he was responsible. The job of Flag Officer Second-in-Command consisted of a constant programme of exercises at sea and a social roundabout ashore, but somehow he made time to write home at length not only to Prue, but to the three children. These letters he typed in triplicate, sending Mark, Victoria and Hugh the top copy in turn—and a very full account they received of the more entertaining side of a Flag Officer's existence as he moved around the ocean, and around the ships under his command.

Episode One of the exciting serial told how, on a 'subsunk' exercise, the new Admiral transferred his flag from the cruiser *Belfast* to the Australian destroyer *Vampire* together with his staff and the Chinese valet, the quicker to reach the scene. The ships searched vainly for some time, and the sub eventually revealed her presence on the bottom by releasing a 'smoke' float and surfacing. After which the Admiral decided to transfer himself, his flag and his valet to the submarine HMS *Tactician* for the trip back to Singapore. Yang helped to serve supper with great éclat, and as *Tactician* headed up harbour at about 10 pm, she made sure the Admiral's flag—a rare sight in a submarine—was floodlit for all to see.

In early August, with *Belfast* off Pulao Tioman, Michael organised a barge picnic for 'assorted Lieuts and the like' who swam ashore to a deserted beach 'rather Robinson-Crusoe-ish, in that one had the impression that no human foot had trodden there before' and shortly afterwards transferred his flag to the carrier *Albion*, with her mixed complement of Sea Hawks, Sea Venoms, Skyraiders and helicopters. There they celebrated the 'Glorious Twelfth' in great style, with a party of 'beaters' bursting in on the Admiral's bridge demanding to be paid, half a dozen 'guns' dressed in heavy tweeds coming up on the forward aircraft lift and popping off at imaginary birds. Finally, a grouse fell from the sky (actually thrown down from Flying Control) and was picked up and presented to the Admiral; it had been in the deep freeze since the previous year and made a splendid supper. Afterwards a film was shown called *Hole in the Head*—'quite appropriate as one of my guests was the Fleet Dental Surgeon'.

During the dog watches on passage to Hong Kong, Michael took his daily 'constitutional' up and down the flight deck where he was accompanied by any members of the ship's company who felt like joining in. One by one, they retired exhausted. Once arrived in Hong Kong, he joined the Chief Petty Officers in their bar at the China Fleet Club for a drink, and when *Albion* gave a children's party, was among the first to test out the chute rigged for them between the flight deck and the hangar

From Hong Kong on to Subic Bay in the Philippines and a reminder of bygone days with the Americans who were 'almost too efficient and tend to smile by numbers' but gave everyone a good time. 'Bit of a drama' on the way, when a Sea Hawk pilot ejected from his aircraft about thirty miles from the ship. Turned out that a 'fire-warning light' had come on, and the *Manual* says 'eject if it doesn't go out after five seconds'. Pilot said he counted to seven, 'but I daresay it was rather like playing hide-and-seek and he counted from one to seven as fast as he could go'. Short episode in the USS *Hancock* which had 'some super jets, much better than anything in *Albion*; and when *Albion* steamed into Singapore 'for a three-thousand mile service', the FO2 fired a salute of seventeen guns to the Commander-in-Chief; 'a bit wet really as I saluted him from *Belfast* about six weeks ago, fifteen guns. But in the meantime he has been promoted to full Admiral so we have to do it again. Luckily he is not likely to be promoted Admiral of the Fleet just yet.'

In Michael's letters of late September, there are hopes that everyone is happily settled at school, that Mark's plan for a barge holiday the next summer will work out : but 'how expens. is it?' and 'how are you going to hoist Mum in and out?'—and a plot is revealed to 'get Mum out here for a short while this term'. However, before she arrived, *Albion* damaged her aircraft catapults and spent some time en route for Trincolamee exercising her helicopters, equipped with their submarine detection devices, or sonars. Their method of operation was admirably described for the children (and, incidentally, for laymen of all ages) : 'They go and hover in a likely place, then lower a large ball into the water. From this ball they shoot out a lump of sound (BEEP!) which, if it hits a submarine, is reflected back. So what you hear if there isn't a submarine is "BEEP . . . rumble rumble . . . gurgle gurgle . . .", but if there *is* one there, you hear "BEEP . . . rumble rumble . . . gurgle gurgle . . . *beep*!" And depending how long the BEEP has been away before it comes back as *beep* you can tell how far off the submarine is. And what you do is raise the ball briskly and move smartly over to above the place where you know the submarine is lurking and drop something NASTY in the water which sinks the submarine, which is one to you. Yesterday I thought I would have a bash at this, and really got on a treat (with a bit of help from the Observer). Heard my BEEP coming back as a beautiful *beep*, and when we "attacked" we were not very far from the right spot.'

In the same letter, Victoria got a ballet poem for her birthday :

> *Lift her up tenderly,*
> *Raise her with care,*
> *Catch hold of one leg*
> *And a handful of hair;*
> *Swing her round savagely,*
> *And when this palls,*

Heave ho! Away with her
Into the stalls.

There was a pause in the letters to the children during November and December 1960, for thanks to 'The RAF turning up trumps' and various other helpful circumstances, Prue was able to fly out and join Michael for a few weeks, and, in his own words, 'The TRIP turned out to be a super success'.

Prue inspired great affection in Michael's current flagship, *Bulwark*, as her Executive Officer, J. D. (Ginger) Cartwright recalled : 'She probably did not know how much she influenced us and in particular four of the biggest rogues we had in the ship. For her to come aboard was of course a considerable physical problem. However our Boatswain and Chippie rigged up a sedan chair which could be carried or hoisted, and we picked the most stalwart seamen we could find to act as "bearers"—they *would* have to be the ones with almost the worst shoreside records. But so long as they were on duty for the Admiral's wife, their record was impeccable. The canteen manager of the Singapore Naval Base Canteen simply couldn't understand the change in them, until I explained the reason !'

Even before Prue's arrival, the Le Fanu touch helped to influence *Bulwark*'s ship's company, who had been going through an unhappy period, and within a week of Michael's arrival, a more cheerful atmosphere once more prevailed. Soon after he joined the ship, he addressed a 'clear lower deck' of the ship's company, 848 (helo) squadron and 42 Commando, and endeared himself to the Royals by remarking that to him 'the ship seems full of very large Royal Marines. Every time I pass one, I keep saying to myself . . . "I'm senior to him, I'm senior to him !" ' He also caused some amusement by his method of insisting that he should be recognised and properly greeted when ashore. 'It's more than likely,' he said, 'that from time to time you may see me around the dockyard in, to say the least, casual civilian clothes. Take a good look at my face, and if you recognise it, salute. But above all, salute if you see me in town with a marvellous looking piece on my arm. If you don't, she'll *never* believe I'm an Admiral !'

There were, however, moments when Michael perhaps would

have preferred not to be saluted. One Saturday afternoon in the autumn of 1960 the Royal Fleet Auxiliary *Gold Ranger* was proceeding gently along the Johore Strait when her Captain was summoned to the bridge by his Officer of the Watch who had spotted a water skier approaching the ship at speed in the opposite direction. Grabbing his binoculars, Captain Stapleton at once recognised the FO2 being towed by his barge, and stopped main engines. As the barge sped past the big ship, the Captain stood smartly to attention and saluted his senior officer, who waved cheerily back, lost his balance and immediately fell into the drink —much to the concern of the Captain, who could see the Admiral struggling in the water, with his Coxswain and Flag Lieutenant coming to the rescue. Some time later Admiral and Captain came face to face at a gathering on shore. 'Stapleton, my friend,' said Michael, 'what is your explanation for capsizing me in the Johore Straits? Next time you pass an Admiral on water skis, stop your engines by all means, but do *not* salute! You owe me a gin, I think.'

Such aquatic sports were laid aside for a time while Prue was in residence, in favour of a little high living ashore. In Singapore they stayed at Admiralty House, which was placed at their disposal while the C-in-C was away; and in Hong Kong, as a peaceful retreat from the daily and nightly social rush, they stayed for several weeks with hospitable business friends at remote Sheko. The bright lights of Hong Kong rarely went out, certainly not for Michael and Prue, who in the course of many parties were joined one night at the Hong Kong Club by the Chief of Staff and his polio disabled wife, Judy Ferguson Innes. The arrival of this convoy of disabled ladies was long remembered by Club members.

It was after Prue's return home that Michael took 'Fergie' to sea on an exercise, where they were delayed by Typhoon Alice; Judy received a message via HQ: 'Please tell Judy that we are having another night out with Alice, signed Michael.'

Prue went back to England in time for Christmas, with instructions to sell the house in Petersfield and look for something within a few miles of Whitehall. The news of Michael's next appointment as Third Sea Lord and Controller of the Navy had reached Singapore while they were having breakfast together at Admiralty House. It was naturally a moment for rejoicing and congratulation, but after some discussion, Prue found herself 'rather feebly' dissolving into tears at the thought of uprooting from Petersfield and embarking on the London scene. Michael waited for a suitable pause to brace his partner with 'Love me, love my job.' He was full of good resolutions (in response to Prue's anxiety) about not over-working, but in fact was eager to return to 'that outfit' and 'push it along a bit perhaps, though there are a lot of insoluble probs, and I will have to try and not go up the twist trying to solve them.'

But for another few months, such problems could be left to themselves. At Christmas 1960, in Singapore, Michael was missing Prue and the children badly, but instead of 'sitting on board getting sloshed and twisted' he decided to borrow some boats and take a party of junior ratings from each ship in harbour out on a picnic.

After Christmas, things rapidly became more eventful again. The destroyer *Caprice* intercepted an SOS on New Year's Eve from an old Panamanian freighter, the *Galatea*, which had gone aground on a coral reef some two hundred miles off the coast of Borneo. It was just the sort of saga Michael knew the children would enjoy—and he resumed his letters to the three with a full account of it:

'*Caprice* was told to go and see what she could do ... The weather was very bad but one by one they got the crew off, using a rubber dinghy and the ship's whaler ... Unfortunately, the ship's Captain, quite an ancient chap, got washed off the dinghy and was thrown against the side of the ship ... the *Caprice* did extremely well, particularly in those dangerous waters which are so studded with rocks over thousands of square miles that the charts say you shouldn't venture in ... those who were rescued were glad the ship had sunk (apart from the Captain business) as she was nearly fifty years old, leaky and scruffy ... One thing I forgot. The only slightly annoying thing was that the RAF, who are absolute hounds for publicity, and not too scrupulous about telling the truth, put out a lot of rubbish to the papers which gave the impression that they had done the rescue with a little minor assistance from *Caprice*. Of course, though they'd been there, they did nothing except give a little moral support. However the great thing is that twenty-one men were saved. Take care of yourselves and don't go near any greasy reefs in the China Sea in later life.'

On 2 January, Michael transferred his flag to HMS *Hermes*, whose Captain, David Tibbits, was 'a soul-mate from way back'; and in this congenial company he led the Fleet on further exercises with the Americans at Subic en route for another visit to Hong Kong.

It was surely only a 'soul-mate' such as Tibbits who knew how tiresome Michael found the colonial atmosphere of Hong Kong. He did not admire people who 'strutted', and the Governor's 'court' seemed full of them—'useless tin gods who should be driven out and given real work to do' was how he summed up the race of Hong Kong ADC's. Invited with Tibbits to dinner at Government House, Michael discovered that, while the Governor would probably wear a dinner jacket, everyone else would feel obliged to wear full mess dress with medals and orders, with ladies decked out in tiaras if they had them.

During the afternoon, Michael said to his Flag Captain: 'I don't go much on this outfit! Outside the three-mile limit, I rate as high as the Governor from here to Aden; why should I throttle myself in a boiled shirt while he sits in comfort? If I decide to go tonight in mess "undress" with a soft shirt, would you be willing to do the same?' David Tibbits agreed, and when they arrived at Government House, the Governor appeared delighted. 'How nice,' he said, as he greeted them, 'to see you in that rig. I cannot understand why everyone has to be so dressy here!' Out of the corner of his eye, Tibbits caught a glimpse of an outraged ADC, but otherwise the evening was a great success.

On board *Hermes* too, Michael displayed the same impatience with protocol, though he respected Tibbits sufficiently to anticipate 'a bit of a wigging' from him on one occasion. The first Tibbits heard about it was when someone appeared on the bridge around noon one day in January 1961 and said, 'The Admiral is in the forward mess hall eating his lunch from the queue!'

This was a new one on the Captain, though whenever his Admiral was quiet, he had come to expect that something would happen sooner or later.

Before long a rather apologetic Admiral appeared. 'You've heard, I see. So sorry, David, but I couldn't tell you, could I?' 'How did you fix it?' asked the Captain. 'I put my Marine Orderly (he was known privately to Michael as Marine Fred) in the queue and lurked about on deck at the top of the ladder. When he reached the food, I slotted in! I had a ghastly moment when I wondered if I should have brought my own knife and fork. The chaps were a bit stand-offish at first and I had a ghastly fear that I should look a bloody fool eating my lunch by myself with my fingers. However, they soon rallied round. The food, incidentally, was excellent!'

'Well, it's the first time it's been done, and now no Admiral can ever do it again,' said the Captain firmly. He knew perfectly well that Michael could get away with things that would be a disaster if attempted by others. 'Part of his secret,' Tibbits said later, 'was that he thought of simple, original things first.' One of the simplest was his by now well-established habit of taking flight deck walks and welcoming the company of anyone who might care to join him; with the result that the humblest member of the ship's company felt the Admiral was concerned for his welfare.

Senior officers were just as impressed. Ian Campbell, who was Commander (Air) in the ship, became extremely worried about the lack of flying time for his aircrews after a long period of Fleet exercises chiefly concerned with such matters as replenishment at sea. Eventually he decided to approach the Admiral and point out to him the facts of aviation life. He found Michael on the Admiral's bridge engaged in the embroidery (petit-point) which often occupied him at sea, and had apprehensive visions that his name might be sewn in (à la *Tale of Two Cities*) for future reference : 'Promotion, no; guillotine, yes.' However, when told of the Air Department's worries, the Flag Officer Second-in-Command's immediate reaction was to order *Hermes* to detach from the 'RAS' serials, so that flying exercises could continue. Ian Campbell was astonished to find a Flag Officer who would react so instantly and, in Ian's view (of course) so logically.

The saga of Michael's doings was continued all through the first six months of 1961 in letters home to 'the three'. Mum was praised, early in February, for getting a house, a good-sized one in Stonehill Road, East Sheen, 'within a stone's throw of Richmond Park'. 'The first thing I'll do when I get home,' wrote Michael, 'will be to get on the roof and see if I can chuck a stone into the park. If not I will tell Mum she has tricked me; upon which she will say that I am not a very good stone-thrower, which is true.'

In Hong Kong, a Marine Corporal driver had to be sacked for unpunctuality, which made Michael *very cross indeed*... but Trincomalee, in Ceylon (now Sri Lanka) was much more congenial, as the FO2 prepared to sail on a series of joint Commonwealth exercises.

'We sally forth on Monday about 4 am and after various contests with submarines and aeroplanes have a major battle with the remainder of the party who are coming up from the Australia direction: furthermore NO ONE KNOWS WHAT IS GOING TO HAPPEN, as all the details of what is going on and who is supposed to clobber who are wrapped up in little envelopes which one opens when one is told. Actually I know what is inside the envelopes, and I daresay some crafty Indians have got a lap ahead by steaming open their envelopes ahead of time. Not that it will help them all that much as the most important envelopes are issued to Admirals only! As long as no ships clout each other in error it will be OK. The whole thing is called an Ocean War Game, and it really is like a game, except that one has to take it rather seriously.'

Early in March, 'Pop' ('not the musical variety') transferred his flag again to the cruiser *Belfast* whose new Captain, Morgan Giles, made 'a v.g. impression', unlike the ship's new 'not very switched on' ship's company.

In an inter-ship competition to drop a lifebuoy and recover it with a ship's boat, *Belfast* came last, when the lifebuoy sentry threw the lifebuoy over the side without realising someone had secured it to a guardrail. Result: 'the thing fell back with a sickening crash, bursting an expensive lamp and window in the side'.

Soon after Michael joined he was inspecting the ship's company at divisions and instantly recognised, in the second rank, a lad who had been his 'doggie' at *Ganges*—cue for long conversation. And the FO2 formed the habit of acting as voluntary unpaid 'rum bosun' for one of the messes—known as 'the Jungle Mess'. He would queue up with the representatives of other messes for the rum issue and when he returned to the mess with a large jugful to be shared between the members entitled to rum—he was rewarded with 'sippers' for his pains.

Off to the coast of Borneo for more exercises with the Americans with the usual 'two and half pounds of operational orders' including some really dreadful warnings about medical hazards ashore which Michael passed on to the children, with the hope that Richmond Park offered fewer terrors than Borneo, where, according to the American orders, 'Malaria, tuberculosis, intestinal infections and scrub typhus are the most troublesome diseases. Harmful marine life consists of several fish which are poisonous to eat (Speckled Moray eel, jack-fish, puffer, yellow snapper, cowfish, Yellow Dung Eater, and some species of barracuda) and dangerous creatures such as sea snakes, catfish, sting rays, jellyfish, sea urchins, sea snails, Estaurine Puffer, sharks and crocodiles. Harmful creatures ashore consist of insects, scorpions, centipedes, leeches, crocodiles and poisonous snakes (cobras, green vipers and banded kraits). The Rengus Tree can cause extreme irritation. All food and water must be regarded as contaminated.'

'I'm glad,' wrote Michael, 'that it is only Captain Franks's Marines that are going ashore. I'm sure if I landed I would drop into a Rengus Tree and be extremely irritated, particularly if I was then offered for lunch a tasty fillet of Yellow Dung Eater.'

Nothing deadly resulted from the Borneo exercises, however; and in April Michael kept his ships busy on individual exercises in the practice area near Singapore while he himself carried out a series of sea inspections, for example, as the children learned, of the New Zealand cruiser *Royalist* : 'We devised a situation whereby the Captain was suddenly confronted with "enemy" aeroplanes to shoot at, a mutinying cruiser to fire shots across the bow of (what bad grammar) and being torpedoed by a submarine which then surfaced and had to be boarded. We threw some funnies in for amusement, such as getting the seamen to make an obstacle course, and the stokers a swimming pool. They did well and I think enjoyed themselves, as when I left, all the Maoris in the ship had put on native dress and gave me a Maori farewell, though this may have been polishing the marble a bit in aid of a good report, what!'

In May, typhoons 'Alice' and 'Betty' kept the Flag Officer Second-in-Command busy with some awkward decisions about how best to dispose his ships. 'Typhoons generally curve around in one direction or another and you have to guess which way they are going to go. Better still is to steer a course which will take you clear of them whatever they do. I thought I would keep my ships at sea when "Alice" threatened as there is not much percentage in sitting in Hong Kong through a typhoon . . . and when she struck I was two hundred miles away to the south-east. Jolly good place to be. "Betty" was bigger than "Alice", with winds of 150 mph at the centre, and I'd hate to have been driving the *Water Violet* (which I see is the name of our canal cruiser this coming summer hols) up the Formosa Strait in that.'

Many memories of the war were revived for Michael on a visit to Japan while 'Betty' was blowing herself out. There, the demanding list of formal visits was relieved by a round of golf, during which the caddies had to try and stop crows from picking up the balls, which they were in the habit of doing in large numbers. By mid-June Michael was looking forward intensely to becoming 'Flag Officer Second-in-Command, East Sheen, instead of Far East Fleet'.

After the trip back to Singapore from Japan, during which the Fleet carried out numerous exercises and some of the ships, four at a time, amused themselves by playing 'Floating Bridge' by radio, Michael was relieved by Vice-Admiral John Frewen, and he was free to leave for home; but not before he had been cheered to the echo by the ships under his command and treated by the Fleet, as befitted a Chinese Admiral, to a traditional-style Chinese firework display by way of farewell.

Thus ended his remarkable year as Flag Officer afloat. Most of the tales which have survived tell of the lighter side of his activities, of those incidents which made an unforgettable impression on those who served under him at this time. But behind the scenes lay long hours of thought and planning, for Michael lost no opportunity of exercising his ships and keeping them in a high state of efficiency and preparedness. This task he carried out in all respects to the high satisfaction of his Commander-in-Chief, who on Michael's departure recommended him for a major Fleet Command in due course.

6—DG * *

FIFTEEN

The 'Thing' Man

After a summer holiday during which Michael happily played
second-in-command to Prue on board their barge, since she was
quite capable of taking the helm and it required two agile legs to
deal with locks and similar canal hazards, he returned to the
Admiralty in mid-September 1961 for about six weeks to under-
study the then Controller, Sir Peter Reid. On 25 October, he
was promoted Vice-Admiral and on 1 November, at the age of
forty-eight, he became the youngest man to occupy the office
of Controller of the Navy and Third Sea Lord for seventy
years.

The Controller is answerable for virtually the entire material
of the Navy—a burden which, as we have seen in an earlier
chapter, had become so great by the late 1950s, that the Controller's empire was split into three major Departments, dealing
respectively with Ships, Weapons and Aircraft, each headed by
a Director-General. At the same time, the Fourth Sea Lord
became responsible to the Controller for dockyards and Fleet
maintenance in addition to his traditional job of looking after
general and armament stores and victualling.

Having been the first 'Director General Weapons' and therefore one of the creators of the new set-up, Michael was well
acquainted with the organisation of which he now assumed overall command. He knew that a main purpose of the re-arrange-
ment had been to leave the Controller himself more freedom to
concentrate on major problems of policy and development—and
in the early 1960s these problems were indeed daunting.

Describing in a speech the basic dilemma of all Controllers,
Michael quoted with approval a newspaper editorial which read:

We are governed by the rule of change, yet we are compelled to maintain a Navy at a certain standard of strength; the problem is to produce always the best fleet without knowing exactly what are the best ships, or being able to provide these in sufficient numbers. Every so often we find our latest achievements apparently out-dated, and yet we cannot venture to discard them altogether because we do not know exactly what to put in their place and we cannot—neither do we have the money to—extemporise a new fleet at a month's notice.

'If you think that was written today,' Michael then told his audience, 'you're wrong. It was written a hundred years ago.' And he went on to describe the many baffling factors he had to cope with: 'I suppose my job as Controller, and it is shared by all the Board of Admiralty, is to provide the country with the most modern well-balanced Fleet with what we can squeeze out of the Treasury. In tackling this problem we are subject to plenty of pressure: from rapid scientific progress; from lack of money; from lack of men; from the increasing need for technicians; from those who think we should have more hulls and less sophisticated equipment; from those who think we should have fewer hulls and more sophisticated equipment; from those who think our hulls should have a shorter life; from those at sea who think they should have an extra 5 knots, more endurance and twice as many more modern equipments and also go green with envy when they see what the Jones's next door have, and from those who, even now, still question whether we need a Navy at all.

'The Third Sea Lord is responsible for the ships, the aircraft, all the weapon systems, all the research and development which goes before and all the refits and modernisations which come after. In this connection the Fourth Sea Lord is responsible to me for the dockyard side of the work, which is jolly nice of him on account of he's senior to me.

'To do their job, the Third Sea Lord and his team have to translate the dreams of the "think-men" of the Naval Staff into things—ships, weapons and aircraft that we can afford, and to get them off the production line when they're required. Having got them, we then have to keep them running for as long as is humanly possible. We have to ensure that we are getting value for some two hundred plus million pounds per year of the country's money.

'The Third Sea Lord's team includes the following varieties of bods : Naval Officers, both Executive and Technical of various specialisations, Constructors of the Royal Corps of Naval Constructors, Civilian Electrical Engineers, the new Admiralty Engineering Service, the Royal Naval Scientific Service and assorted civil servants. All these with their varied outlooks and temperaments have to be kept working together, to be kept happy in their work, to be given purpose and kept enthusiastic. And the whole machine has ramifications and tentacles stretching into most corners of industry.

'All this produces a constant stream of problems : problems of organisation, man management, industrial relations, co-operation, the lot. I believe that in the Canadian Rockies there is an official known as the Bear Controller—he gets no sympathy from me.

'Just to ensure that there is no confusion, the one thing the Controller doesn't control is the Navy. They always send someone to keep the Controller under control ! He just does what everyone else tells him to do in the way of producing hardware, such as submarines, aircraft carriers, frigates and weapon systems. Now and again he says that they don't want that or they ought to want this. No one takes the slightest notice.'

No one had taken the slightest notice, or so Michael thought at the time, of the report he had produced, just before he went to the Far East, on the organisation that would be required to build Polaris submarines in Britain. 'It fell so flat,' he later recalled, 'that I wondered for a moment if I had been wrong.' In fact he had been right; the Polaris report was to provide the basis for the Navy's biggest building achievement for years. During Michael's first year and a half as Controller, however, the report remained in cold storage while other matters clamoured for attention.

By far the most important of these was the question of a replacement for the aircraft carrier *Victorious* which was expected to end her useful life in 1970. By the middle of 1962 detailed designs were well under way for a big new carrier of some 50,000 tons, designated CVA 01; it was the first opportunity the Navy had had for some twenty years of designing a carrier from the keel up, and every permutation of size and layout had been considered. The ship, as finally conceived, would be capable of accommodating three complete squadrons of the coming generation of naval aircraft and would incorporate many new ideas; she would cost about eighty million pounds. Even if the government gave the go-ahead for her construction, was it the best way to spend so large a proportion of the Navy's budget? Would it not be better to place the emphasis on a 'balanced fleet', with perhaps one or more smaller carriers? Within the Navy, there grew up a sharp division of opinion.

Admiral of the Fleet Sir Varyl Begg recalled that when he became Vice-Chief of the Naval Staff in 1960, the whole of the Admiralty Board were in favour of a new generation of big carriers: it was the era of the huge American carriers such as the *Forrestal* and of a world-wide British military presence, which clearly implied a world-wide maritime strategy. But by the time Begg left the Board to become Commander-in-Chief Far East in April 1963, he and others had begun to question whether the large carrier concept might damage the maintenance of a balanced fleet, particularly in view of the long-term manpower projections which had by then become available. But the First Sea Lord himself, Admiral Sir Caspar John, was a convinced advocate of the big carrier, and he had no more wholehearted supporter than Michael as Controller. His period in command of HMS *Eagle* (or, as he put it, a 'Bird' class carrier!) had no doubt influenced him in favour of a big ship—and indeed many aviators in the Admiralty at this time felt that the only member of the Board who both understood the importance of air power at sea and was ready to argue their case at the highest level was Michael Le Fanu. However, as with Polaris, so with CVA 01 at this stage—both awaited government decisions.

In the meantime, there was progress in less controversial areas. It was generally agreed that if the Royal Navy was to maintain a world-wide operating capability, in spite of the reduction in available shore bases, then the question of Fleet support—of replenishment at sea—assumed a crucial importance; and in 1962 an extensive building programme was put in hand to replace the ageing Fleet Train with new purpose-built ships. The result, by 1970, was a Royal Fleet Auxiliary of some forty ships of the latest design—an achievement of the utmost importance in which Michael took a close interest. (In Aden, in 1967, he had a chance to see how the plans of the early sixties were working out in practice when he visited the new Royal Fleet Auxiliary *Stromness*: he was delighted to see that the lifts, the closed-circuit TV, the specially designed fork-lift trucks, were all performing as intended.)

As for the Fleet itself, it was steadily assuming its future shape. The 'Leander' frigates were coming off the slipways, and in November 1962 came an occasion full of memories for Michael when the new *Aurora* was launched at John Brown's shipyard on the Clyde. This was a launch Michael took very much into his own personal care; Prue was invited to perform the ceremony, and the old *Aurora*'s Gunnery Officer laid on a special train for scores of former shipmates, among them the Chief Bosun's Mate and the padre, Arthur Green, who led the prayers for the new frigate. It was a tremendous party.

The new 'County' class of guided missile destroyers were also coming into service. In the month of *Aurora*'s launch, the first of these large destroyers, HMS *Devonshire*, was commissioned, full of the most sophisticated equipment. All of it came, in one way or another, within the province of the Controller of the Navy, right down to the question as to whether these ships should be fitted with three or four portable saluting guns. As Controller, Michael had fewer chances than formerly to break into verse, but the solemn matter of whether three saluting guns would be adequate provided such an opportunity. On the relevant minute he wrote:

> *From Greenland's Icy Mountains*
> *To India's coral strand,*
> *The natives see the Counties*
> *Parade a squeegie band.*
> *What ho! The spicy breezes*
> *Blow off o'er Ceylon's isle*
> *And every prospect pleases*

But DGD (Director, Gunnery Division) *is vile.*
For hark! the Master Gunner
All gloriously attired
Says 'Pardon: re salute, sir,
Three PSG's misfired.'
In vain with lavish kindness
You tempt me from the groove.
Controller in his blindness
Proposes to approve.

To which another member of the Admiralty Board, the Second Sea Lord, added :

This deep investigation
convinces me full well—
Three PSG's for Counties
Approved by 2SL.

Sometimes colleagues calling on the Controller after office hours would find him seated at his high desk with a single sheet of paper before him, working out some rhyme to enliven the record of a solemn meeting, but more usually the late hours kept in the office were the result of an overload of work.

In Michael's case, the door at such times was always open to anyone who might have a problem to discuss; nor was his office staff, often called upon to work late hours, forgotten. Beryl Gibbs, Michael's personal assistant at this time, found her three years with Michael 'the hardest (workwise)' of her career. But they were 'perhaps the happiest. He was a marvellous leader; his own enthusiasm was infectious. We all felt part of the team and the Admiral never forgot the most junior of his staff.' All of them treasured the small but personally chosen Christmas gifts, appreciated the interest Michael showed in everyone as an individual, and remembered the night when they'd all been snowed under with work and Michael himself came into the office bearing glasses of sherry on a tray as a gesture of thanks.

When out of the office, Michael avoided formality whenever he could. Generally without a coat, he would often be seen striding along the embankment at lunchtime taking a breath of fresh air before plunging back into the afternoon's work. One day a junior colleague took shelter from a sudden downpour at the refreshment stall next to Charing Cross Underground station, and was enjoying a cup of coffee and a bun, when he felt a dig in the back accompanied by the words, 'Move over, cock!' There was the Controller of the Navy, rain pouring off his bowler and old naval raincoat. He seemed to know all the cabbies and other regulars of the stall by their first names and a good many details of their personal lives. 'I often come here for a bite,' he said, as the two men left together for the office, 'in fact, whenever I can get away from all those ghastly official lunches.'

Michael was able to get on his own terms with most people, whatever their position. The brilliant and formidable Director-General (Ships) at this time was Sir Alfred Sims, who, perhaps on account of his musical Welsh accent, became 'Sims the Ship'. Other officials of the Ship Department at Bath were addressed by ecclesiastical titles; thus the Director in Charge of Frigate and Destroyer Design, Ken Purvis, became the 'Archdeacon', and 'Dearly Beloved Archdeacon' he still was in 1970, when Michael wrote to all his friends telling them that the onset of leukaemia would prevent him from becoming Chief of the Defence Staff (an office equivalent to 'Pope' in their private language).

With fellow 'bishops' on the Admiralty Board, Michael could behave with even less inhibition. As Controller, he sat as a member on the *Fleet* Requirements Committee, chaired by the Vice-Chief of the Naval Staff, which decided what ships the Fleet needed. These roles were reversed in the *Ships* Requirements Committee, where the means of meeting the Fleet's needs were worked out. Some differences arose over a particular class of ship, and one day Michael, wearing a rather scruffy tweed suit (one of his greatest admirers described him as the worst-dressed naval officer he had ever known) marched into the office of the Vice-Chief of the Naval Staff with a double-handled banner reading 'VCNS is being beastly to the Controller!'

This was an amiable way of dealing with a difference of opinion. Michael was not always charming on such occasions; if thwarted, he was capable of showing his disapproval with what some thought a lack of grace. And he could be very sharp with anyone who appeared to underestimate him. In March 1962, during a visit to the Admiralty Engineering Laboratory at West Drayton, he was shown a demonstration rig in the noise and vibration section. All went well until it was mentioned that the rig had been displayed on the Royal Navy stand at the recent School-boys' Exhibition. 'Ah,' said Michael, as he moved away smartly to the next exhibit, 'suitable for showing to schoolboys and Admirals, eh?'

At official meetings, Michael's unorthodoxy made itself felt through injections of humour whenever he felt the proceedings were becoming dull. Most people welcomed them with relief, but some Service and Ministerial colleagues thought him unduly impatient of discussion. Not given to compromise, he sometimes appeared intractable to those who had to make a workable policy for the Navy among all the complex pressures of Whitehall.

As First Lord of the Admiralty, Lord Carrington found Michael difficult to work with at times, simply because he was so downright in his views—one of the qualities, as the First Lord realised, which made him so magnetic a leader. Carrington never forgot his thoughtfulness during the strains imposed by the Vassall Admiralty spy case in the summer and autumn of 1962. At that difficult time, Michael would suddenly appear in the First Lord's office when meetings were done for the day, plonk a bottle of wine down on the desk and dispel some of the tension with good company.

Apart from being the best of companions in private, Michael was in great demand as a speaker at public functions of many different kinds; and it was to a gathering of marine engineers ('When in danger or in fear, always blame the engineer!') that he described his state of mind towards the end of 1962 when a momentous development for the Navy was about to occur.

'There I was,' he said 'on December sixteenth, quietly contemplating that, despite the many difficulties we have in the hardware world, the Navy—my Navy—your Navy—was in pretty good nick. The *Ashanti* and the *Devonshire* had had some troubles with their steam turbines, but they were coming good on the whole. *Dreadnought* had had her first run to sea, the carrier design was coming along very well. We were, I thought, slowly getting to grips with the problems of the Fleet's reliability and availability and, I thought, whatever new problems come our way, and they whistle past my ear 'ole every hour on the hour, we have a pretty good Board of Admiralty to deal with them. Just when I was indulging in these smug reflections, the telephone rang and a voice said "Le Fanu? Ministry of Defence here. The Minister wants you to go to the Bahamas tomorrow. Happy Christmas." What I said back was, "Me no savvy, master. Me Lee Fan Yew, me happy go Bahamas long Chinese New Year. Not Kismis, my missy no likee!" Of course I went to the Bahamas with the Minister and the Prime Minister, and he came back with Polaris.'

This was Le Fanu-ese for the meeting which produced the Nassau agreement of 21 December, 1962. The United States had decided to cancel further development and production for their own air force of the 'Skybolt' missile which, in 1960, had been offered to Britain to extend the effective life of the V-bomber force. President Kennedy suggested either a cost-sharing 'Skybolt' programme for Britain alone, or, as an alternative, the use by the RAF of the 'Hound Dog' missile. On grounds of cost and technical problems, Mr Macmillan, for Britain, turned down these suggestions. Instead, building on the goodwill carefully nurtured by Lord Mountbatten among American submariners, it was decided that the US would make available Polaris missiles without warheads for the Royal Navy. Britain would build up at an estimated cost of three hundred and fifty three million pounds, a force of Polaris submarines as part of the NATO nuclear deterrent, a force which would not be used independently of NATO unless 'supreme national interests' were at stake.

Now Michael's Polaris plan came into its own. It was the blueprint for what he himself called 'the toughest job our Navy has ever tackled in peace': within a month of Nassau, where Michael is said to have reassured the Prime Minister by telling him, 'It'll be all right—I've got friends,' the government had decided to build up to five nuclear powered Polaris submarines, each equipped with sixteen of the new 'A.3' missiles which could carry a British-made nuclear warhead some two thousand five hundred miles. Such submarines remain 'the ultimate deterrent', to quote the title of a book by Commander N. F. Whitestone, since they can range the oceans on constant patrol virtually without fear of detection and each of them packs a punch much heavier than a squadron of World War Two battleships.

The first of Britain's Polaris submarines, designed at Bath by a team led by Sir Rowland Baker, was to be operational by 1968, when the Navy would begin to take over from the RAF the nuclear deterrent until then operated by the V-bombers. In fact, by 1968 all the four Polaris submarines which eventually constituted the Royal Navy's programme, had been launched—a triumph of skill and planning: every stage of the building programme which lasted nine years overall, was completed on schedule. Full use was made throughout of computer technology, not least in the American-style Programme Evaluation Research Task and Review Technique (PERT) employed for overall control of the task.

It was Michael who had specified this and who had outlined the project—team organisation that would be needed to carry the task to a successful conclusion, cutting through the normal hierarchies of the Admiralty and civilian contractors alike. But although, as the 'hardware merchant', he had overall responsibility for the programme, it was directed by Vice-Admiral H. S. 'Rufus' Mackenzie, the submarine specialist who was appointed Chief Polaris Executive. He it was who had to co-ordinate the work of hundreds of American and British firms, providing a base at Faslane on the Clyde for two thousand men and their families, as well as the huge 7,000-ton submarines themselves together with all their intricate equipment and all the support facilities they would require.

In March 1963, Michael warned the Institute of Marine Engineers of what would be involved in 'slotting a highly complex and sophisticated weapon system into a highly sophisticated and complex nuclear submarine design, not yet proved at sea. Furthermore, the resultant submarine weapon system has the unique feature of having to stay at sea for very long periods, one hundred per cent reliable and one hundred per cent available. We are going to require from our own people, in plain clothes and in uniform, and from our contractors, extraordinary efforts of mind and will, if we are to honour, as we must honour, the Navy's pledge and the government's pledge. This is a big, big deal, and the biggest part of the deal—in which the marine engineers are going to help us—is on the reliability front—there must be no temperamental pumps playing up and no double-acting valves on the blink. We have got to set new standards of design and workmanship. We are going to enjoy it enormously; enjoy using every bit of brains and endurance we have, and every bit of the press-on spirit.'

This entirely positive approach was a source of inspiration to everyone connected with the Polaris programme on both sides of the Atlantic. In January, Michael was in the USA again to follow up the Nassau agreement with discussions as to how the programme was to be implemented. Now he had to deal with the legendary Vice-Admiral Hyman Rickover, 'father' of nuclear-propelled submarines.

A taciturn gentleman who was capable of being extremely rude to people he did not like (an attitude which seemed to extend to most of the human race), he had astonished all observers by agreeing to let Britain have the nuclear propulsion plant for our first nuclear submarine, HMS *Dreadnought*. This had been achieved largely through the unsparing diplomatic efforts of Lord Mountbatten, First Sea Lord at the time, who was said to be the only British naval officer to whom Rickover would speak.

A fine prospect for Le Fanu, who had unfortunately made matters worse when he first met Rickover by answering bluntness with bluntness. There was obviously some urgent fence-mending to be done; fortunately a brief meeting arranged between the two men extended to two hours, after which they both emerged wreathed in smiles, and Le Fanu became the second British sailor with whom the mighty Rickover agreed to parley.

In fact, Michael's contribution to Britain's successful Polaris programme, and to the spirit of co-operation with which it was carried out, was widely recognised in the US Navy, as the American messages of condolence after his untimely death made clear; though it is also true to say that Americans were sometimes nonplussed by Michael's often humorous approach to high level discussions on professional matters.

No such embarrassment was felt in these islands. There were well-remembered visits to the two main shipyards involved in the building of the Polaris fleet: Vickers-Armstrongs at Barrow in Furness, where *Resolution* and *Repulse* were built, and Cammell Laird's at Birkenhead, constructors of *Renown* and *Revenge*. Encouragement and praise for the efforts of the shipyard teams was always forthcoming when it was deserved: Michael had time for everyone who produced results and not excuses, and, in the words of Sir Leonard Redshaw, chairman of Vickers, 'never used strong words where he felt he could achieve the same object by jocular comments and the creation of a will to work for him'. He made a habit of carrying around in his pocket small bars of chocolate which he would toss, often to quite distinguished gentlemen, as rewards for work well done. As he remarked at the Yarrow centenary dinner in London: 'There's not many who've gone to a party like this with their pockets stuffed with "nutty"!'

Michael even made a hit at the Vickers annual apprentice prizegiving, a notoriously difficult occasion—for once the cash prizes had been given out, the apprentices were bored and anxious to get out to their 'locals'. Sometimes there were jeers and catcalls during the speeches, and a very audible jingling of prize money to show no more talk was wanted. In 1963, Michael was invited to be the principal guest speaker and Ernest Brokensha, Principal Naval Overseer at Barrow, took care to warn him of what he might be in for. Thus prepared, he attended in full uniform together with his Naval Assistant, John Treacher.

Once the prizes had been presented, the usual row started up. A director was foolish enough to address the audience as 'boys' and was almost shouted down; but when Michael's turn came, he pushed aside the microphone, strode to the front of the stage and boomed out in his rich voice words to this effect: 'Men! Tonight I represent the Royal Navy. No connection with Speedy Gonzales (referring to a Vickers VIP of swarthy appearance) and none whatever with all that lot (with an imperious sweep of the arm encompassing the assembled directors). I'm here to introduce you to "Jet" Treacher, former holder of the world jet speed record . . .' and so it went on, without notes, without hesitation, and the Controller sat down to a great roar of applause.

Nor had he lost his touch with the Navy's lower deck. Once, as he was arriving at Barrow in Furness to a reception by the top brass, two sailors happened to be passing just as Michael was uncoiling himself from the Vickers Jaguar which had been sent to meet him. He was still in the act of putting his cap on as the sailors, spotting all that gold braid, chopped off a smart salute. Unable to give a proper salute in return as he got out of the car door, he gave a cheery wave and shouted, 'Mornin' Jack,' which delighted the sailors no end.

Visits to the Ship Department at Bath were of course frequent, and normally all concerned would wear civilian clothes. But on one occasion the naval officers serving there were surprised to hear that the Controller's next visit would be 'in uniform'. This announcement of course was sufficient to ensure a good turnout of doeskin on the day, but the reason for it remained a mystery, except to the inhabitants of Peasedown St John, Radstock, not far from Bath, where lived a friend of Prue's, Doris Phillips. Doris, like Prue, was a polio victim, and one day she had asked Prue for a photograph of the Admiral in uniform. Michael decided to go one better. After his meetings in Bath, he had driven off to Radstock, on the way converting to full dress, stopped the car well short of Doris's prefab to give the neighbours a good eyeful and complete with aiguillettes, medals and sword made his way up the path to her front door. He hadn't forgotten the photograph either.

Not all of Michael's surprise visits were so welcome. Once he had a little time to spare, and was offered a trip down the Tyne in one of the Harbour Commissioner's launches. Near the mouth of the river he spotted a fishery protection vessel lying alongside and decided to make an impromptu inspection. At first, the half-dressed sailor who was the only man on deck, appeared to be quite unable to haul in the identity of his visitor, but by degrees the truth apparently dawned. As the onlookers in the launch could see, the ship was transformed in a matter of minutes from a chaotic shambles to something approaching an RN ship. As soon as this was accomplished, Michael decided to leave, and

as the Commissioner's launch drew away, waved cheerily to the
flabbergasted crew, who never forgot that it pays to expect a
Sea Lord at any hour of the day or night.

In June 1963, Michael's services to the Royal Navy were
recognised in the Birthday Honours list; he was appointed Knight
Commander of the Order of the Bath—and soon afterwards he
and Prue went to Buckingham Palace for the investiture. Among
the hundreds of letters of congratulation there was one they
specially valued. It came on a small sheet of paper, and was
written in a hand that was beginning to look a trifle shaky. D'or
wrote : 'You will know how much I am thinking of you today.
You may also have discovered that I am rather nervous of very
prosperous people. However prosperous you two get, it will never
spoil you. With this compliment—truly sincere—ringing in your
ears, I end up. Your proud and loving mother and mother-in-
law, Georgiana Le Fanu.'

Michael did not change with the success that came to him.
However punishing his schedule—and he once said that travelling and not work is the fatal ingredient of a busy man's life—
he made time whenever he could for his family. The residents
of a Lake District hotel were intrigued one year to see a red-
headed man and a lady in a wheelchair poring over Ordnance
Survey maps after dinner each night—and only later discovered
the nature of the joint expeditions they were planning. Prue
would drive Michael to some pre-selected spot and while he
embarked on a ten-mile mountain walk, would drive round to
meet him at the other end several hours later—a routine repeated throughout their holiday.

During free weekends at home, a new walking plot developed,
this time with Victoria. The process was known as 'Thamesing'
and consisted of walking the entire length of the Upper Thames
from Putney Bridge in instalments, whenever time could be
spared. Again it was Prue who acted as chauffeur—dropping the
pair of them off, and picking them up at the end of the day,
miles further upstream.

Michael also found time for family on trips overseas. His cousin
Philip Le Fanu, in Australia, was struck by the ease with which
Michael dispensed with the officials sent to meet him on arrival

in Perth and set off almost at once with Philip for a couple of days of family relaxation. Dressed in blue issue shorts, socks and sandshoes, he scored a great hit in the local pub with his capacity to communicate with everyone.

No one seeing him in such relaxed circumstances would have dreamed of the responsibility he carried, and the considerable worries of his work at the time, particularly in connection with CVA 01.

The first hurdle was to get a government decision to design and develop the big new ship; the matter was considered at two Cabinet meetings of the Macmillan government in the summer of 1963 and in July, after weeks of tension in the Navy, the go-ahead was given. A year later the commitment to build the ship was formally announced and, if all had gone well, tenders from shipyards would have been invited by 1966. However, in October 1964, a Labour government was returned in the General Election, and a new Review of Defence expenditure was instituted.

Cuts were inevitable; the problem the government had to face was how to get the best value for the money they were prepared to spend, and a central point at issue was the problem of air cover at sea and for sea-borne landings. This boiled down to a battle between the Royal Air Force and the Fleet Air Arm ('the battle of the blues') and feelings ran high on both sides. In January 1965 a distinguished soldier, Field-Marshal Sir Gerald Templer, was appointed to head a committee to investigate the most efficient and economical use of air power. Co-operation between the RAF and Fleet Air Arm in the matter of new aircraft, notably the prototype vertical take-off fighter, the P1154, had proved virtually impossible to achieve—and by this time the RAF desperately needed re-equipping. All its front line aircraft were rapidly becoming obsolete: and in spite of a new low-level role for the V-bombers, the approaching loss of the nuclear deterrent to the Navy's Polaris fleet added to the RAF's determination to fight this round and win it.

The RAF deployed their arguments with great skill—with greater skill, many think, than the Navy was able to muster. There are sailors who still suspect that the Australian continent was moved five hundred miles to the west in the process, to prove the ability of land-based air power to cover any conceivable landing operation anywhere in the world! And within the Navy itself, during the year 1965, opinion was acutely divided. Increasingly, things looked black for CVA 01. If the Navy was only to have one new carrier, where in the world would it be stationed? And was there any chance that the Navy would be able to man more than four carriers in the seventies? Had not Marshal of the RAF Sir Thomas Pike been right in his suggestion, when Chief of the Air Staff, that the Navy would do better to go for a smaller carrier?

Michael remained unflinchingly in favour of the big one. It was on the drawing board; he felt totally committed. The Templer Committee thought otherwise. The blow, when it fell in the Defence White Paper of February 1966, was indeed bitter for the Navy. The RAF was to get, in due course, four to five hundred aircraft covering almost the entire spectrum of its roles; on the other hand, CVA 01 was not to be built, the Fleet Air Arm was to be run down and, although *Ark Royal* was to be re-fitted, the Navy's existing carrier force was to be reduced to three and be phased out by the mid-seventies, on the premise that in the late seventies, the government could foresee no possible landing or withdrawal of British troops taking place which could not be covered by land-based aircraft.

So committed did they feel to the cause of the carrier and the Fleet Air Arm, that both the First Sea Lord, Sir David Luce, and the Navy Minister, Christopher Mayhew, resigned. Whether Michael would have done so had he still been Controller in 1966 is not certain, for in November 1965, shortly after he was promoted full Admiral, he took up his appointment as tri-service Commander-in-Chief in the Middle East, based in Aden—then at the height of the troubles which were to lead to British withdrawal.

Michael and his family had known of his next job for some months, and the prospect was causing some anxiety to his mother. In spite of the long hours and heavy responsibilities of his life as Controller, he had managed to fit in many trips up the M1 to see D'or, who was inevitably succumbing to the frustrations of old age. Her gradually failing eyesight caused increasing difficulty in living alone, and forced her to accept the ministrations of a series of housekeepers—never an easy adjustment for someone of her independent and forthright character. Eventually the advantages of a home for elderly people seemed to outweigh the struggle to maintain a serene atmosphere at Bradgate Road, where the mistress could no longer reign supreme.

Reluctantly Michael discussed the future with his mother who, true to tradition, accepted with dignity and courage the wrench of leaving her home. She moved only a short distance from Bradgate Road, and so her countless friends were still able to 'step right in' for a chat; after a time she came to terms with 'this contraption'—the talking book machine—and passed many hours listening with enjoyment to books of her choice.

In July 1965 she fell and fractured her hip and a few days later died peacefully, gallant and lovable to the last. Fate, in fact, had chosen an opportune moment for her death, for D'or would not have ceased to fret, had she lived, at the thought of her family disappearing to a country becoming notorious for bomb outrages and terrorism.

A word of warning about his new job was offered to Michael in that same month by Lord Mountbatten who, as Chief of the Defence Staff, had appointed him to it. Quite unexpectedly, the private conversation to which Michael had been summoned seemed to be less concerned with the dangers and difficulties of his task as unified Commander than with his known style of leadership. Mountbatten wished him luck, but added this firm advice : 'Not too many practical jokes, Michael, the Air Marshals won't like them !'

SIXTEEN

Commander-in-Chief (1)

The lot of the armed forces during the dismantling of the British Empire has been an unhappy one in many parts of the world, but nowhere more so than in the Middle East during the mid-sixties. From his headquarters in Aden, the Commander-in-Chief was responsible for an operational area which extended from the Persian Gulf to Southern Africa and included the Indian Ocean islands of the Seychelles and Mauritius; India and Pakistan were part of an even more widespread 'area of interest', which also covered all the Middle Eastern States, among them Egypt, Syria, Jordan, Saudi Arabia, Iran and Iraq.

Among the many commitments Michael took over from his predecessor General Sir Charles Harington in November 1965 was the maintenance of the Beira patrol and the offer of military help to Zambia following the unilateral declaration of independence by Mr Ian Smith in Rhodesia; the need to ensure a smooth handover of power in Swaziland, Bechuanaland and Basutoland, all about to assume independence; and the requirement to observe, though not to challenge, the growing activities of the Soviet Fleet in the Indian Ocean.

Throughout the whole area, the 'wind of change' was blowing strongly, demanding from those in authority a precarious balance between firmness and readiness to move with the times, not least in South Arabia and in Aden itself, where independence had already been promised by 1968 and where several warring factions were at work trying to assure power for themselves when it came.

However pressing the problems were elsewhere, the C-in-C's attention was constantly directed to the condition of his central

base, vulnerable to terrorists within, and dependent for vital
supplies, particularly oil, on the long sea journey round South
Africa after the Suez Canal was closed in the six-day war : at
one stage reserves of fuel were down to a single day's supply.
Michael's two years in Aden, culminating in the final withdrawal
of the British, were an anxious time for all concerned. The
responsibilities of a large command had to be discharged against
a background of growing uncertainty and successive changes of
policy.

One thing at least was clear : the concept of having a major
base in Aden was rapidly proving untenable, under pressure
from the strongly running tide of Arab nationalism, hostile world
opinion as expressed in the United Nations, and a growing
shortage of the necessary funds as well as the political will to
support a world-wide British presence.

By the end of 1965 the position in Aden had become extremely
tense. In 1959, in an attempt to create a stable political structure
in South Arabia to which power could eventually be handed over
by Britain, and which could be expected to act as a defensive
buffer around a continuing British base in Aden, a Federation
of South Arabian States had been set up. This Federation consisted of nearly all the States of the old Western Aden Protectorate; but its effective functioning was baulked by the
calculated obstruction of Aden and by the determination of the
three States of the old Eastern Aden Protectorate to hold themselves completely aloof from it. In the words of one expert :

'For a number of reasons the Federation never justified the
hopes placed in it by its architects. The bitter relationship with
Aden, the stubbornness of the Eastern States, the hostile attitude
of Arab nationalist movements elsewhere in the Peninsula and
the propaganda disseminated by Egypt would have made it difficult enough for an efficient administration, whose members were
in sympathy with one another, to carry out the normal processes
of government. And the Federation, crippled by internal dissen-
sions and manned by rulers who, with two or three exceptions,
were quite unfitted to wield the powers vested in them, could not
bring itself to tackle any of the important issues—constitutional,
political and economic—that faced it. It commanded little con-

fidence in South Arabia, and none whatsoever in the other regions of the Middle East. The Federal rulers were resentfully aware that their adherence to the British had earned them the scorn and mistrust of the greater part of the Arab world; all the same, they were determined to hang on to the advantages they had secured from their relationship with us, that is to say, British money and protection from Egyptian colonialism, for as long as they possibly could.'

Into this wobbly structure the Crown Colony of Aden itself was brought in March 1963, a sophisticated community which had no wish to associate, much less share its wealth, with the feudally governed Federal tribesmen. The Adenis felt they had been shanghaied into the Federation and deeply resented it. They preferred the idea of complete independence, with possible access to a revised federation later.

While Britain was engaged in trying to create a South Arabian organisation which would be self governing and yet remain favourable to a British presence in return for British protection, there were numerous agencies at work intent on achieving the end of colonial rule and influence by other means.

On 10 December, 1963, a bomb was thrown at the High Commissioner, Sir Kennedy Trevaskis, and a group of Federal Ministers gathered at the airport. It fatally wounded the High Commissioner's adviser, George Henderson, and the incident—it marked the start of the armed 'revolutionary struggle' which was to continue in Aden for four years—led to the declaration of a State of Emergency throughout the Federation, including Aden State.

Among the many political groups active in Aden and in the Federation, by far the most formidable were FLOSY (the Front for the Liberation of South Yemen) and the NLF (The National Liberation Front).

FLOSY, directed and financed by the Egyptians from its headquarters in Cairo, liked to refer to itself as 'the sole legitimate representative of the people of South Arabia'. It was primarily an urban organisation and carried little weight outside Aden; it made frequent references to trade unionism and to democracy, and so was able, in spite of its campaign of assassination, to surround itself with a spurious aura of respectability which did not fail to take in those willing, and even anxious, to be deceived. FLOSY's ambition was to be in full charge of the trade union movement in Aden, but when it came to really intense pressure it could not measure up to the NLF.

The NLF, in its origins, consisted of men of the wadis rather than urban agitators and misfits. Each of the States had its quota of outlaws, malcontents and broken men; there were fugitives from justice, those properly or improperly dispossessed of their inheritance, members of families at feud with the reigning Sultan and, perhaps the biggest element of all, those who had no employment, no land, and no skills to offer other than a precise knowledge of the terrain and a genius for guerrilla warfare. They were admirably fitted for the role they were to play in the last couple of years of British rule for they had been fighting amongst themselves and fighting authority since pre-Islamic days. NLF members in Aden could be described as rural dissidents who had come to town; by 1965 they had succeeded in dominating half a dozen of the major trade unions. It took the British authorities some time to realise that the NLF had found a way of sinking their individual and tribal differences in a common cause; they had also penetrated the Federal regular army and Federal Guard to such an extent that these bodies (for all the protestations of their British officers) could not be regarded as very reliable.

Early in 1965, a South Arabian conference attempted to achieve a revised Federal Constitution, the surrender of British sovereignty in Aden and independence for the Federation by 1968. When it collapsed the British, with the acquiescence of the United Nations, established a constitutional commission to study the question on the spot. Aden responded by declaring the members of the commission prohibited immigrants, and the attempt had to be abandoned. In September 1965, under the pressure of increased terrorism, violence and intimidation, the British government suspended the Aden constitution and the High Commissioner, Sir Richard Turnbull, became 'the government of Aden'.

This was the situation when Michael arrived in Aden in

November of that year, accompanied by Prue. They were at least well rested, for they had enjoyed a fortnight at the end of September in the canal boat *Merlin,* with Prue at the wheel and Michael as an active crewman, leaping ashore as required to deal with lock gates. They did not succeed entirely in brushing aside thoughts of what was to come, for it was while listening to the radio in the *Merlin* that they heard the news of the suspension of the Aden constitution; a reminder for Michael of the responsibility he would soon assume and for Prue of the upheaval she was about to face. As Michael wrote to a friend, 'She likes the domestic nest and does not altogether relish being C-in-C-ess complete with spanners.'

Nevertheless, amid a flurry of mid-November snow they left London in the P and O liner *Orsova,* with Prue in her fur hat waving rather gloomily to Mark and Hugh as their figures on the jetty receded into the grey distance. Gradually the increasing warmth of the Mediterranean restored them both to high morale, and they made the most of a quiet and relatively private voyage, since Michael had 'specially requested a table for two, negative Captain's table and all that lot'. From the ship Michael sent a signal to Aden about his reception there which gave the staff (engaged in elaborate preparations for his arrival) an advance clue about the style of their new C-in-C: 'Don't bother about any special arrangements. I'm relaxed and I hope you are.'

Faced with a precarious situation which might at any moment deteriorate still further in a number of alarming ways, Michael's first priority was to establish a feeling of calm confidence among the thousands of British troops and their families who now came under his command, and in this approach Prue played a full part. Very soon after their arrival, Michael was to be seen pushing Prue in her wheelchair around the busy shopping area of Steamer Point, mixing with all the other service families, or down the hill from the Commander-in-Chief's house to the bathing beach where the C-in-C would lift his wife into the sea for her daily swim. As the internal security problem became worse, such expeditions had to be undertaken with great care, but an appearance of casual normality was maintained for as long as possible.

The C-in-C's staff very soon got used to the idea that the Le Fanus disliked unnecessary fuss. Soon after his arrival Michael said he would like to have an informal look round the administrative side of his headquarters. When he arrived he was met by some twenty officers and NCO's who were to conduct him round. This was clearly not to his liking, but he suffered the retinue until they came to a tiny office containing a single typist. Michael went in by himself and closed the door. After about half an hour, the escorting party felt they ought to ease the Commander-in-Chief out of the office to continue his tour, but on opening the door they found the girl by herself with the window open. The C-in-C had disappeared through it to continue the tour as he had originally wished—by himself.

The same desire to dispose of pompous formalities applied to the constant round of parties in which the C-in-C and his his lady were necessarily involved. Not long after they had established themselves in Aden, a note was circulated to the effect that Admiral and Lady Le Fanu were fully paid up members of the MEATYLADS (Middle-East-Anti-Thank-You-Letters-After-Drinks-Society). At one reception at Command House, the guests who had been invited to meet the C-in-C were baffled as the time came to leave by the fact that he had apparently not put in an appearance. 'Ah, but he has,' they were assured by a member of the staff, 'and he spoke to every single one of you!' Michael had decided to dress as a waiter and mingle with his guests while serving them with drinks personally! But woe betide anyone who mistook an unconventional approach for a casual attitude towards good manners. Punctuality, for example, was invariably expected—when the Commander-in-Chief issued invitations—and these were many, bringing to Command House as wide a range of guests as possible, from visiting ministers and touring theatrical stars to junior officers and their wives and many of the British civilians working in Aden.

Command House, perched on a high promontory at Steamer Point, was an old-fashioned colonial bungalow of immense character. To the west, it overlooked the colourful panorama of Aden harbour with the dramatic crags of Little Aden beyond. At sunset these were silhouetted against a background of brilliant colour, as the C-in-C's guests had supper on the terrace among oleanders and bougainvillaeas, or danced under the stars to the strains of *A Swinging Safari*.

Further up the hill were the houses of the Air Force and Army commanders, the AOC and the GOC, while below, near the beach, was a curious circular house built on top of a gun emplacement which was the residence of the Flag Officer Middle East. But outside the guarded enclave of this headquarters area in which visitors must have felt that nothing could shake the security of British rule, men women and children were exposed to terrorist attacks which the security forces found increasingly hard to control.

Michael was not personally involved in security operations in Aden. As Commander-in-Chief he was of course concerned with the whole area of Middle East Command, as were his three Service Chiefs. Under the GOC (Major-General Sir John Willoughby and subsequently Major-General Philip Tower) responsibility for the Army in Aden was exercised by the Brigadier Aden Brigade (Brigadier Louis Hargroves and later Brigadier Richard Jeffries). But Michael lost no opportunity to make personal contact with the troops. Not for him the lofty seclusion of Steamer Point if there was the slightest chance of getting out and meeting the men who had to tackle Aden's troubles face to face.

His willingness to 'have a go' was sometimes an embarrassment to commanders in forward areas who knew only too well the risks he was running. They were by no means always happy to let the C-in-C go on foot patrols up-country in the exposed Radfan, which he nevertheless did, sometimes returning in the early hours.

Graham Mills, the army Chief of Staff, had the utmost difficulty in dissuading him from doing a parachute jump into the sea off Aden (usually safe for senior officers because the water provides a soft landing!). Mills only succeeded when he remembered to point out that the glint of buckles on the parachute harness might well attract the sharks which infest the waters around Aden. Sharks or not, Michael was not to be talked out of deep diving offshore, which he greatly enjoyed, when he was not busy acting as unoffical ferry man for the Steamer Point Powered Boat Club.

Sometimes he would visit up-country areas by flying on the routine 'milk run' helicopter from Khormaksar Airfield, and often went unrecognised in his flying gear. A story goes that the aircraft one day put down on a remote heli-pad in the mountains so that an airman could put a couple of packages aboard to be taken back to Aden. Seeing what he took to be a crewman in flying overalls, he offered him the consignment sheet with the words : 'Here you are, mate, sign for these will you?' Michael demurely signed.

But flying as a passenger in helicopters was not good enough for him. He decided to take a course of instruction as a pilot in which he made 'well above average progress to solo standard in spite of adverse weather' and completed nearly sixty hours in Wessex and Sioux helicopters of the RAF, Army Air Corps and Royal Navy. Thus during the last few months of his period in Aden, and subsequently as First Sea Lord, he was able to pilot his own Wessex.

As for the official car—initially a black Austin Princess nick-named 'the hearse'—Michael was known to enjoy taking the wheel himself. It is said that after one long and tiring day, he told his driver, CPO Cross (who, like Michael, was subsequently to die of leukaemia) that there was yet another trip to Khormaksar airfield to be done. 'I'm fed up with driving you, sir,' said Cross, half-seriously, 'I need a transfer!' 'Right,' said the C-in-C, 'you sit in the back and I'll take the wheel—only you'll have to wear my cap and take the salutes.'

The switching of uniforms was a favourite Le Fanu ploy to keep people on their toes and create a little amusement in the often grim lives of the Aden garrison. Usually things were well planned, but Michael's first visit to Aden Brigade did not go quite as intended. He drove there in 'the hearse', which was later exchanged for a less conspicuous vehicle, and on the way decided to change places with a sailor in the escorting jeep which was bringing up the rear of the convoy. The sailor duly donned the Admiral's cap and tunic, while Michael, in the sailor's rig, climbed into the jeep. At a security checkpoint further along the road the Princess was allowed to pass through but the jeep was stopped. When the car arrived at the parade ground there was the guard of honour and the Brigadier, and out stepped the sailor to be greeted in the appropriate manner for a C-in-C. Alas, the real C-in-C was not instantly at hand to put matters right, and an awkward pause ensued before the jeep rushed up and the right man appeared to explain.

But such a contretemps was unique, and Army units enjoyed Michael's visits to them. Colonel J. A. Aylmer, of the First Battalion Irish Guards, expressed Michael's impact on his soldiers thus : 'It is not often that a Commander-in-Chief means very much to the individual guardsman, but in Aden the Admiral was known and trusted by them all, and his visits to the battalion or any part of it were eagerly looked forward to by everyone. His leadership and cheerful presence got down to every Irish Guardsman, and in circumstances where the political purpose was obscure, this meant a lot to all of us.' The Le Fanu touch was no less sure with the children of servicemen. Richard Allison was eight years old when the C-in-C came to inspect his Cub pack. 'Hullo,' said Michael, 'you've got freckles, just like me !'

The C-in-C, to demonstrate his tri-service function, wore a khaki uniform with four stars pinned to the collar of his shirt and only the gold-braided cap declared him a senior member of the senior service; one day he lost this on a helicopter journey to the forward airstrip at Habilayn. One of the crew members had hung the Admiral's cap in the rear of the cabin; but on take-off for the return trip, the port door of the cabin had been left open as the aircraft was to drop some loads en route, and out blew the Admiral's cap as the aircraft left the ground. A horrified glance behind by the crew revealed the magnificent object blowing along a primitive runway made of compacted sand and old sump oil. The pilot was duly informed, and with some trepidation broke the news to his distinguished passenger, who merely smiled and produced from the pocket of his overalls an American baseball cap which he happily wore for the rest of the day.

Often Michael chose to wear a rig which gave little clue as to his identity. Bill Kelly was RAF Chaplain to the Khormaksar Beach Hospital and went there one day to visit a number of badly wounded men. When he arrived there was, as he recalled, 'absolute uproar everywhere, with even the very ill smiling broadly or laughing outright at the antics or jokes (or both) of a gingerish man standing in the middle of the ward wearing a dishevelled shirt and a pair of slacks. I had never met the man before. But as I entered, he came towards me and took my hand: "My name's Le Fanu," he said, "and I thought I'd just pop in and say hello to the boys." When he left a few moments later, his presence remained with the ward. No penicillin could have bucked up their spirits half as much as "Ginger's" unheralded visit. He succeeded brilliantly because he was the epitome of courtesy always, and because he thought the world of those who served with him in a common cause.'

This was unquestionably true. Michael immensely admired the courage of the ordinary soldiers, sailors and airmen under his command, entrusted as they were with an almost impossible task, and he made his sympathy clear. Speaking to the 4/7 RDG (Royal Dragoon Guards) he made play with the oddity of seeing an Admiral in the Aden hinterland. 'I'll be the only one, though,' he said, 'in accordance with your regimental motto, First and Last!' His constant visits up-country, he told them, made the Sea Lords wince, but he couldn't resist this chance to show off his 4/7 stable belt. Now they were going back home to serve in Northern Ireland: there they would have to face another sort of dizzy, and fight another war with their hands tied behind their backs. As for their journey back, how would they be travelling? Maybe they would consider adopting temporarily the motto of the Royal Marines: 'Per Mare, Per Terram'—by horse and by tram!'

It is to be hoped that the Admiral on this occasion wore his 4/7 stable belt in the correct manner: he certainly had gone to some trouble to ascertain what this should be from their Commanding Officer, Lieutenant-Colonel R. C. Ford, MBE. 'The Admiral would be obliged,' ran a naval-style message from Command House, 'if the Commanding Officer would state whether the fastening of the belt should be worn amidships and if so whether the straps should be trained on the port or starboard beam; alternately if the fastening should traditionally be worn on a relative bearing of red or green nine zero and whether the straps should point for'ard or aft. The Admiral would be distressed to learn of a regimental tradition which decreed that the fastening should be worn over the stern as he fears that this would be anatomically beyond him.' The Commanding Officer was quick to reply to the Commander-in-Chief in Army parlance 'From the twelve o'clock position with zero set on the traverse indicator, the Admiral should go left one thousand six hundred mils. He should now ensure that the straps are pointing towards the engine decks. If these two actions have been carried out, the belt should be locked in position. The Commanding Officer would like to reassure the Admiral that only by an unacceptable error in his calculations would the Admiral find himself fastening his belt in the six o'clock position.'

These up-country visits were by no means always social. In one area, British troops were living in a joint camp shared with a Federal Army unit, and a very awkward situation arose when a grenade was thrown into a canteen used by the British, causing a number of casualties. Ugly suspicions were aroused which could have had very widespread repercussions. In the temporary absence of the GOC, Sir John Willoughby, on whose energy and decisiveness the C-in-C was happy to rely, Michael flew to the scene of the trouble with the Army Chief of Staff Graham Mills, and attended a potentially explosive conference between British and Arab commanders. 'All concerned,' Mills recalled, 'were flabbergasted to see an Admiral appear in a remote and scorching desert but he very quickly took control of the situation, worked out a compromise acceptable to both sides and then walked round talking to both British and Arab troops. I remember clearly the calming effect this confident, ebullient, red-headed sailor had in that part of the Radfan. There was no doubt who was the boss, though the book would have shown that the Arab troops, though operating with the British, were not technically under command.'

These outings had to be undertaken in what time remained from a busy routine at headquarters involving constant communication with the High Commissioner and with the Ministry of Defence and the government at home. Each of the three Services had its own commander and staff, except for the functions of Intelligence, Contingency Planning, Movements and Provost staff which were centralised under the C-in-C and co-ordinated by the Chief of Staff, Brigadier 'Roly' (later General Sir Roland) Gibbs. At 8.30 every morning, the Admiral was briefed by his personal staff, and on Mondays this briefing was long and exhaustive. On Tuesdays there was the C-in-C's policy meeting, on Wednesdays a similar gathering chaired by the High Commissioner. On Saturdays there would often be a general briefing which included a lecture on some subject of current interest. In between there was a more or less constant stream of important visitors to be dealt with, meetings to discuss contingency plans (the Command had to be ready to evacuate British nationals in several countries should the need arise), the drafting of numerous signals.

At the start, Michael's manner in official business struck some of his staff as remote, and such remarks as 'he's on the bridge, we're in the saloon!' were exchanged among them; this in fact was little more than an acknowledgment that Michael was in charge—there was never any doubt about that. As time went on they assessed him as an outstanding chairman, 'listening, questioning, weighing up and directing so that everyone was clear about what was to be done and why'. With those who had to deal directly with him, he was straightforward, sometimes bluntly so. He expected those under his command to know their jobs and to know the answers. If they did, he trusted them completely and allowed them to get on with their jobs without interference. His quick brain enabled him to grasp the essentials of an extremely complicated situation and to retain a grip on what was happening—but it was never an oppressive grip. However baffling and exasperating the shifts of government policy were to one who was responsible for security, order and many thousands of British lives, Michael made it a main plank of his policy to avoid any kind of rift with the High Commissioner, whether Sir Richard Turnbull or his successor Sir Humphrey Trevelyan. Not an easy matter when it came to discussing the degree of force to be applied in a given situation, or the extent to which the police, infiltrated as they were by the terrorist organisations, should be trusted with information.

As always, one of Michael's main forms of relaxation—and one of his main opportunities to think—was walking. Occupying the centre of the Aden peninsula is the peak of Shamsan which rises to 1,784 feet between Steamer Point and the Arab town of Crater. Michael would stride to the top of this mountain, taking with him any visitor who happened to be staying at Command House or the bodyguards who were allocated to him at any particular time. Many a soldier or Royal Marine must remember making this ascent at a high rate of knots—so high in fact that when a Shamsan Challenge Race was held in March 1966, Michael (though refusing to be a competitor) was first to the top! No wonder the first record to be dedicated to him by the Forces Broadcasting Station was *Climb Every Mountain*.

Among those who were hi-jacked into these testing excursions were the master of a Royal Fleet Auxiliary and two sailors from a Tribal class frigate. The sailors were strolling gently through the town one day when a gentleman in slacks and an open-necked shirt asked if they'd like to accompany him on a short walk. Several exhausting hours later they said goodbye to 'Ginger', as they'd been told to call him, and only realised his true identity a few days later when a bemedalled figure was paying an official visit to the ships in harbour.

Michael always expressed his gratitude to those who had to accompany him in the course of duty. Thus, after the guard had been changed on one occasion, he wrote to Major D. E. Miller, Commanding Officer 'C' company, King's Own Royal Border Regiment: 'It has been very agreeable to have your Charlie, with smatterings of Bravo I understand, around my location. They have struck me as a very cheerful, on the ball, smart outfit —Scouses and Marras alike. My particular thanks are due to those who escorted me safely round Aden and galloped the Jebels so willingly. The following names come to mind—and my apologies for any I have missed:

Pte. Wally Hilton
Pte. Dick Bridge

Pte. Chubby Chambers
Pte. Johnny Acton
and Cpl. (Scoop) Woods.

'Please present my compliments to your Colonel when you meet, show him this letter, and thank him for all that his fine regiment has done for us in this rather hairy situation.'

These energetic walks over Shamsan or the Jebel Jihaff, overlooking the forbidden territory of the Yemen, were almost the only sparetime activities in which Prue was not able to share. Spectators at the inter-services rugby final, for instance, saw the large official car of the Commander-in-Chief arrive, to an appropriate welcome, after which the C-in-C personally went to the boot and got out the wheelchair so that they could make their way together to a place on the touchline. And Prue was much engaged on her own account with work for SSAFA, with the Guide troop, with deep-sea fishing and with entertaining Lady Turnbull's painting class when they gathered for lessons on the colourful terrace of Command House. All this apart from a demanding programme of official entertaining. Guests were accommodated in the annexe, where Michael's talented ADC, Lieutenant Roger Hicks, had his quarters.

At Christmas, 1965, Mark, Hugh and Victoria were able to fly out and join their parents. Together the family travelled in the C-in-C's Andover aircraft to the Wadi Hadramaut some two hundred miles north of Aden and some four centuries back in time: they enjoyed their visit to this (at the time) peaceful medieval valley and also to Beihan. It was a happy holiday in spite of the many problems which surrounded Michael, and a welcome interlude before news reached Aden in February 1966 which disturbed the C-in-C's peace of mind in more ways than one.

ove): With a cub pack in Aden

A moustached and mystified Harry
Secombe on his visit to Aden

(*Above*): Michael with Colonel Colin
Mitchell

A typical Le Fanu prank: clad in Air
Quartermaster's uniform, Michael bid
AOC Andrew Humphrey a surprise
farewell

): 1967: Michael with the Soviet
hief of Naval Staff, Admiral
rshkov at Massawa, Ethiopia

HMS *Hermes*, 1968: 'Distinguished
Chinese observer recovered on deck'

1 May 1970: Michael with
David Owen and senior colleagues at a
'brood in'

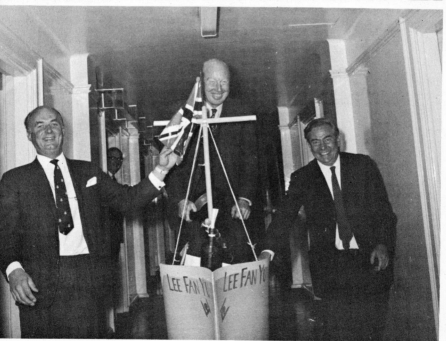

(*Above*): 30 June 1970: one of Michael's
last official engagements—the
commissioning ceremony of *Sparkle*,
one of the first boats in the world to be
built specifically for the handicapped

3 July 1970: LeF retires in style, with
Captain Charles Denman,
Secretary, and Captain Martin
Wemyss, Naval Assistant

"Deputation from the Lower Deck, sir. We want a word with 'Old Ginger'."

On 31 July 1970 the final tot of Royal
Navy rum was issued
(*Southern Sentinel*)

Retirement: Prue and Michael at
Stonehill Road (*Westminster Press*)

The three: Mark, Victoria, Hugh

SEVENTEEN

Commander-in-Chief (2)

The Government Defence White Paper published in February 1966 not only spelt the end of the proposed big new carrier CVA 01 (with which Michael had been so closely involved as Controller) and the ultimate phasing-out of aircraft carriers in the Navy; it also stated that after the departure of the British —scheduled for 1968—there would be no continuing British base in Aden and therefore no Defence agreement with the Federal States.

Michael took the blow to the Fleet Air Arm very badly. Normally he was calm and good-humoured, and held in check the hot temper which is often associated with red-headed people. Now it burst forth. He began to draft a signal to the Ministry of Defence about the importance of carrier support off Aden, and by inference in all similar situations, which would, Michael's staff knew, give deep offence in some quarters if it were dispatched. Fortunately, his temper cooled in the process of composition, and still further in the course of a long thinking walk, after which he agreed to a substantially modified draft. The news, however, led to a period of strained relations with the RAF (though the RAF had themselves suffered a cutback in their front-line requirements) until Michael regained his customary composure.

As far as the immediate situation in Aden was concerned, the announcement that there would be no defence agreement with the Federation after independence had much more serious consequences. 'Now' (in the words of Sir Richard Turnbull) 'in a world of violence and conjecture there was only one certainty: that whatever government might ultimately be in command, it would not be a British one; there was no longer any advantage to be secured in supporting us, and everybody had to look for a new band-wagon upon which to secure a safe seat'.

The problem of maintaining law and order in such circumstances would obviously be acutely difficult, not least because, while the movements of the British would be reported widely to the opposition, the authorities would find it more and more difficult to find reliable sources of information about the terrorist organisations, each of which was anxious to establish itself as the most likely successor after the British withdrawal. British policy was now to make the Federation 'a democratic state capable of surviving economically and in terms of its own defence in the Middle East' and to ensure that Britain left South Arabia with what dignity could still be maintained.

The problems which now confronted the Commander-in-Chief and his service commanders were: the reorganisation of the Federal Army and the Federal Guard—a formidable project which involved the formation of new units, an intelligence service and the Arabisation of all supporting services, and the creation of Federal naval and air forces; the maintenance of law and order in a situation where the police could no longer be relied on in an anti-insurgency role; and the planning of the run-down of the British base. All this, of course, was set against the background of the Command's responsibilities outside South Arabia.

Though good at delegating authority, Michael decided to take a close personal interest in the withdrawal programme. John Whewell, who started a tour in Aden as a member of the Army Work Study Group in March 1966, very soon found himself part of a Joint Progress and Analysis team which, at the C-in-C's personal wish, produced and monitored a Network Analysis programme for the withdrawal and redeployment of the Command. Network Analysis was in those days a relatively new concept little used in the Services. 'Here then,' wrote Whewell, 'we had as C-in-C a manager using all the aids of modern management to achieve his objectives.'

Clearly Michael was applying in Aden the techniques he had already established for the Polaris building programme. There was a vast chart in the war room which showed what should happen in every part of the British domain in South Arabia on every day leading up to the time Britain was scheduled to leave. This chart was, in the words of one of his staff, 'Admiral Le Fanu's pride and joy. He could show quite simply whether the plan was progressing and point out the times when certain things had to be completed so that the main plan was not jeopardised. It was of considerable use to those of us who had to implement the plans for withdrawal and redeployment of the Command in the Gulf.' It was also of great use in briefing important visitors.

Late on the evening of 3 July, the Minister of Defence, Mr Denis Healey, and his wife arrived for a short visit, and on the following day he was briefed in the war room before attending a 'stag' lunch at Command House. One of those present recalled how 'the Admiral opened the briefing but left the limelight to his staff. He emphasised that we were bedevilled by the absence of a definite departure date and said that until this was forthcoming he had ordered planning to proceed on the assumption that withdrawal day was to be 1 January, 1968. He then praised the work of the forces, particularly the soldiers on foot patrol and told the Minister it was not appreciated at home that we were involved in a dirty, bloody war in which we were having to fight with both hands tied behind our backs. It was the only time I saw the Admiral almost "blow his top".'

Over the buffet lunch, the atmosphere was more relaxed; Michael found the Healeys 'easy and engaging' but allowed a would-be funny remark by the Minister about Admirals and aircraft carriers to 'fall into a leaden silence' and made it quite clear that when he returned home he would be leaving the British in Aden with nothing more than 'a can of worms'. This was very much the line he pursued with a parliamentary delegation which came to Aden in mid-September 1966. 'You will readily appreciate,' he told them, 'that we are fighting a dirty, treacherous, dangerous, disagreeable war—a war of treachery and hate and thuggery and unease. We are not fighting against the Arabs, or the left or the right; we are fighting a small number of unprincipled thugs. Some may say that this is a war which should never have been fought. Maybe. But we are under an obligation to try to maintain stable government here. We are hugely fortunate that this war is being fought by a fine body of young men : we can deliver the goods for HMG. That's what we are hired for; but we need all the support we can get. And when I say "we" I hope you will find here a good deal of "we" and "us", not only between the three services but between the other ministries, the High Commission, commerce and such of the local people as the threat enables us to communicate with.'

Meanwhile during the hottest months of 1966, while the plans for evacuation were getting under way, Michael had embarked on a series of visits to various parts of his command. In the spring he had been to Bahrein, Kenya, Zambia, and Perim; in May there was Mauritius and the Eastern Aden Protectorate. Whenever possible Prue had accompanied him, but in June she flew home temporarily on medical advice, to avoid the humidity of the Aden summer. Michael paid a very brief business visit to London at that time, forming the impression that Whitehall had little idea of the pressure under which the troops were operating in South Arabia. Then it was back to an incessantly busy round in Aden and further visits elsewhere—in mid-July to Swaziland, Basutoland and Bechuanaland, about to become independent as Botswana that September. There Michael was deeply impressed with Seretse Khama and his wife Ruth and was able to discuss the question of British assistance to Botswana after independence.

Business apart, the social round at Command House continued incessantly, and was described in 'spicey' detail to Prue in letters home. The visit of the President of the Methodist Conference was the occasion for 'a Methobuff : quite a good job lot with a Rev. flavour. 4 Free Churchers, 3 Anglican. Tried to raise Father Ambrose-BP/Little Aden R.C.—but couldn't.' In fact the Rev. Douglas W. Thompson fell sick, but the 'Methobuff' took place notwithstanding; when he did arrive, 'quiet, v. intelligent, sense of humour, relaxed', his visit was marred by the shooting on Sunday 24 July of two RAF sergeants in the Crescent—the kind of sharp jolt which was only too apt at this time to shake Aden's attempts at normal life.

A day or two later the Commander of the Hadrami Bedouin Legion, Pat Gray, and his wife were shot near Mukalla in the Eastern Protectorate—'a pretty shaky place'. The hunt for the murderer, Egyptian air attacks on Beihan and pressure from London to bring Service families home sooner than planned kept Command House at full stretch late in July, but Michael managed a flying visit to the aircraft carrier *Victorious*—'a very battery-charging outing'. He was also busy planning, to provide some light relief from more serious matters, a double birthday party on 2 August for himself and Captain 'Splash' Carver who had been at Dartmouth with him and was his exact contemporary. It was to be a 'child's birthday party, though not grub and grog of course, with crackers and a balloon for all on departure (hope to have Dick Turnbull easing out with balloon in hand). There will be two small cakes, one with five candles, the other with three, inscribed Splash and Leffy, small presents and sorbet for pud.' It turned out to be hilarious.

'After the joint we served squeakers for no particular reason, then the cakes and sorbets, crackers, caps, etc. No lingering by the gents and soon after reuniting with the ladies, an up-country sheik came to pay his respects on "Splash". Complete with head-dress, skirt and all. Petty Officer Sawkins! (The "major domo".) All his idea, and extremely well done and comical. He made his futah (skirt) out of one of the Combined flags that fly on the mast. Then some maddish games, not too long. Prizes for everybody and departure with balloons. BFBS played a request for me : *You've got your troubles, I've got mine* was the tune.'

Birthday over, it was time for a spell of leave at home before returning to Aden by the end of August and embarking on a further series of visits.

On 3 September, Michael left for Basutoland which was about to become independent as Lesotho. In the capital, Maseru, he found the resident British 'had rather let go the end and were leaving the about-to-be-independent Africans to sort things out. I wouldn't put the chances of a peaceful transition to independence at better than evens. Talked firmly to everybody who would listen.'

Back in Aden, one of his first tasks was to send off to the Chief of the Defence Staff, Field-Marshal Sir Richard Hull, a 'news letter' about events in the Command from November 1965 to June 1966, though the whole thing was, as Michael said, 'thoroughly OBE, Overtaken by Events (I sometimes wonder if it wouldn't be smart to institute an Honourable Order of Events—Mesmerised by Events, Knighted by Events and Ground Down by Events). As I write the Gulf is quiet, the Yemen is more confused than ever, Aden escalates and over Africa there is an unnatural calm. In general terms I remain cynical, relaxed and confident that the endearing, indomitable forces for which I am responsible to you will somehow sort out this lot. Our motto: "Have Conkers, will extricate".'

In mid-September, the British staged a show of force in the Eastern Protectorate ('bit of a gamble, but I think it will be beneficial'), which coincided with the visit of the parliamentary delegation. 'Their plane was two hours late—our fault—and their hand baggage was left in Bahrein. Also they got fed three meals in six hours, including our buffet. So I've had to work double plus overtime to retrieve the sit. with personal attentions and charm galore. RAF in the doghouse in a big way.' But the visit, once started, went smoothly and the MP's were 'appreciative'. However their stay was not without its moments of amusement for Michael: 'While they were jawing to their constituents at one stage, I asked a Corporal who'd just emerged from an interview with an MP what party he belonged to. He said "Labour. I'm Liberal myself, but he talked very nice so I may go Labour next time." I happened to know that he'd been with Neil Marten, Conservative MP for Banbury.'

At the beginning of October, Prue returned to Aden, when Michael had just got back from a visit to Bahrein and Sharjah (the transfer of Middle East Command to the Persian Gulf, a very big task, was already beginning) and almost at once he was off again to see the soldiers at Jebel Jihaff. Trafalgar night, 21 October took him on board HMS *Fearless*, proposing 'The Immortal Memory': 'I think we are in danger,' he said, 'of erecting a sort of oratorical museum around Lord Nelson. If he was here today, he would for sure be a fully paid-up member of the GWI Club—the Get With It Club—and he would be casting around for fresh ideas, new angles to snatch victory from these Arabian quicksands.

'I find it hard to conceive what he would have made of the kind of dispensation under which I work, but I've no doubt that he would have fixed it and found the equivalent of embarking the entire Middle East Command, shoving off to Africa, sorting out Rhodesia and reporting back to Whitehall three months later. Instead of which I am at the instantaneous teleprinter command of the Westminster Palace of Varieties. Actually, this command set-up works a treat and when I was last at home I was happy to pay the Chiefs of Staff a small tribute by reading out to them one of those advertisements for eggs, except that I substituted Ministry of Defence, or MoD, for egg: "Happiness is MoD shaped," I began, "MoD is full of promise, of deliciousness and nourishment. MoD is lovely to look at; delicate enough for the most fastidious, filling enough to keep grown men quiet. Days which start with MoD are more perfect than those which don't. You can say what you like. But I say "Happiness is MoD shaped".'

All this was the lighter side of Michael's life; whenever he could persuade his staff to let him take the risks involved, he put in an appearance at the front line—he would suddenly arrive by helicopter and join a patrol on a cordon and search operation, and make his presence known wherever things were difficult. Out in the Radfan, the men of 45 Commando, Royal Marines, had been on their feet in disagreeable circumstances for several days when Michael came to see them. Their Chaplain, Ray Roberts, dressed in crumpled denims and not looking in the least like a Naval Chaplain, was staggered when Michael walked up to him in the desert and continued a conversation they'd had five years earlier.

According to Roberts, it was on a visit to the Radfan (and not on the dockside) that one of the best known Le Fanu incidents occurred. On one occasion, wearing his khaki uniform with four stars pinned into the shirt peaks, he gave a hand to an airman who had a lot of stores to unload from an aircraft. The airman had not recognised the face or understood the unusual badges of his companion, but finding that the older man was not doing terribly well, exhorted him with the deathless injunction, 'Come on Ginge, get a bloody move on!' 'What did you do?' Roberts asked him later. 'Exactly what I was told to,' Michael replied, 'I got a move on!'

At Christmas 1966, Mark, Hugh and Victoria came out for the holidays which the family spent in Kenya, and in his New Year message printed in the Forces' newspaper *The Dhow* Michael looked back on the year with some satisfaction : 'Many demands have been made on us. Demands for swift action, for skilled action, for brave action, for patient enduring and watchful action. To all these demands the response has been cheerful, instant and professional. I am much in your debt.' 1966 ended with the security forces in South Arabia by and large in control of the situation, but the situation was soon to become much more dangerous and difficult. Michael's attention had to be focused more and more on Aden and its problems as 1967 got into its ugly stride; but in February there was a visit abroad which had its lighter aspect.

The annual passing out parade from the Ethiopian naval college had become, over the years, the occasion for an assembly of ships of all nations and a Naval Review which was something of an international 'face' competition. In 1967, the French sent their Chief of Naval Staff and the Soviet equivalent, Admiral Gorshkov, was also there. Michael arrived in the Tribal class frigate *Nubian*. 'A small ship,' wrote Michael later, 'but we had a very good hole card in the shape of our Wasp, and I was able to say, when the Emperor saw the helo, "would your Imperial Majesty care to get airborne?" So he had a half-hour trip round the harbour piloted by the *Nubian*'s man, one Lieutenant Belgeonne who happily was bilingual in French, the Emperor's principal language. Fortunately there was no engine failure and when he returned we took him down to the wardroom for English tea with muffins. The next day the assembled Fleet staggered off to sea in the wildest disarray. The Service toffs like myself were embarked in the Ethiopian flagship which had the most gorgeous royal apartments from the roof of which we viewed the proceedings, and in the dining room of which we had a gold-plated lunch. I spent a lot of the time, as I had done on the previous days, talking to Gorshkov. We kept off political matters and mostly talked Service shop. I didn't tell him anything above Secret ! We had a photograph taken together, and by this time Gorshkov, who had been rather prickly to begin with, had realised that I was a bit of a comedian and as soon as I approached him would go to laughing stations. I must say the snapshot hardly reflects this, and I can only tell you that one of his staff said they had seen him smile more in three days than in the previous three years. As a souvenir of this occasion I was presented with about half an acre of Ethiopian carpet which eventually found its way to my home at East Sheen where it may be inspected by the curious.'

Michael returned to Aden from this outing to find that the situation there was rapidly deteriorating.

Every possible plan had been explored for revising the Federal constitution in a way which would be acceptable to all parties; the government had even agreed to the sending of a United Nations mission to recommend ways of setting up a central caretaker government while a new constitution could be agreed and brought into operation. Whitehall stuck for a long while to the idea of holding elections but, in the words of the High Commissioner, 'In the Federation, where every man went armed and tribal feuds were endemic, the notion was not a practicable one; and in Aden, not even the opposition could agree on an appropriate franchise, indeed the very mention of the subject was apt to lead to civil disturbances.'

The differences between Aden on the one hand and the Federalis on the other became ever more irreconcilable, and early 1967 saw a rapidly escalating pattern of violent incidents. 'What in 1965 had been undisciplined groups of demonstrators bent on starting small fires and interfering with the sewage system, had transformed themselves into skilled exponents of street fighting, using weapons of heavier and heavier calibre.' The extent to which the Federal Army had been infiltrated was revealed in March when one of the Arab battalion commanders was killed by a mine and his funeral was attended by members of his battalion not in uniform and by known members of the NLF, in which it proved the commander had been a leading figure.

It seemed at this stage that Britain's exit from South Arabia might well have to be a defended military withdrawal rather than a dignified ceremonial departure; and in an effort to ensure that there would be a disciplined force in existence to hold the ring

during and after the departure, George Thomson went out to
Aden in mid-March to offer the Federalis a temporary continua-
tion of British protection. This attempt ran counter to the feelers
that were being put out by the High Commissioner towards a
meeting with the anti-Federali nationalist leaders, and was likely
to prejudice British relations with the UN mission which was
then imminent. In the event it was turned down by the Federalis
in the hope that the offer would eventually be expanded into a
full-scale defence agreement. Both the High Commissioner and
the C-in-C, though much impressed by Thomson, were relieved
that they did not have to operate what they both felt would have
been an ill-fated plan.

U Thant's announcement about the UN mission was the cue
for an increase of violence in late February and through March.
Several horrifying incidents killing civilians caused Prue to decide
to fly home for Easter instead of the family coming out to a very
restricted environment at an age when they felt they wanted freedom of movement. Her decision caused Michael some embarrassment, for all events in Aden were now subjected to exhaustive
coverage by broadcasting and the Press and already he had to
survive criticism for allowing the 'Lollipop' flights to bring out
hundreds of Servicemen's children for the Easter holidays.
Thanks to the vigilance of the security forces, no incident took
place involving Service children, and to Michael's relief they all
departed safely for home. Prue flew back to a social round which
could now only take place under armed escort; and to the most
disastrous week so far in this year of turbulence.

On 1 April, the colony was hit by the worst rainstorm in living
memory, causing widespread floods and the failure of electricity,
telephone and water services. Michael signalled to the Chief of
the Defence Staff in London:

'Since dawn today Aden has suffered the biggest deluge since
Noah was CDS (Chief Deluge Survivor). We have a raft of
administrative problems, and Aden communications centre is
out of action. We have no news about arrival of UN mission or
anything else much. Allah obviously has a message. Another
thrilling instalment tomorrow, by dove if necessary.'

The next instalment contained little to amuse Whitehall, however. On 2 April, while members of the Services and Ministry of Public Buildings and Works were at work repairing the flood damage, a general strike began, to coincide with the arrival of the UN mission. On 3 and 4 April, there were grenade and small arms attacks causing many casualties in Crater, Maalla, Sheikh Othman and Khormaksar as they did on 5 April, which also saw the arrival in Aden of the rock 'n' roll star, Wee Willie Harris! On 6 April, the violence was still widespread and on 7 April the 'gunfight at the Sheikh Othman corral' was filmed by a television news team.

This was the roughest day that the security forces had yet had to face. There were no less than one hundred and thirty-six small-arms attacks and close on one hundred grenades were thrown. The GOC got the impression that a determined attempt was being made to evict us from Sheikh Othman. One particularly tiresome circumstance was that here the opposition were firing for much of the time from a mosque, which British troops were not allowed to enter. Eventually, members of the Federal Army went in, thus winning for themselves much admiration from the British. On this day the UN mission departed, on the eighth the strike was over, and there was a return to an uneasy normality.

During the week there had been a total of two hundred and seventy-seven incidents, resulting in many deaths and injuries and in the arrest of two hundred and forty-seven rioters—an orgy of violence in which the rival terrorist organisations had demonstrated their power and provoked the British to 'repressive' action, at a time when in fact Britain was only too willing to abdicate, if only the various factions could be made to agree on an acceptable formula for the future.

Michael congratulated all concerned on their steadiness under the stresses of that first week of April. 'There must be other difficult days ahead. But the resolution, good humour and professional skill that have been demonstrated during the past week show that we have nothing to fear. Well done all!' The C-in-C did not have to become involved with the UN mission, whose representatives came from Venezuela, Mali and Afghanistan, and who were utterly opposed to the Federal government—indeed they refused to recognise its existence, or to meet its ministers, and the members of the government of Quaiti State in the EAP threatened to resign if it attempted to visit Mukalla. The Adenis for their part refused to meet the mission; the UN team were prevented from making a broadcast against the Federation and as a result left the next day. Their report to the British government, hostile as it was to the Federation, created a further impasse for the authorities.

A week after the departure of the UN mission, Lord Shackleton came to Aden to take up a special appointment as Resident Minister of State with special responsibility for South Arabia. A month later there was an abrupt replacement of the High Commissioner, Sir Richard Turnbull being relieved by Sir Humphrey Trevelyan. Whatever need there might have been for this, the C-in-C felt that Turnbull had been monstrously treated, and made a point of organising a full ceremonial farewell for him, although he had been advised not to do so. On his arrival in May, Sir Humphrey re-emphasised Britain's objectives as laid down by George Brown in the House of Commons on the eleventh of that month:

1. the orderly withdrawal of British forces and the establishment of an independent South Arabia at the earliest possible date;

2. to work in close consultation with all concerned, and especially with the United Nations, for the establishment of a broad-based government by the time of Independence;

3. to leave behind a stable and secure government in South Arabia.

It was clear that Britain would now attempt to involve organisations other than the Federal government in a settlement. There was a preference in favour of FLOSY but in appealing on 19 June for 'all patriotic parties' to come forward for discussion, Sir Humphrey stated that the NLF was no longer outlawed. On the same day it was announced in the House of Commons that Independence Day had been set for 9 January, 1968.

Once the new High Commissioner was installed, Michael made it his business to see that he was supported no less wholeheartedly by the Forces than Sir Richard Turnbull had been.

Early in May, against a background of ever-growing violence, the evacuation of Service families began.

However, intent as they were on keeping normal life going, Michael and Prue were at that very moment engaged in a three days' visit to remote and primitive Socotra, south-east of the Gulf of Aden. The C-in-C was sponsor of a Service and scientific expedition to the island, and although the time for this might have seemed inopportune, the island had never been completely explored and 1967 seemed as good a time as any to do it. Peter Boxhall, the expedition leader, never forgot the cordiality of the Le Fanu welcome at Steamer Point both on their way to Socotra and when they returned. As they were about to leave Aden finally, the expedition presented to Michael and Prue the remains of the expedition flag, which had been patiently made for them by the typists on the Admiral's staff.

The Socotra trip was one of the last expeditions Prue was able to take part in; she departed for home early in June, this time with no prospect of return. Michael's first letters to her reported constant contact with the new High Commissioner who was 'optimistic and a great chatter', and worries about the effect on the mood of the local workers when tugs and lighters in the harbour would need to be requisitioned for the loading of British gear. In fact the terrible outburst of violence which came in mid-June had nothing to do with this. The outbreak of the six-day war between Egypt and Israel greatly increased the unrest throughout South Arabia. This in turn caused a series of disastrous misunderstandings which led to fighting between the British and the newly formed South Arabian Army and South Arabian Police; it resulted in the deaths of twenty-two British soldiers and thirty-one wounded.

The worst encounter took place on 20 June in the Arab town of Crater, when the Royal Northumberland Fusiliers suffered heavy casualties in attacks led from the Armed Police barracks. For political reasons, strongly advanced by the High Commissioner who was most concerned to reduce tension wherever possible, the Army refrained from reoccupying Crater forthwith, as they doubtless could have done, and what was virtually a siege developed. The terrorists were in occupation of the town, which was ringed by units of the army, angry and frustrated that the rule of 'minimum force' had been so rigidly applied and that they were not to be allowed for the moment to re-establish their authority in Crater itself.

Since Crater was within mortar range of Khormaksar airport, it was vital that it should be in friendly hands during the latter stages of the British evacuation, and everyone from the C-in-C down were eager to 'oil back into Crater' if at all possible. As he wrote to Prue, he found the High Commissioner 'bleakly pessimistic', but Michael was encouraging the new General Officer Commanding, Major General Philip Tower, to take action : 'The going back was a question of timing, very delicate, and as you can imagine, a good many fingers were crossed.' In the event, the return went better—and much further—than anyone had expected : on the night of 3 July, after careful advance patrolling, Lieutenant-Colonel Mitchell led the Argyll and Sutherland Highlanders with the armoured cars of the Queen's Dragoon Guards (flying the red and white hackles of the Northumberland Fusiliers) back into Crater. By dawn on the fourth, having encountered relatively little opposition, he had established his headquarters in the Chartered Bank, henceforth re-named 'Stirling Castle' and from there, in an operation exhaustively covered by Press and television, to whom he granted every facility ('to ensure'. in his own words, 'that the higher command would not get away with another disgraceful abandonment of their responsibility to the soldiers entrusted to their care') he exercised effective control of the town until the British finally left Aden.

The forthright manner of Mitchell's actions, and the prominence he acquired in the eyes of the British public, certainly made him a problematic figure for 'the higher command'. The new GOC decided to shift the limelight away from Mitchell by pointing out to the Press that as General Officer Commanding *he* was responsible for the re-taking of Crater. This unhappily resulted in a *Daily Mail* story to the effect that there was a split between the military and the High Commissioner, who had not, it was alleged, known in advance what was happening. It was exactly the kind of situation ('rifts in top Brit. lutes') that Michael had been at pains to avoid. He and the High Commissioner immediately issued a public statement that the responsibility was their and congratulated all concerned.

Though motivated by a desire to re-assert the unity of the Army, General Tower had unwittingly given the C-in-C the impression that he was using a brilliantly successful tactical operation as a personal publicity vehicle. Matters were, however, beginning to mend until, on 13 July, General Tower held, on his own initiative, a formal inspection of the Armed Police in their barracks at Crater. The Argyll and Sutherland Highlanders occupied strategic positions covering the parade in case of trouble, which did not occur. General Tower intended by this action to assist the High Commissioner's policy of cooling the political situation. But once again the wrong impression was created, for neither the C-in-C nor the High Commissioner had known of the parade in advance and the Press once again exacerbated the situation, when the *Daily Mirror* wrote of 'the British Army consorting with murderers'.

Another action of Colonel Mitchell served to widen the rift within the command still further. In an uneasy situation in Crater, and under instruction from Army headquarters to use less tough methods, Mitchell decided to issue the instruction as a written order to his troops, but added a statement that he did not agree with this policy and, if more casualties were caused as a result, it would not be his fault. The paper found its way on to Michael's desk, and he decided to deal personally with what he saw as arrant disloyalty to higher command.

Colin Mitchell has told how he was summoned to the GOC's house where General Tower was sitting on a windowsill, immobilised through straining a cartilage, and how the C-in-C, normally 'a man to look you straight in the eye', on this occasion read out a prepared statement, without once looking up. It was to the effect that Mitchell had behaved disloyally, but that he would not be sent home, as he deserved, on account of the effect this might have on the morale of his troops. It was, however, to be regarded as a warning. Although obliged, he felt, to deliver such a warning, Michael did not cancel the visit to Crater he was due to make on 27 July: in fact it passed off very well. The C-in-C showed Mitchell a letter he had sent to London a few days earlier in answer to complaints about Highland brutality in Crater, telling the Chiefs of Staff that he had every confidence in the troops, who were showing remarkable restraint. Mitchell was impressed.

Michael made the Argylls' occupation of Crater an opportunity to extend his walking routes (and perhaps to show in his own manner his solidarity with the soldiers there). He formed a habit —somewhat tiring to his ADC, any unwilling house guests and his sentries, who were called upon to act as escort—of rising at 4 am, being escorted from Command House round through Crater by the Argylls and then walking over the Jebels to Shamsan Col and down again to Steamer Point in time for breakfast and a beer.

A more far-reaching result of the Highland Regiment's conduct of affairs—whether 'firm' or 'restrained' it was highly effective— was that the centre of terrorist activities shifted to other areas such as Maalla and Sheikh Othman; but the pressure of violence remained high. During July there had been an abortive attempt under Husain Ali Bayoomi to form a caretaker government involving all parties, but the NLF and FLOSY had refused to participate. By September, the South Arabian government had ceased to function, as the NLF took over the Sultanates and Sheikhdoms of the Federation outside Aden and by October they had control of the Eastern Protectorates which had not joined the Federation.

When it was clear that the Federation had disintegrated, Sir Humphrey Trevelyan, after consultations in London, declared that he recognised the 'nationalist forces' as representatives of the people and that he was ready to negotiate with them. While this volte-face was taking place, the C-in-C had to continue with the business of the whole Command and also bring forward the evacuation of troops in Aden, hopeful that despite the many uncertainties of the situation the final date of 9 January, 1968 could be met and perhaps improved upon.

Meanwhile, Michael too had his share of Press attention, and willingly yielded to mild pressure from the *Daily Express* on the lines of : 'Give the boys a break—If Bob Hope Can Go to Vietnam Why Can't Our Stars Go to ADEN!' by welcoming the initiative and inviting Tony Hancock and Hughie Green and subsequently Bob Monkhouse and Harry Secombe to lunch at Command House. Light relief apart, he was now deeply involved in the progress of the evacuation plans. There were numerous complications on the shipping front, 'what with boycotts, no canal and this and that' and several ships were being worked with military labour: 'All Army and Navy auxiliaries except one large cargo ship which we have chartered. We have to put 10,000 tons of stuff into her for the UK. Baggage, ammunition, all sorts. We supplement the expert Royal Corps of Transport people with any gash soldiers or airmen we can lay our hands on. Thought it would be a good idea to find out at first hand how this was going, so yesterday Stephen (Stephen Taylor, the new ADC) and I went down incognito and tagged ourselves on to a party of Marines. Spent about 3 hours down in the hold loading ammunition. Quite a sweat. I was drenched in a few minutes. But well-organised fluids. My colleagues towards the end of the stint were using their favourite adjective, adverb, noun, even more freely than usual. Instead of 'let's put the f. box f. there' we got 'f. let's for f's sake put the f. box f. there, f. it'.

Many people remembered the incident clearly, not least the NCO who had been given two extra hands and told the taller of the two, 'Right then, Ginge, you get stuck in with that lot'—and a senior officer who knew that men from 45 Commando were working on cargo handling and saw approaching him what he took to be two very scruffy half-naked Royal Marines, without berets and looking extremely dishevelled. He was about to give them a monumental blast when he recognised one of them as the C-in-C, and promptly saluted. 'I've been giving your lot a hand on board,' said Michael, 'they're doing a good job!'

His birthday in early August also provided some light relief amid the anxiety. The naval staff bought him a cigarette lighter in the form of a small cannon which they filled with fuel, and buried with a cigar in an enormous parcel which was smuggled (not without difficulty in view of the security precautions) on to the C-in-C's desk. It was accompanied with an ode which read:

All the sailors in Araby are
United with one Ginger Tar

> *Whom they hope will have fun*
> *With this son of a gun*
> *To illumine his birthday cigar.*

The reply was not long in coming :

> *Fifty four is a bit of a jar*
> *But the blow is made softer by far*
> *By the kindness you've done*
> *And the gun that I've won,*
> *So a red-headed sailor says 'Ta'.*

The departure of Field-Marshal Sir Richard Hull from the post of Chief of the Defence staff at about the same time was another opportunity for verse. . . . Michael sent him a parody of Omar Khayyám :

> *Herewith a can of worms, a standby dhow*
> *A flask of wine, some cavaliers, some chow*
> *And signals singing in the wilderness—*
> *Ah wilderness were paradise enow.*

> *They say that soon Sir Elworthy will keep*
> *The Chair where you, Sir, Labour'd long and deep*
> *And Healey, great Reviewer, S of S,*
> *Stamps o'er your head but cannot break your sleep.*

> *So when you read in Mirror or Express*
> *Of how we're in another fearful mess,*
> *Come join our batter'd caravanserai*
> *(A baton's very handy for IS).*

But early in August, too, the question of internal security in Aden was causing some difficulty with the High Commissioner. Sir Humphrey Trevelyan had become convinced that the troops resented the policy of restraint they were told to pursue and were blaming it on him. Michael had to persuade him that all involved were solidly behind him and that there was no question of disloyalty. This he was able to do, before departing for a fortnight's leave at home. When he returned, it was to find that the Federation was rapidly crumbling, that the up-country situation had disintegrated and, as he wrote to Prue, the Eastern Protectorate was 'wonky. So we must look to our moat, as they say in the classics. It is all a ferocious muddle and I am concentrating on getting all Brits. out in one piece.' Extrication from the Eastern states was 'delicate' while there were constant meetings between the C-in-C and the High Commissioner to review the rapidly changing situation.

Backed by a letter from the C-in-C, Sir Humphrey Trevelyan went to London to urge action on the government, and when he came back it was clear the Federalis were to be abandoned in favour of the NLF and FLOSY. The problem remained as to which of those two horses should be backed. Privately Michael hinted 'we are going to have a dash at the NLF (not more than five hundred fils each way)'. The danger of a civil war 'with both sides united only in being anti-Brit' was ever present; in fact there were bitter arguments which flared up eventually into five days' fighting between the NLF and FLOSY over the question of forming a government in which both organisations could be represented. As for the British, in Michael's words 'we are straw clutching as usual. Slightly complicated by the fact that Nasser and Feisal are busy clutching another straw, to wit—down with NLF. For different reasons they are pushing a FLOSY/Sultans/South Arabian League deal. Dotty.' But in September there was a peaceful lull, for which the security forces were very grateful.

In the middle of the month Michael heard that, after Aden, he was to become the next First Sea Lord. The news did not come entirely as a surprise to him, and he told Prue he thought he would accept, provided she did not object. 'Your happiness means more to me than First Sea Lord or anything else'; but 'I am pleased,' he went on, 'because Granny D'Or in heaven will be rejoicing and I hope a few people on earth will also derive pleasure. And if it comes off there should be an extensive hol. to be had.' Michael made it a condition of acceptance that they should not live in the First Sea Lord's flat in Admiralty Arch, which would have made problems for Prue : they would continue to live at Stonehill Road.

Meanwhile in Aden, C-in-C and High Commissioner had established a smooth 'Modus Vivendi'. 'Humphrey with his history of offering *advice* likes to send "assessments" or "thoughts" all the time; I with my background of *doing* things like to offer no opinions beyond those necessary for action, get into no trenches and offer no hostages to fortune. We are in a "do" situation so I have a contribution to make. On the other hand we are dealing with the Foreign Office which Humphrey can handle better than I. So we get on very well.' Certainly Trevelyan went down very well with the troops and sparkled at the many encounters with them which Michael organised.

By the end of September Michael was able to report that the British had 'oiled out of Sheikh Othman and Mansoura' and that all was going well for 'Absquatulation Day (new word, ABSQUATULATE : to decamp)'. He was confident enough to include in his weekly Sitrep to the Chiefs of Staff an advertiser's supplement which read : 'Crown Colony of Character near Red Sea in sought-after position . . . owner going overseas, open any offer for quick disposal . . . recently modernised regardless of expense by present occupier and includes : "Government House", a large modern residence facing sea, suit Chairman of people's National Liberation concern. Also "Command House", suit senior diplomat o.n.o., and unique circular residence converted from gun emplacement suitable for reconversion to gun emplacement . . .' The internal security situation still remained relatively quiet, and among many other social engagements, the C-in-C dined with the Argylls in Crater : 'where they are comfortably set up. They are a nice bright lot and, as the Colonel was more or less under control, it was all very pleasant.'

In October, while lengthy discussions took place in Cairo between the NLF and FLOSY, tension continued to mount in Aden. 'I have an idea,' wrote Michael, 'that both sides are bent on having a go at each other to their mutual disadvantage and destruction, and are determined that the blame shall be laid on us.' Sir Humphrey Trevelyan went to London to consult with the Foreign Secretary leaving Michael hopeful that the date for evacuation could be advanced. A large armada of naval ships and transports was beginning to assemble off Aden, and at the end of the month the headquarters moved from Steamer Point to Khormaksar airfield.

For a naval newspaper called *The South Arabian Sun*, Michael wrote a message of greeting which expressed the hope that the sun would shine but that its setting would not be too long delayed; and on 29 October, when the AOC (Andrew Humphrey) left for his new Persian Gulf headquarters he decided a farewell prank was called for, if only to prove that Air-Marshals did not object to practical jokes.

It was a Sunday afternoon, and most of Aden's VIP's had assembled at the airport to bid farewell to the AOC. The C-in-C was not in evidence and this caused some mild surprise, though Humphrey had in fact told him not to bother to come, as he would be returning in a day or two. After the usual formalities in the lounge, the whole party emerged to watch a very good fly past of all the available RAF aircraft. Then, wrote Michael, 'they sauntered across to the Andover, which was pointing to the right as seen from the lounge, so that they had to walk round the tail to get to the entrance steps. A good deal of chat ("how kind of you to come and see me off" sort of thing) as they paused for a final word by the rail. All this overheard of course by the immaculate Air Quartermaster (bow tie, etc.) who was standing at the foot of the ladder with his back to them. Eventually amid final farewells Andrew mounted the steps, and Air Quartermaster saluted and after saying "Goodbye, sir" in a louder and louder voice eventually caught Andrew's eye just before he disappeared. Of course he came back down and we had a great chuckle.'

Early in November, a number of rapid developments took place. Following five days of fighting between the NLF and FLOSY, largely centred on Mansoura, Saif Dhali, head of the NLF political bureau, announced that the NLF was in full control of South Arabia and demanded negotiations with Britain. Political detainees were released, and the NLF ordered the surrender of all arms to the authorities prior to negotiations with the British in Geneva. The final exodus of British forces was now imminent : 'a complex but tidy operation which would appeal to you', Michael wrote to Prue. 'We are going out in one large complicated heap in the last few days. The only thing you would not care for is the number of jokers in the pack—to wit we do not yet have a definite date for final departure—we do not know whether Khormaksar will be under mortar fire—do we get all the civvy Brits out with us or leave them behind? and so on. There are still some interesting decisions to take.'

All through November Michael remained closely in touch with the High Commissioner, as no one could be certain when or whether some new alarming development might occur. In Michael's view, the Foreign Office was dilatory in giving Sir Humphrey permission to deal direct with the NLF. 'Here we are,' he wrote, 'balanced on a razor's edge and all they can do is treat it like a question of precedence at a garden party!' Nor was it easy to get a firm date from the government for independence. It was not until the middle of the month that George Brown announced that 30 November would be Independence Day. Michael was greatly relieved.

On 'W-5' (five days before withdrawal day) he decided there would be a Review of the now considerable fleet which lay off Aden ('good psychologically to make a bit of a show'), and embarked on a last round of farewell visits, including one to Sharjah on the Persian Gulf, where he was well received by the Ruler. The naval Review, with the High Commissioner steaming past the lines of ships in HMS *Appleton*, was a great success on 25 November, and then: 'time is running out, to-morrow should be the last day in this house at Khormaksar. Then to Bahrein and then you-know-where!'

On 27 November the keys of Government House were handed over to the NLF and on the twenty-eighth, the High Commissioner and the C-in-C flew out of Khormaksar. On the twenty-ninth, a memorandum of agreement was signed between the British and the NLF, and at midnight, South Arabia became independent under the name of the People's Republic of South Yemen.

Michael was on his way home, like the thousands of other British servicemen who had survived the daunting and dangerous problems of Britain's last years in Aden. As Commander-in-Chief, Middle East Command, he had, apart from the official business of his immensely demanding job, set an example of cheerful leadership which has never been forgotten by those who experienced it. 'The Admiral's real greatness,' wrote Roger Hicks, his first ADC, after Michael's death, 'was that among the pressure of internationally important affairs, he found time to concern himself with the problems of all the ordinary servicemen with whom he came into contact. I am sure this was his outstanding achievement and will be remembered long after his policy decisions are committed to the archives. I suspect too that this is the way he would wish things to be.'

EIGHTEEN

First Sea Lord

The year 1968 opened for Michael with congratulations—on his appointment as a Knight Grand Cross of the Order of the Bath in the New Year's Honours List (a mark of recognition of his work in Aden) and on the announcement that he was to be the next First Sea Lord and Chief of Naval Staff—the professional head of the Navy.

The reaction reported by Roger Hicks, now serving in HMS *Dainty*, seems to have been widespread : 'Wild jubilation here at Portland, accompanied by a rash of highly coloured stories about your past career. I listened spellbound to a fantastic tale yesterday, breathtaking in its audacity, and eventually realised it was "the book of the film" about your visit to Aden Brigade—which proves, I suppose, that the naval bush telegraph is as unreliable as ever.' 'It couldn't have happened to a nicer fellow,' wired Harry Secombe; and Class 4A at the County Junior School, Petersfield, told Michael they were 'very proud that you have come from Petersfield and I expect other people from Petersfield are proud of you too.' The pride and pleasure expressed by Lord Fraser of North Cape was coupled with a warning about the 'difficult time' he was likely to have, as was the message from Admiral Sir John Frewen, that very able and original man who was to end his career as C-in-C Portsmouth, offering good wishes in forthcoming 'battles which will make your days as Controller seem like Christmas parties'. 'A nice job you've landed yourself in,' said Admiral Sir Royston Wright, 'it all stems from a mistaken policy of "getting fell in previous". However I can imagine no better tonic for a hard-pressed Navy; not least because you will demonstrate that it can be fun at the Top.' That this was one of

Michael's intentions there is no doubt—and the prospect rather worried another of his friends, who had first called on him in *Superb* and found him leading the ship's company at a brisk trot round St Mary's Island. 'If the Admiralty Board is treated similarly round Whitehall Gardens,' he wrote, 'I fear the mortality rate among your fellow members will be rather high!'

The realisation that Michael was the man to restore morale in the Navy at a time when the Service was at odds with itself reflected credit on his predecessor, Sir Varyl Begg, who had had the deciding voice in choosing him. Begg's had been the unenviable task of reshaping the future Fleet in the light of the carrier decision and no one could have carried it through with a more single-minded devotion to duty. Sir Varyl, second to none in his love for the Navy, had faced political realities and in so doing won immense respect from his colleagues in Whitehall and in the Fleet. But although he could have stayed on for another year as First Sea Lord, he felt that the Navy now needed an injection of self-confidence, requiring talents different from his own. Michael possessed them. Though more complex and far-seeing than many thought, he realised that the task of cheering everybody up was not the least of his duties as First Sea Lord, and he prepared for the task with his customary energy.

The early months of 1968 provided Michael with a chance to think and to discuss with friends how he should tackle the new job. Earlier in his career there had been a switch round in plans for promotion which had resulted in his becoming Controller instead of Vice-Chief of the Naval Staff, an appointment normally held by future First Sea Lords. Therefore in some respects Michael lacked the experience of the Chiefs of Staff Committee from which others in his position had usually benefited. This was one factor which led him to decide to emphasise his role as Leader of the Navy and First Sea Lord ('Though I'm not a Lord, and I don't go to sea as often as I would like, I *am* First!')—rather than concentrating chiefly on the Whitehall battle under the more recently bestowed title of CNS—Chief of Naval Staff. Fortunately in Vice-Admiral Sir Peter Hill-Norton, Michael inherited a forceful and efficient Vice-Chief; and Hill-Norton was succeeded by the very able Vice-Admiral Edward Ashmore (later

Sir Edward) whose appointment Michael himself had approved while in Aden. Both men were eventually to become First Sea Lords, and both admirably deputised when Michael was absent on other duties or, towards the end, on sick leave.

It was soon clear that Michael intended to make no change in his personal style to conform with the grandeur of his new position. Not long after his return from the Middle East, he had to attend Whitehall de-briefing sessions, and on at least one occasion was seen to leave with bicycle clips on his trousers, ready to cycle back to East Sheen.

Even as First Sea Lord designate, he was determined not to be tamed by the pomposities of high office, and, as always, made time for ordinary people. An accounting problem had arisen regarding his pay, and he telephoned the pay office in Portsmouth to make some enquiries. After the difficulty had been straightened out, Michael wrote to the Officer-in-Charge and asked the name and service details of the Wren Writer who had assisted him. There then followed, practically by return of post, a handwritten letter addressed to her personally : this was rapidly passed round the office and caused an immediate upswing in morale. It was in such small but significant ways, long remembered by those concerned, that Michael exercised his gift of leadership.

The quality was appreciated in February 1968 by the men of the submarine HMS *Onyx* in which Michael embarked for a week, dressed in his own individual "dress of the day"—open-necked shirt and (on the bridge and casing) Admiral's reefer. His now receding ginger locks gave rise to a disrespectful limerick:

> *To send us an Admiral as spare*
> *We reckoned at first was unfair*
> *But now he's been seen*
> *We're a little more keen—*
> *For at least we can't get in his hair!*

At about the same time he received a valentine from the men of 759 Squadron which was a reminder of the almost extravagant hopes the Navy entertained of him when he became its professional head :

O Mighty one whose August Power
Will shield us all in danger's hour,
This Service save, nor let decline
And be our own true Valentine!

Michael was well aware of these hopes, but took a more detached view himself, as he explained in a letter to a friend. 'I fear a lot of people expect me to work miracles and unscramble miscellaneous messes. It *won't be* that way—the powers of the Board in general and the First Sea Lord in particular have been badly eroded—but of course I'll do my best. It occurs to me that a lot of very fine incumbents have kept their noses devotedly to the Whitehall grindstone and where has that got us? Anyway it gives me the excuse to get out and around a bit.' By way of preparation for this, Michael took a helicopter pilot's course at the Royal Naval Air Station at Culdrose in July, but before doing so he set aside five weeks of his leave to tour the East Coast of the United States with Prue, a trip they had always hoped to make ever since Michael had tasted the American way of life in 1945. They visited relations and wartime naval friends, returning home in time for Michael's date with the flying instructors.

When he started work at the Ministry of Defence on 12 August, his appointment was greeted in the *Guardian* as 'surprising and absolutely right—the Navy could do with a bit of a heretic', but it must be recorded that Michael's unorthodox approach was not universally approved among senior officers and politicians. There were those who felt he should have been content to plug away at the 'Whitehall grindstone' and to leave the skylarks to those in less responsible positions. Taking his publicity-worthy activities at their face value, and failing, perhaps, to understand their true significance as a means of projecting the Navy's cause, his critics saw him as superficial and too impatient of the demanding detail of a Chief of Staff's job. But Michael had thought his approach out thoroughly, and he swung into action along the lines he had planned.

Early in 1968, the government had announced its intention of withdrawing from the Far East, though a naval presence was to be maintained there, as a contribution to SEATO, and would be quickly reinforced if necessary. To draw attention to the Navy's ability to fulfil this requirement—and also to emphasise the importance of the Fleet Air Arm which was already being run down —Michael flew eight thousand miles to Singapore, within a week of taking office, in the back seat of a Buccaneer jet bomber, having learnt enough in a quick pre-flight course to carry out the duties of Navigator to Lieutenant-Commander Jeremy Nichols. The flight attracted the immediate interest of the Press as Michael had intended. The newspapers quoted with relish the signal from the Commander Far East Fleet after the First Sea Lord's aircraft had made a safe landing en route for Singapore on the deck of HMS *Hermes*: 'Distinguished Chinese observer recovered on deck and Advises Vice-Chief of Naval Staff to relax'. Two days later, they reported how, in the course of a week's tour of naval establishments, Lee Fan Yew the 'Chinese Admiral' called once again on Lee Kwan Yew, Singapore's Prime Minister, renewing the acquaintance begun in the Far East some years before.

Back in London Michael lost no time in reminding the inhabitants of the MOD main building of the Le Fanu touch. At about four o'clock on Friday afternoon a Wren—now Mrs V. A. Blackwell—was working in a Royal Marines office when 'a gentleman appeared in the door carrying a bundle wrapped in brown paper and, with all respect, although he was wearing a pin-stripe suit he did look a trifle scruffy. I decided he was not a naval officer and he did not really look like a civil servant. I asked if I could help him, and he replied, "No, I don't think so", but then he proceeded to ask a number of questions about work load, number of people in the office, job satisfaction, hours, whether we enjoyed our work, etc. This continued for some minutes; the visistor would not take a seat and I was busy wondering who he was and why the questions. The Sergeant then returned to the office, and, probably noticing our inability to cope efficiently with the visitor (who, by the way, seemed perfectly at ease) enquired, "Can I help you sir?" "No thank you," was the reply, "I'm just having a look round on this floor." After asking the Sergeant some probing questions, the visitor backed towards the door saying, "Well, it's after four and you should all be off. I won't delay you further." "Excuse me, sir," said the Sergeant quickly, "may I ask your name?" "Certainly, my name's Le Fanu. Good afternoon." And he was gone, before the astonished occupants of the office had time to say goodbye.'

On the desk in his own office on the sixth floor he placed a card with the admonitory message: 'There they go and I must hurry to catch up with them, for I am their leader.' The door, as often as not, was left open between the inner and the outer office, where Captain Charles Denman as Secretary and Captain Martin Wemyss as Naval Assistant exhibited the same ready welcome to visitors as their master. But the appearance of bluff and non-chalant humour belied in both men sharp brains and a passion for efficiency. Denman well knew from personal experience, while Assistant Secretary Ian Sutherland and June Light ('the office machine—36-24-36') quickly learned that Michael's complete trust implied that each must bear a high degree of individual responsibility.

On the surface there appeared to be less work than under previous First Sea Lords; there was certainly less paper. Lengthy minutes were replaced by LEFgrams; the Admiral took no papers home in the battered old suitcase inscribed 'Rear-Admiral Le Fanu' which he used in place of a briefcase; able as he was to digest information at high speed, he quickly made himself master of the reports submitted to him.

Charles Denman, in an article written for *Reader's Digest* after Michael's death, described the first Tuesday morning briefing session prior to the Chiefs of Staff meeting that afternoon. The usual crowd of specialists had gathered in the First Sea Lord's office, expecting to be cross-questioned about the reports they had submitted. Michael said that he had read them and began to go through the agenda. 'Item 1: Understood, Item 2: Understood, Item 3: Understood, Item 4: Understood, Item 5: Understood, Item 6: What the hell are we all doing here?' He cut a meeting which had normally lasted two and a half hours to twenty minutes.

There were those who felt that such a dashing approach, while admirable in some ways, left little chance for subordinates to have a say. In fact Michael soon demonstrated his interest in

other people's views by establishing the First Sea Lord's Debating
Society. From time to time he would decide on two subjects for
debate, and detail suitable speakers. An early motion was that
'There is no place in a modern Navy for the Seaman Officer';
another that 'This house considers there is no place for the Board
of Admiralty in Modern Management'. One officer had defended
the board by recalling that even Jesus had had a board of management in the twelve Apostles, and in summing up the debate
the First Sea Lord said, 'We have heard some interesting views
this afternoon, and I have come to the conclusion that my Relief
as First Sea Lord will have to be either an idiot or Jesus Christ.
Gentlemen, I would ask that even though you think him the
former, you should treat him as the latter.'

That Michael should have made such a remark in jest may
have been an indication that even in his early days as First Sea
Lord, he had in mind the possible future direction of his career.
As early as mid-1968 he was already being tipped as the next
Chief of the Defence Staff. It was the Navy's turn, and Michael's
personal reputation after Aden stood high. He viewed the prospect with a certain misgiving, feeling that talents foreign to his
own were needed to integrate the three Services under their political masters; but he hoped that if the job came his way, he might
be able to do for the Armed Services as a whole what he intended
to do for the Navy—to put them back on the map in no uncertain terms.

The more aware the public became of what the Services were
called upon to do, the more pressure would be brought to bear
upon the government to provide them with the necessary backing
—and the more recruits of the right kind would come forward.
In due course he hoped the Chiefs of Staff would play a greater
role as policy makers. But all depended on the support of public
opinion, and this could only be won through a new emphasis on
public relations, beginning, against tradition, with the Navy:
'We may be the Silent Service, but there's no need to be dumb!'
Wherever he saw a chance to influence opinion, the new First
Sea Lord would accept an invitation to speak, and such invitations were numerous, for people remembered how well he had
filled the after-dinner role in his days as Controller.

One of Charles Denman's main functions was to prepare the material for Michael's speeches, following the First Sea Lord's principle : 'I never tell stories but say ordinary things in a funny way.' For this reason it is impossible to reproduce on paper his effect on a gathering of dinner guests—so much depended on gesture, nuance and timing—and always within the froth of absurdity there was the message he wanted to punch home. But Charles and he did invent some amusing lines. On one occasion, when introduced effusively, Michael replied, 'I thought for a moment I was being confused with *Saint* Michael, perhaps because his name is sewn into my underwear.' We can still enjoy 'FOMAS, the Flag Officers' Mutual Admiration Society (FOMAS washes whiter)' and the 'Westminster Palace of Varieties featuring nightly entertainment at "Healey's Hacienda", where the Higher Organisation for Defence ("known as Nearer my God to Thee") gathers in the MOD'. There, 'guys wander round the corridors with dazed expressions on their faces wondering where they stand—in more ways than one.'

'Actually,' Michael admitted, 'I'm all right Jack. I have an office from which I can spend my days gazing at boats on the river and dreaming of salt sea spray and all that jazz, and I haven't changed my title—just had it abbreviated—an occupational hazard in this place. Under my more old-fashioned title—First Sea Lord—I think I should point out that although I do get the occasional letter referring to "Your Lordship", and one recent one started off "My Lord" (I think that was an expression of surprise), I realise that I, too, have bosses and have to go around murmuring "Yes Minister", "Quite so Secretary of State", and even "I entirely agree, Prime Minister"—but quite often I am left alone to get on with the job of streamlining the Navy—and making it more efficient—on Healey's diet of LIMMITS.'

And what did Denis Healey as Minister of Defence make of his Chief of Naval Staff? He found him charming and very good company but did not think he was cut out to be a Whitehall warrior. 'He was a great leader of men and in wartime would have been a splendid First Sea Lord—in some ways he was the "Monty" of the Navy.'

Lord Carrington, Mr Healey's successor in 1970, dissented only from the latter part of Mr Healey's assessment. As for Michael, he disguised neither his dislike of political control over the Services nor his distrust of politicians in general, though he took trouble to educate them in the ways of the Navy. This applied particularly to Dr David Owen, who had been appointed Minister for the Navy at the age of twenty-nine in July 1968.

In 1969 Michael was asked to preside at an RN Club dinner in honour of the Admiralty Board and had to welcome the Navy Minister among the guests: 'Doctor David Anthony Llewellyn Owen—Dai the DREADNOUGHT, Owen the Admiralty. *Who's Who* has him down as being born and bred in the suburbs of Guzz (Plymouth), but don't be misled. Anyone less like a dozy Devon dumpling I have yet to meet. There is no danger in any of us old sweats lying back and thinking how well we're doing, believe me. For this, I in particular, and the Board and the Navy in general, are very grateful to Chairman Harold for putting him in charge. As for his Welsh credentials—I must admit that I have not yet heard David singing *Sospan Fach* when confronted with our own particular variety of Chaos in the kitchen. But with a name like that in the Chinese Year of the Daffodil and the Leek, he can't go far wrong.'

After working for six weeks with Sir Varyl Begg, whom he much admired, Owen was at once aware of the change of approach when Michael took over as First Sea Lord. Owen enjoyed his breezy manner, greatly appreciated the wedding gift from the Board of a silver ashtray inscribed with the words 'From the Crew', and found himself in agreement with Michael on one of the most important questions then before the Board, concerning the future pattern of the Fleet—the shape of the proposed new cruiser.

Sir Varyl Begg and Peter Hill-Norton as Vice-Chief of Naval Staff were opposed on grounds of cost to any major change in the proposed plans for a relatively conventional vessel; Michael and David Owen were among those who wanted the ship to have a 'through-deck'—a flat top—and thus be capable of flying Harriers. Though this in effect would lead to a new generation of aircraft carriers, everyone was most careful not to say so in public;

and although the project might ultimately lead to a revival of hope for a Fleet Air Arm and Michael kept a model of a Harrier prominently displayed on his desk, he would firmly tell visitors who expressed interest that he did not much care about the colour of the uniform of those who might fly the aircraft, so long as it landed on his ships.

It was not until 1973 that the 'through-deck cruiser' to be named HMS *Invincible* was ordered, but its shape was decided during Michael's time as First Sea Lord, bringing the promise of a return to fixed-wing flying in the Fleet. A similar process of planning must have been taking place at much the same time in the Soviet Navy which before long was to surprise some observers by starting an aircraft carrier programme.

Meanwhile, after her three-year refit, *Ark Royal* returned to the Fleet in 1970, as did her sister ship *Eagle*, and HMS *Blake*, the converted helicopter cruiser, proved herself well in sea trials. The guided missile destroyers were continuing to come off the slipways, together with the frigates which are the workhorses of the Royal Navy in the seventies, and the nuclear-powered Fleet submarines which are its Capital ships. The construction of Fleet submarines had been halted in order that the 'Polaris' submarine programme should be completed on time, but now the rate of production of these most important vessels picked up.

While these and other vital matters were under consideration at meetings of the Admiralty Board—where the First Sea Lord, wearing as often as not a bright coloured 'psychedelic' tie, would preside quietly, listening with care to the arguments of others before voicing his own opinion—he also continued to get out and about as often as possible.

In December 1968, on the principle that 'a few hours doing the job is worth weeks reading about it in Whitehall' he joined the Hull trawler *Joseph Conrad* on passage to Iceland, after which he transferred to HMS *Belton* of the Fishery Protection Squadron and was brought back to Leith : it was all part of a plan to 'unite the professionals of the sea'. The outing, incidentally, provided Michael with a chance on the journey to Hull to share the driving of his car with his official driver, Ron Stirling. A welcome relief, no doubt, for Michael's driver was kept very fully employed, partly owing to the First Sea Lord's decision to live at East Sheen rather than at Admiralty Arch.

Wherever they went, Michael was always anxious to return if possible to East Sheen the same night. This meant long hours at the wheel for the excellent Ron, who in a very short time became a friend to all the family and a particular support to Prue in the never-ending official round—helping her in and out of awkward naval aircraft or prospecting the easiest wheelchair route through many a London hotel. Michael had deliberately chosen to have a civilian, rather than a Marine, driver as he thought it unfair that a Serviceman should be expected to work unlimited hours without overtime pay. As it was, when hours extended, as they frequently did, well beyond the working week, Michael showed much consideration towards Mrs Stirling and would always enquire, 'Is it all right with Lena if we work this weekend?' When First Sea Lord he called to see the Stirlings more than once in their Greenwich home, on one occasion after a Greenwich wedding, amazing their young son by appearing in a top hat.

Although not using a Service driver, he made a point of visiting (as no previous First Sea Lord had ever done) the Regent's Park barracks of 20 Squadron, Royal Corps of Transport who supplied all the official cars, a visit which was greatly appreciated; and he would often, with Stirling's agreement, place the car at the disposal of other Service people if he thought this would be helpful.

As ex-officio president of the RN Football Association, he regularly received tickets for important matches at Wembley. On one such occasion he sent the car to Paddington to pick up the Petty Officer who was captain of the RN soccer team, while he himself went to Wembley by tube; and on another day he gave his own tickets to a junior Captain on the staff, coupled with use of the official car.

When embarked himself, Michael liked a turn of speed. Never reluctant to go one-up in a comradely fashion on the RAF, he was pleased when, on the road back to London from a State occasion at Windsor, his car passed that of the Chief of the Defence Staff, Air Chief Marshal Sir Charles Elworthy. Alas, a few minutes later Michael's car was pulled up for speeding, and it was the RAF's turn to glide past with a gracious wave.

After the constant round of travelling, Christmas leave 1968 was a welcome break, beginning with silver wedding celebrations and a gathering of many relations and friends at Stonehill Road.

Not long after he returned to the office, the First Sea Lord decided it was time for him to get airborne again. From the Royal Naval Air Station at Yeovilton he flew in the back seat of a supersonic Phantom jet piloted by Commander Antony Pearson, to Naples for talks with the Commander-in-Chief Allied Forces Southern Europe (Admiral Horacio Rivero), an expedition which brought him a model of a Phantom, inscribed 'Naples for Lunch, 26.2.69' and a share of Press attention which rivalled the coverage given that week to his daughter Victoria. She was appearing with the Prince of Wales in a revue put on by the Dryden Society of Trinity College, Cambridge and found immediate fame as the girl dragged offstage by Prince Charles with the words, 'I must say I do like giving myself heirs!'

Michael's efforts to 'put the Navy on the map' continued at a hectic pace all through 1969, involving such 'knockabout turns' (to use Prue's phrase) as descending by wire on to the Royal Marine-manned entry in the Round Britain Powerboat Race. There were no limits to Michael's wish to 'Have a go', and his colleagues sometimes intervened if they were quick enough to discover the First Sea Lord's intentions in advance. Thus the Commandant-General, Royal Marines, managed to scotch a plan for a parachute jump on a visit to the Royal Marines at Poole— a disappointment to the Marines, for they had prepared a special helmet marked on top with a cross and the words 'Dig Here!' No one, however, could stop him donning a frogman's suit on the same visit and doing some diving.

Later in the year, in a heavy gale, the First Sea Lord celebrated his election as an Elder Brother of Trinity House by going out in the Trinity House vessel *Stella* to visit the *Seven Stones* Lightship and by taking the wheel of a 12,000-ton freighter as she made her way up the Thames to the King George V Docks. On some of his less spectacular enterprises, he took the Admiralty Board— including the Navy Minister—with him on what he called 'brood-ins', to HMS *Mercury* for instance, and later to the

RNAS Yeovilton—all part of his campaign to bridge the gap which he felt existed between Whitehall and the workers.

Media people were astonished to find how accessible the professional head of the Navy now was; in fact he was so ready to be interviewed that Lord Fraser once expressed surprise to Michael because he had not seen him on television for a week. He was interviewed by the author of this book for the BBC and for the Navy's annual Scrapbook film *Scranbag*, in the course of which the Admiral expressed confidence in the Navy's future and, asked what would happen if things went wrong under his regime, replied by taking off his cap and placing a bowler hat firmly on his head.

A member of his staff who took Michael to lunch with the Editor of the *Daily Mirror* was thanked subsequently for bringing along the Navy's public relations man; Tom Pocock of the *Evening Standard*, having accompanied 'the most off-beat' First Sea Lord on a Thames excursion in a BP tanker, found him 'fresh minded and forward thinking. Unusual, even eccentric, but behind all the jokes a serious professional with a reputation for ruthlessness.'

To Pocock and to anyone else who would listen, from professionals at the RN Staff College at Greenwich to members of the Little Ship Club, Michael spoke in direct terms of the threat which made a strong Navy a necessity for Britain. He would point to the startling increase in the Soviet fleet and changes in its deployment pattern, implying a major shift in the balance of power. Though we could not hope to match them in numbers of ships or weapons, we could still provide a substantial deterrent, and this the new Navy was well able to do, with the force of Polaris submarines becoming operational and the growing number of nuclear fleet submarines, not to mention a substantial force of cruisers, frigates and destroyers, assault ships, mine counter-measures craft, patrol craft and (while they still remained in the Fleet) aircraft carriers; all backed up with an efficient fleet of support ships.

But there were major problems—not least the 'missile gap' in the medium and long ranges caused by the future absence of carriers and the need to recruit enough of the right kind of young men. They must be persuaded that the future Navy 'will not be based at Margate or Broadstairs but will have a real role. We are still critically dependent on our overseas trade and our Merchant Navy—lose that and we lose all, including the National Health Service and our pensions. At the end of the day, and under God's good providence, it is still upon the sea that the well-being of this country does chiefly depend. So you see, there is plenty to do, though fewer to do it, and it will be very worthwhile and rewarding.'

'I would be grateful if you could help,' Michael told the Royal Naval Association, 'by banging out the message till it hurts :

> *The law of the Navy still says*
> *Six days shalt thou labour*
> *And do all thou art able*
> *And on the Seventh*
> *Holystone the deck and paint the cable—*

But they get Music while they Work nowadays ! And I'm told Jack has in his ditty box a wig to cover up his NAAFI hair when he goes ashore. And the field-gun crews get faster every year—so not to worry !'

Michael instituted periodic gatherings of retired officers so that they could be kept informed and be recruited in a propaganda role; serving officers were issued with two successive editions of a small classified handbook labelled PIM ('Position and Intended Movement')—this led later to the creation of a 'Board Bulletin'. It was good, Michael thought, that the Fleet should have matters clearly laid before them by the Navy's top professionals, rather than having to wait for the politicians to produce another White Paper. Consistently Michael tried to make people at all levels feel that their views counted, and he would listen as attentively to the conversation round the bar as he consumed a lunchtime sandwich at the Ship and Shovel as he would to the arguments of the Admiralty Board.

His touch with the young remained as sure as it had been at *Ganges* and he made a tremendous impact in September 1969 when he visited the boys of the training ship *Formidable* at Portishead. He went aboard one of the 32-foot cutters in Portishead

Dock and suggested that he should take an oar and pull his weight. 'The Admiral took stroke oar, port side,' reported the *North Somerset Mercury*, 'then turned to his bench-mate, Steven Nicholls, and recalled that when he was a boy, the starboard oarsman always set the stroke. He was told that this was still the custom, and the lads were thrilled and delighted to hear the First Sea Lord remark : "All right, mate, you're the boss. I'll follow you !" Afterwards the boy whose place Michael had taken could hardly contain his excitement : "He sat on my spec (thwart), my spec I tell you !" '

The young at Bradford Grammar School responded with the utmost enthusiasm to Michael's speech day address on 'Courage' —it was, said their Headmaster, 'like a cheerful and invigorating breeze on a sultry day.' Even the Le Fanu young were used to benefiting from their father's willingness to help. A few years earlier, his younger son Hugh had taken on a paper round during the holidays, but when invited one Sunday to go on a particularly attractive fishing expedition, he accepted Dad's offer to deliver the papers instead !

At every level, at home and overseas, Michael devoted himself to the cause of 'the Maritime Affair'. In mid-1969 he was in America, where he was regarded by many senior officers who remembered his work with the Pacific Fleet as 'one of our own'— and where there were visits to the headquarters of the Supreme Allied Commander Atlantic, to Cape Kennedy, to Bermuda and the Caribbean. Later in the year, the First Sea Lord visited Germany, Australia and New Zealand. The antipodean visit, in which Prue was able to take part, was an immense success. What Michael had to say about the future pattern of British co-operation in the defence of the Far East was of the utmost interest to the Australians and New Zealanders; as for Prue, it was, in a sense, a return home, for she had been at Marsden School, Wellington, some thirty-five years previously, a fact which added a strong touch of local interest to the arrival of the Le Fanus. Everywhere they made a tremendous impression—Michael with his professional grasp and easy good humour, and the pair of them through their apparently nonchalant approach to Prue's disability.

This particular quality had to survive a tough test when the Comet which had taken them out to the Far East went unserviceable and had to be replaced—if they were to arrive at Wellington on time—by a Hercules transport aircraft. Michael, needless to say, turned the incident into verse :

> At Canberra, jealous of Lady Lef's polio,
> The Comet says 'Ow, I've got pains in me oleo!'
> So while a spare's sent for and other Things tried
> It's really a question of bumming a ride.
> The Far Eastern Air Force display their abilities
> By providing a Herc—with no female facilities.
> An Elsan however is hastily run up
> And the ladies enjoined not to drink after sun-up.
> So at last in New Zealand the party arrives
> For some there are staff talks, for others the dives!

The visit to Australia and New Zealand had followed on the public announcement that Michael was to be the next Chief of the Defence Staff. This was widely reported in the newspapers, together with a good deal of speculation about the possible return of fixed-wing flying to the Fleet when the vertical take off Harrier (which had undergone sea trials, closely watched by the First Sea Lord, in August) was sufficiently developed.

The growing technological complexity of naval warfare gave rise to much discussion at this time about the question of the daily rum issue which had been introduced into the Navy in 1731. This was widely regarded as one of the sailor's most cherished privileges, although it was not a universal view, and a growing body of opinion in the Navy felt that rum should go. The matter had been discussed for some years, and had certainly been raised again during Sir Varyl Begg's time as First Sea Lord. He felt, however, that he already had so much unpopular news to communicate to the Navy, that the rum decision had better be shelved for his successor. As Second Sea Lord (the 'man man') Admiral Sir Frank Twiss was greatly in favour of abolition and Michael agreed that the institution of the midday tot, with its outdated ceremony and resultant drowsiness in the afternoon, was unsuited to a modern Navy.

But it was not a simple matter to do away with the rum issue. The Admiralty Board seriously debated the possibility of mutiny if and when the announcement should be made, and there were differences of view among the Board as to how the decision should be implemented. The government felt it could not be a political decision, for to do away with so time-honoured a tradition would have been to court grave unpopularity. The Navy Minister, Dr David Owen, was reluctant to be involved, and was unwilling to 'bite the bullet' on the matter, to quote his own words, unless a reasonable beer ration could be provided for the junior ratings and chief and petty officers could be given drinking privileges similar to those provided for officers. He also argued for the provision of two and half million pounds for naval welfare funds by the Treasury in lieu of the amount provided for the purchase of rum. All these points were eventually agreed, and on 18 December, 1969 a signal went out announcing that the last issue of rum in the Royal Navy would take place on 31 July, 1970.

Michael, as Sir Varyl Begg had known, was just the man to weather the storm of criticism that broke. To those who challenged the decision he pointed out that a large tot of rum in the middle of the day was not the best medicine for those who had to handle the Navy's electronic mysteries, emphasised the more democratic drinking arrangements which would replace rum, and gaily dubbed himself 'Dry Ginger'.

That autumn he and the 'office machine' concentrated on organising an entirely light-hearted occasion—the reunion of fellow members of the Benbow Term at Dartmouth and their wives, which took place on board HMS *President* in November 1969. Men like Commander John Nicholson, who had been on the staff of the college at that time, were also delighted to receive invitations; and Michael did his utmost to ensure that all the invited guests were able to be there. Delayed in Gothenburg by a dock strike, Lieutenant-Commander Anthony Buckle had cabled that, although he would do his best to travel by another route, he was unlikely to arrive in time. This was not acceptable to Michael, who discovered that the only alternative ship would put in at Immingham on the late afternoon of the day in ques-

tion. When he arrived there, Buckle was astonished to find a
large staff car on the dockside awaiting him: he missed the
dinner, but not the after-dinner conversation of his old friends.

For Prue a highlight of that autumn was the re-commissioning,
on 18 November, of the Frigate HMS *Aurora*, which she had
launched; but privately, as the relentless social and professional
round continued, she was becoming anxious about the pace of
her husband's activities. After Christmas spent at Sheen, Michael
set off early in 1970 for a visit to the Far East, in the course of
which he paid personal visits to thirteen ships in three days, calling on five messes in one ship in the space of forty minutes. Everywhere he radiated cheerful confidence, but in the barge between
visits, his Naval Assistant noticed that he was shaking with
exhaustion. He contracted a bad cough which he could not shake
off and was reluctantly forced to consult the doctors who insisted
on an immediate rest: he and Prue were flown by the RAF to
Cyprus where they spent a fortnight at the Dome Hotel, Kyrenia.

After a week, Michael was able to tackle mountain walks and
recovery seemed to be well on the way. Unwell though he had
been before leaving for Cyprus, he had not neglected to telephone
the Duty Commander, Colin Robinson, at the Ministry of
Defence, to thank him for his efforts in making efficient last-
minute arrangements for the journey—yet another gesture of the
kind which assured the First Sea Lord of a warm welcome when
he returned to the office, apparently restored to full health.

The pressure was on again, with unabated force. There was
another round of Harrier trials in HMS *Eagle* in March, flying
visits to Lundy Island (delivering a bottle of whisky to the light-
house crew) and to Malta in April (in the back seat of a
Buccaneer) and a hectic burst of activities in early May, including
a visit to HMS *Ganges*, the launch of HMNZS *Canterbury* at
Yarrow, a *Howe* reunion, a 'brood-in' by the Board at RNAS
Yeovilton and a much publicised descent in a helicopter on to
the Cunard liner *Queen Elizabeth* in the English Channel. On
this occasion it was very apparent to friends that Michael was
far from well; he agreed to be examined by naval doctors shortly
afterwards and, after consultations and x-rays, they recommended him to enter King Edward VII hospital in London for

further tests. Here, Sir Ronald Bodley Scott confirmed the true cause of Michael's troubles : he had leukaemia.

At once, all was changed. Though there was no reason to suppose that, with care, he might not live for some years, it was clear to the doctors that Michael's days in office were numbered; it would not, in their view, be possible for him to become Chief of the Defence Staff. During the last weeks of May when he was on sick leave and different treatments were being tried out, he had all too much time for considering his situation and future; but eventually, after a blood transfusion, his optimism and energy returned, even to the extent of imagining that he could still become CDS.

During June, no one except Prue and his closest friends knew of his illness. He continued with his demanding round of engagements, still radiating to those who did not know him well, the old confidence and gaiety.

However, after various visits to Sir Ronald Bodley Scott Michael gradually realised the bitter truth that he could not become CDS and would be forced to retire at the beginning of July.

When the new Minister for the Navy, Peter Kirk, came into the main building of the Ministry of Defence after the Conservative victory in the election of June 1970, almost the first person he met was Michael, who at once had to break the news of his impending retirement. It was in Kirk's words 'a bad blow for the new administration. And yet the one outstanding memory I have of that interview was of the courage and cheerfulness with which he faced up to what must have been a terrible blow to him.'

A few days later, in the course of a two-hour conversation Michael was able to brief the new Minister on the future shape of the Navy in a way which impressed him deeply. On 22 June the time came for him to write an official letter of resignation to Lord Carrington, and with characteristic thoughtfulness he wrote reassuringly, too, to a vast number of friends before the news was announced in the Press.

'I have contracted a disease of the blood known as Chronic Lymphatic Leukaemia', he explained in the printed part of the letter. 'This is by no means as ominous as it sounds and is so well contained that I am currently one hundred per cent fit and active. There is however a possibility that at some time in the future I might find myself able to operate only at something less than one hundred per cent. In these circumstances I thought it would be unfair to the government, myself and others concerned to take on the job of Chief of the Defence Staff which requires maximum effort for, normally, a three-year term. As I have said, I am currently one hundred per cent fit and active and am now looking round for something else to do.'

Receipt of this letter brought gloom to many a household, and it brought a flood of letters, none more touching than the one from Miss Annie Kemp of Bedford, his mother's daily help when Michael was a boy, who said, 'Perhaps you have been doing too much. It must be a big job just being Sea Lord, let alone being Chief of Defence. I think that when one reaches the ticklish age of over fifty, we all have moments of feeling downright ill, and if you could have a good rest now you can yet do more good work ...' The good work in fact had continued (though perhaps at a slackened pace) through June. When the Royal Naval Football Association was holding its AGM in Whitehall, Michael, as president, invited them all up to his office for a lunchtime drink. When they arrived at reception and explained who they were and why they'd come, the girl at the desk exclaimed, 'The Admiral is always doing silly things like this, I do wish he wouldn't!' But the members of that committee never forgot the gesture; for them it was a sign of an almost revolutionary rapport between the rulers and the ruled in the Queen's Navy. The members of Michael's personal staff felt much the same when they were all bidden to a farewell party at Stonehill Road.

On 30 June, Michael presided with Prue over the commissioning at Tower Pier in London of a special ship—the very first boat in the world to be designed and built for the handicapped. A catamaran named *Sparkle* because she was built with funds raised by SPARKS—Sportsmen Pledged to Aid Research into Crippling Diseases she was designed to provide over 350 square feet of free manoeuvring space for wheelchairs, and her sails were rigged for handling by a chair-bound crew. As almost the last official engagement in Michael's career, it is difficult to think of a more fitting occasion.

On 3 July Michael retired as First Sea Lord, and on the same day was promoted Admiral of the Fleet; thus congratulation was able to take the place of condolence. From every branch of the Service in every part of the world, the messages of good wishes and thanks poured in, one of the neatest from the Far East: 'There is not a man or woman in the Fleet who is not sad at your going and grateful for all you have done as First Sea Lord and for so often making us laugh and feel better. All our good wishes are yours and we hope that the Chinese Admiral of the Fleet will find time to visit these waters again. We will bottle our last tot against the day.'

Rear Admiral C. C. H. Dunlop, Head of the RN staff in Washington, summed up the Navy's feelings when he wrote: 'Now you've hauled down your flag, and flattery is no longer suspect, may I tell you what a tremendous thing you did for us all. Admiral Begg had one of the roughest Whitehall battles to fight that I have ever seen. He won through; but at the cost (through no fault of his own) of being unable to tell the Navy. Only your great personality could have restored to its old sense of purpose a Navy whose faith in itself had nearly been shattered This you did for us in a way which will make the Royal Navy for ever indebted to you and will ensure for you a golden place in the lists of our First Sea Lords.'

Michael's sendoff from the MOD was memorable indeed. I seemed that thousands had left their desks to bid him farewell after he had been wheeled out in a specially constructed ship or wheels, and, as one who was present said, 'they were only representative of all the affection in the Fleet'. But there was 'positively no moaning at the bar', and Michael's final word to the Flee was in keeping with the rest of his career—cheerful and to the point:

> *Most farewell messages try to tear-jerk the tear from the eye;*
> *But I say to you lot*
> *Very sad about tot,*
> *And thank you, good luck and goodbye!*

NINETEEN

Cultivate Courage

Many of those who had come to admire Michael in the course of his career respected even more the way he lived out his brief retirement : one day at the centre of affairs, fêted and acclaimed, the next a private citizen deprived suddenly of brilliant hopes by an illness which, however well controlled, must ultimately prove fatal. The shock of being pitchforked into civilian life where prospects of further employment might well prove dim (Michael was always ill-content with idleness)—called for a major effort of readjustment.

However, there were to be no complaints, no 'beefs'. He assured the countless people who wrote to enquire about him that he considered himself lucky and that he was confident there were plenty of good youngsters coming along to sort out 'the Andrew'. As for the CDS job, he reminded himself in a few scribbled lines of verse that he had had to forgo what, after all, might well have proved another 'can of worms' :

> *I'm a maladjusted drop-out late of Whitehall,*
> *I'm an Admiral of the Fleet who's in a mess;*
> *But there are times, I must confess it,*
> *When I really rather bless it*
> *That I'll never now be known as 'CDS'.*
>
> *For it's 'CDS, there's trouble in Anguilla'*
> *And 'What are you going to do about the Rock?'*
> *So it's really little wonder*
> *That from time to time you blunder*
> *And the Foreign Office says 'You made a cock!'*

A First Sea Lord can always say 'I'm Guv'nor—
Here's Navy List to prove it, more or less';
But CDS's Channel
Of Command is only flannel,
So I'm glad I won't be known as CDS!

For it's 'CDS, the Cabinet is worried;
Sir Alec is particularly cross.
Yes, I know you know it's Sunday
But it cannot wait till Monday
And, after all, the PM is the boss . . .'

Given reasonable luck, Michael's doctors thought he could well live for another five years; and, as his health for the moment, with the help of cortisone, seemed reasonably good, he borrowed his brother-in-law's caravan and set off with Prue for several weeks' tour of Dorset and Wales, finding in the Brecon Beacons inspiration and hope through his favourite pursuit of mountain walking. He rarely spoke of his illness, preferring, as had always been his way, to press on with living.

Back home after the holidays, Michael now had leisure to prove that Stonehill Road was no more than a stone's throw from Richmond Park. This was an ideal starting point for long walks, often to the home of Lord Fraser of North Cape near Hampton Court, or to the Mitcham vicarage of the Rev. Arthur Green, the former Chaplain of *Aurora*. On these Mitcham expeditions, Michael made a point of carrying the price of a phone call in his pocket, in case he should suddenly feel unwell and in need of a lift home. In September, looking cheerful and fit, he led a twenty-mile charity walk around Richmond Park and along the river which raised twenty pounds for mentally handicapped children.

But walking was not enough. Soon Michael bought a kayak canoe and, after taking expert instruction, set off on ambitious solo trips on the Thames. With a cheery wave en route to anyone who might be watching from the windows of the Ministry of Defence main building (where the buzz soon got around that an Admiral of the Fleet was sometimes to be seen paddling his own canoe), Michael—after a careful study of the tides—made round trips lasting six hours or more down the river from Richmond to Greenwich and back. When tired from such pursuits, there were sedentary tasks at home—bringing up to date the family's 'pub' book which eventually contained three thousand names of pubs, all different, and all personally spotted over the years by a member of the Le Fanu family. An excellent photographer, Michael also bestowed immense care on the family photograph albums and scrapbooks—an example of the systematic way he had always approached any task, great or small.

However, such occupations could not satisfy one of his temperament for long. With characteristic gusto he enlisted for the House Maintenance Course (known in Service circles as the 'bricks and mortar' course) at the Army Resettlement Centre at Aldershot. The course, as its name implies, is concerned with painting and decorating, bricklaying, concreting, plastering, carpentry and so forth, and is intended to enable retired senior officers to maintain their properties without incurring large repair bills on retirement pay.

On the first morning of the course, Colonel Anthony d'Reilly and two other Colonels noticed this 'white-overalled matelot' alone at a table during the coffee break and asked if they might join him, though they had no idea who he was—a retired Commander or Captain, they thought. When asked by the staff to form a working team of four, they did so—at which point the Army men discovered the identity of their companion.

In d'Reilly's words: 'Multiples of colonels tend to be fairly unimpressionable groupings and we were not exceptions to the rule. However "our" Admiral, as he became known, impressed us very much and very quickly. "Call me Michael," he said early on. We couldn't, and compromised with "Admiral" or "Admiral Michael" when he pressed us hard. For the next four weeks we worked together, taking it in turns to do the chores, getting the coffee or tea, with Admiral Michael playing his part to the full. "Cement and plaster" was the first skill we learned, and when we explained that soldiers already knew about shovelling, he set off with the barrow to collect the syndicate sand. We found we were in contact with an outstanding individual—a great human being in so many ways—a leader who impressed even us, and at a time when the situation did not require leadership. It was typical of him that we never realised how ill he was, nor that the reason for his absence on October 27, when he asked me to take notes for him, was that he was lunching with the Queen. He was invariably apologetic when for any reason he was not present; he seemed anxious that we should not feel he wasn't pulling his weight—as if we would! By now we were very impressed indeed, and remained so right through to the final party. It was not until I returned to the MOD for a few weeks prior to retirement that I discovered what a legendary figure we had been dealing with.

'In Aden, he had done nothing less than revolutionise the private soldier's customary view of the naval officer; he is normally thought of as a sarcastic and unreasonable creature who regards soldiers as so many pairs of muddy boots liable to ruin his spotless decks! "Our Admiral" was a great gentleman.'

It fell to Michael to express the thanks of all three hundred students on the course at their final gathering. After expressing gratitude to all the instructors, he ended by turning to the Commandant, Lieutenant-Colonel R. Dock, RAEC. 'As for the Commandant,' said Michael, 'I am sure you will agree he richly deserves—a bar of chocolate!' Whereupon he accurately threw a bar of fruit and nut fully twelve yards down the room to Colonel Dock, who caught it to vociferous cheers from all present—LeF's last recorded 'bar of nutty'. . .

During the resettlement course, Michael found time to respond to an invitation to write an article on leadership in the Services for the magazine *Officer* which had originally been made to him while he was First Sea Lord but was repeated in September 1970. Michael's reply took the form of a letter addressed to Commander J. R. B. Montanaro, RN, of the Navy's Directorate of Public Relations, and began 'Dear Jeremy'. . . the letter turned out to be the Le Fanu testament to the Service he loved.

In the course of it, he advanced carefully-reasoned arguments for the existence of armed forces as 'an honourable part of our society' and went on to consider the kind of individuals the Services were going to need in the future: 'Men and women from all sections of the community and all parts of society; as the old class distinctions become blurred, so the backgrounds of officers become less exclusive. Colonel Blimp takes his honoured place in history, leaving for today the realisation that beneath the military tunic of his successor beats the heart of a first class managerial-type citizen who is very good at *people* ... It is easy to say we want more and better leadership but leadership is hard to define and develop. It is certainly not a skill one can learn from a do-it-yourself book and I know of no rheostat or graphite moderator which can increase the leadership output. I personally believe in doing what comes naturally, within certain fairly obvious constraints ... Service discipline will in the end and for a while make men do as they are told, even though they are wet, cold and frightened. But this is no basis for leadership, which must extract willing, intelligent obedience ... Perhaps then, having said I have nothing to add on the subject, I might add to Lord Slim's list of Courage, Willpower, Initiative and Knowledge as the essential attributes of a leader, one more attribute—the ability to *Communicate*.'

This attribute of leadership Michael himself possessed in the highest degree; through it he influenced the social atmosphere of the Royal Navy, and led the British public to a heightened appreciation of 'the Maritime Affair'.

If, on looking back, we now see the 'Dear Jeremy' letter as valedictory, there was nothing in Michael's style of living when he wrote it to suggest that he was not fully fit and confident of remaining so.

In September he and Prue flew by helicopter to the recommissioning at Plymouth of Mark's ship HMS *Achilles* and early in October, at the moment when, if all had gone well, he would have taken up his appointment as CDS, he was elected Chairman of the Dover Harbour Board, an office traditionally held by distinguished men. Dover was delighted to have him, and looked forward to a promised visit when Michael would have time to meet all concerned. He was in fine form when he crowned the 'Ideal Barmaid' in Whitbread's City Brewery and, later that month, when he was guest of honour at the Hammersmith Hospital Nurses' Prizegiving. On this occasion, he expressed his admiration for those in 'this wonderful Service profession', remarking that they could never expect to receive their full reward on earth and advising them to 'cultivate courage'; he also demanded a prize himself, and ordered gold medal winner Karin Schafer on to the platform to give him a kiss!

There was a visit too, during October, to Dorchester in Oxfordshire where Michael's cousin, the composer Elizabeth Maconchy, was preparing performances of her church opera *The Jesse Tree*. Michael and Prue attended the dress rehearsal, but he insisted on paying more than the performance price for their seats. One of the organisers asked what should be done with the over-large cheque: 'Cash it!' came the reply. And in the pub afterwards, the visitors chatted happily to all the performers, among them the percussionist who was required to produce noises from a variety of unexpected objects. 'I'm delighted,' said Michael, 'to have met the world's greatest performer on the saw and bucket!' The social highlight of October was a dinner on board HMS *Victory* at Portsmouth given by Admiral Sir Horace Law for Michael's closest Service friends. Lord Fraser of North Cape, who occupied a unique place in Michael's affections, was able to be there, and delighted those present by remarking suddenly in the middle of dinner, 'I say, this is a swinging evening!'

In November there was a formidable list of engagements: the new Admiral of the Fleet was in great demand, and whenever he felt the occasion would promote the cause of the Navy, or of general cheerfulness, he accepted. Thus he was guest of the gunroom in HMS *President* on the Thames on 6 November, where he listened with obvious enjoyment to a specially composed calypso and advised the young RNR officers to 'have a good skylark. I was told I couldn't skylark after I was a Lieutenant but I've been doing so ever since!'

In the middle of the month, he was a very popular guest of honour at the Chelsea Arts Club, and the 'life and soul' of a British Legion dinner; he opened the Christmas Fair of the South West London branch of the British Polio Fellowship; was apparently 'in good spirits' at the meeting of Admirals at Admiralty House on the sixteenth and seemed to be 'looking much better' at the Western Approaches Command Reunion dinner at the Dorchester on 20 November, where he remarked to a friend who complimented him on his healthy appearance: 'Nothing like a stiff cortisone and soda twice a day.' The following day he attended the wedding of a friend's daughter.

In the latter part of the month he was kept busy acknowledging replies to his radio appeal on Radio 4 on 8 November in aid of the Soldiers, Sailors and Airmen's Families Association for which he raised over a thousand pounds. He had ended by giving the address of the association for those who wished to send donations, together with his own name, adding, 'It doesn't matter how you spell it'; listeners took him at his word, and responded with letters addressed to 'Admiral Sapper', 'Admiral Avenue', 'Admiral Applenew', 'Admiral Repenu', 'Admiral Lupescu' and 'Old Thingy, SSAFA'.

In the last week of November, Michael set out to fulfil his promise to revisit Dover, where a full programme had been arranged for him and Prue. They met the Mayor and other council members, many of the yachting fraternity, shipping operators and representatives of Trinity House; in fact he inspected the harbour installations in a new Trinity House pilot launch, from which he signalled as follows : 'Trinity House from Dover Harbour Board : Elder Brother Le Fanu, sober and properly Dressed, afloat with flag flying, sends greetings to the Elder Brethren.'

That evening at a cocktail party given by the Harbour Board Michael was obviously unwell but insisted on keeping his appointment to visit Calais the next day. By Thursday morning it was clear that he could not complete his programme and had to be driven back to London by Prue. Bitterly disappointed, he promised to return in January to chair the next meeting of the Board. But that same day he was taken into the King Edward VII Hospital in London, where, in the course of the next two days, he gradually became unconscious and died at 6.30 pm on Saturday, 28 November.

This sudden collapse had been unforeseen, even by Michael's doctor, Sir Ronald Bodley Scott. He afterwards wrote about Michael's last days to Prue : 'The destruction of his red blood cells was proceeding unabated. I made arrangements for an immediate blood transfusion, but as is often the way in this situation, it was difficult to find blood which matched. Clearly nothing we could do prevented this progressive blood destruction and the anaemia which resulted was more than his previously damaged heart could withstand. I have only seen this happen twice before in this disease and nothing can avert the process. Perhaps the only thing we should be thankful about is that for him it was over rapidly, without two or three years of miserable invalidism which would have been more than he could stand.' Sir Ronald then offered the heartfelt sympathy of one who had become a friend as well as physician. 'One had only to know your husband for an hour in order to realise that he was a very special kind of person, an enchanting and impressive man.'

Many hundreds of letters came to Prue after the announcement of Michael's death, all attempting to express his exceptional quality. Shock was mingled with disbelief when his portrait was flashed on the TV screen with the news of his death: so many people had seen him so recently, radiantly alive. His young cousin, Matthew Porteous, who inherited the canoe, perhaps best caught the Le Fanu approach to death. 'I was very sorry to hear about Michael for I was very fond of him. I am doing well in all subjects, especially Maths where I am top'. . . and, after all, as Matthew told his mother, 'It was pretty splendid to be on the News!'

Many of Michael's family and friends must have shared the thought expressed by Matthew's Aunt Jane who 'suddenly felt something I have never felt before, which I have seen written about someone else: he was so alive that his death did more to convince me of immortality than anything else has ever done. It was not a matter of intellectual proof: simply that when my idea of him and my idea of death met in my mind, it was my idea of death which changed.'

The tributes spoke of the 'wonderful courage and inner strength' which had made Michael and Prue together such 'a source of inspiration'; they assured Prue that as far as the Navy was concerned Michael 'had been loved as Nelson must have been', that he was 'the symbol of the happy ending; the right man reaching the top; the victory of friendliness, the common touch, directness and unorthodoxy, over aloofness, pomposity, deviousness and the book of rules'.

Other letters recalled Michael's unstinting work for charities for the disabled, and his innumerable acts of personal kindness.

Arthur Green of the *Aurora* conducted the private funeral service; then, on 15 December, 1970, there was a Memorial Service in Westminster Abbey. Though doubtless the most imposing, it was only one of many such services held in Michael's memory all round the world. They were deliberately simple affairs for the most part, attended by people of all ranks who came as they were, in their working rig, to pay tribute to one who had never had much time for outward show; and for all the grandeur of its setting, the Abbey tribute, too, had a quality which matched the man. The great church was packed to the doors with people who were there not because they ought to be, but because they wanted to be. It fell to Admiral Sir Peter Hill-Norton as First Sea Lord to give the address—according to him, one of the most difficult tasks he ever had to face. He reminded the congregation of Michael's achievements in the war, in *Aurora*, and with the Americans, who said of him 'we could not have had a better shipmate'. He asserted that by the time he was in command of HMS *Eagle* 'most of us in the Navy felt certain that Michael would reach the top of his profession. People saw then that he had the happy knack of getting them to do better than they ever thought they could; and that, despite the unconventional style which was so essential a part of him, he was a master of his own profession; that he was as tough and forthright as he was an accomplished administrator and outstanding leader . . .

'As Commander-in-Chief of all the British Forces in the Arabian peninsula during our withdrawal, he was able to deploy all these qualities, and with them, and with his panache and his infectious sense of fun and gaiety, he inspired and encouraged everyone, Service and civilian, in their thankless daily round and did much to keep their spirits as buoyant as his own . . .

'Many of us will remember him as a young man—but nobody could ever think of him as an old man; he was a man of our time, for whom rank, or age, or class raised no barriers. His charm, sincerity and love of his fellow men gave him that rare quality of the common touch.'

Thus, as the congregation stood in silence while Mark wheeled

Prue, composed and serene, to the door of the Abbey, the world said farewell to Michael Le Fanu. But 'gay and gallant Michael', —the words of Mark's housemaster—had achieved his own kind of immortality. Sir Richard Turnbull sent Prue these lines, from the account in Thucydides of a funeral oration by Pericles:

> *The whole earth is the tomb of heroic men; and their story is not graven only on stone over their clay, but abides everywhere, without visible symbol, woven into the stuff of other men's lives.*

Select Bibliography

A Memoir of the Le Fanu Family, T. P. Le Fanu. Privately printed.

The Royal Navy Since 1945, A. Cecil Hampshire. William Kimber & Co. Ltd (1975).

The Second World War, Sir Winston Churchill. Cassell & Co. Ltd.

The Silver Phantom (*HMS 'AURORA'*), by her Ship's Company. Frederick Muller Ltd (1945).

The Forgotten Fleet, John Winton. Michael Joseph Ltd (1969).

The Book of the 'Howe'. Privately printed.

The Quiet Warrior (*Admiral Raymond A. Spruance*), Thomas R. Buell. Little, Brown Inc. (1974).

Admiral Halsey's Story, W. F. Halsey and Joseph Bryan. McGraw-Hill Book Co. (1947).

Farewell to Arabia, David Holden. Faber and Faber Ltd (1966).

Last Post: Aden 1964-67, Julian Paget. Faber and Faber Ltd (1969).

Having Been a Soldier, Lt. Col. Colin Mitchell. Hamish Hamilton Ltd (1969).

Index

Churchill, Sir Winston, 44, 66
Cleopatra, HMS, 100
Cochrane, Molly, 34
Consort, HMS, 126
Controller of the Navy, 161, 162
Copenhagen, 103, 104
Cossack, HMS, 36, 37
Crater, 191, 203–8, 212
Crossbow, HMS, 101
Crusader, HMS, 30, 31
Culdrose, 132, 219
'Cultivate Courage' motto, 24, 242
Cumberland, HMS, 140
Cunningham, Admiral Sir J. H. D., 46
CVA 01, 165, 176, 177, 193
Cyprus, 233

Dainty, HMS, 216
Dartmouth, 22, 26, 30
Davies, Sub-Lieutenant Rupert, 33
Denman, Captain Charles, 130, 131, 221, 223
Denmark, 103
Denny, Sir Michael, 109, 114
Devonport, 59
Devonshire, HMS, 166, 169
Dorsetshire, HMS, 30
Dover Harbour Board, 241, 243
Dreadnought, HMS, 144, 169, 172
d'Reilly, Colonel Anthony, 239
Driffield, Harry, 138
Duke of York, HMS, 55, 58, 81, 82
Dunlop, Rear Admiral G. C. H., 236

Eagle, HMS, 130–6, 164, 225, 233, 245
Eastern Fleet, 62
Eastney, 35
Edict of Nantes, 15
Ellum, Lieutenant G. F. C., 40, 48
Elworthy, Air Chief Marshal Sir Charles, 226
Ethiopia, 32, 200
Excellent, HMS, 32, 33, 51, 89

Fearless, HMS, 144, 198
Fettes, Peter, 60
Fleet Air Arm, 34, 220, 225
FLOSY, 181, 182, 204, 208, 211, 213
Force 'A', 42
Force 'B', 47

Force 'K', 44–7
Force 'Z', 66
Ford, Lieutenant-Colonel R. C., 188
Fraser, Admiral Sir Bruce, 55, 58, 62, 66, 69, 79, 80–2, 89, 111, 112, 216, 238, 242
Frewen, Vice-Admiral John, 160, 216

Ganges, HMS, 113, 118–29, 134, 136, 159, 229, 233
Gibbs, Beryl, 167
Gibbs, Brigadier 'Roly', 190
Gibraltar, 44
Giles, Captain Morgan, 158
Girdle Ness, HMS, 140
Godmanchester, 23, 30, 31
Gold Ranger, HMS, 154
Gorshkov, Admiral, 200
Graf Spee, 36
Green, Rev. Arthur, 41, 110, 166, 238, 245
'Green Triangle Gang', 23
Gregory, Admiral Sir David, 54
Gunnery, 32, 34–9, 41, 46, 59, 61, 63, 89, 92

Hall, Captain Tim, 115, 134
Halsey, Admiral W. F., 11, 69, 76–82
Hamilton, Captain L. H. K., 39
Hamlet, 11, 41, 117
Hammerfest, 42
Hancock, USS, 151
Hargroves, Brigadier Louis, 185
Harington, General Sir Charles, 179
Harpur Trust, 21
Havock, HMS, 47
Healey, Denis (M.P.), 195, 223, 224
Hermes, HMS, 156, 157, 220
Hicks, Lieutenant Roger, 192, 215, 216
Hill-Norton, Vice-Admiral, 217, 224, 245
Hiroshima, 79, 109
Holloway, R. L., 41
Home Fleet, 53, 54, 58, 99
Hong Kong, 151, 154, 156
Hopking, Sub-Lieutenant, 33
Hopkins, Captain Frank, 131
Howe, HMS, 27, 59–67, 73, 233
Huguenots, 14, 15